THE
SAVAGE
GARDEN

"Ah, but we are splendid devils, aren't we?"
"Hunters of the Savage Garden," I said.

THE VAMPIRE LESTAT
—ANNE RICE

THE
SAVAGE
GARDEN

CULTIVATING
CARNIVOROUS PLANTS

PETER D'AMATO

TEN SPEED PRESS
Berkeley, California

Ten Speed Press
P.O. Box 7123
Berkeley, California 94707
www.tenspeed.com

Distributed in Canada by Ten Speed Press Canada, in New Zealand by Southern
Publishers Group, in South Africa by Real Books, and in the United Kingdom and
Europe by Airlift Book Company.

Design by Catherine Jacobes and Toni Tajima

Library of Congress Cataloging-in-Publication Data:
D'Amato, Peter.
The savage garden: cultivating carnivorous plants / Peter D'Amato.
        p.   cm.
Includes bibliographical references and index.
ISBN 0-89815-915-6
1. Carnivorous plants. I. Title.
SB432.7.D36   1998
635.9'3375—dc21   97–6927
                                                CIP

First printing, 1998
Printed in Hong Kong
4 5 6 7 8 9 10—07 06 05 04 03

*I would like to dedicate this book
to my longtime friend and biz partner
Marilee Maertz, who believes in
the magic of the plants,
and to Eleonore, my mother,
who believes in us.*

CONTENTS

PREFACE

NOT TOO LONG AGO, I was browsing through a local garden center and met with a familiar sight. There at the dark but spacious checkout stand, where nursery managers enjoy placing quick-selling impulse items, sat an open cardboard box of Venus flytraps. The plants were in little pots with clear plastic cups protecting their traps from curious fingers. The box was half empty, and of the remaining plants most had at least a couple of black leaves. Two plants looked entirely dead, and I could see that the soil in a few of the pots was so dry it was shrinking like a dried-out sponge. A small, handwritten sign read: "50% Off."

What a tragedy, I thought. Just then a young boy of about ten pushed up so closely that I had to step aside. "Oh wow!" he cried, "Look Mom, Venus flytraps! Can I get one?" His mother gently pulled him away. "Venus flytraps always die," I heard her say rather matter-of-factly, as she led her son away through the palms and oleander. Venus flytraps always die. I had heard such statements many times before.

I purchased those remaining flytraps and I saved their little lives. They sit now on my sunny porch—ten plants in a large pot. A mass of dozens of lush green and red traps, yawning patiently for food. A few of the traps hold the shriveled carcasses of digested flies. A neighbor just yesterday told me my flytraps were "absolutely beautiful."

With this book I hope to teach people how to grow a Venus flytrap. For if you can grow this plant successfully, a whole world will begin to be open to you. It is a world filled with wonder—a strange, strange world turned upside down; a world of plants that lure, catch, kill, and digest insects and other animals for food.

This fact in itself many people find startling. For while much of the general public may be vaguely aware of the Venus flytrap, they are often rather surprised to learn that this is only one of several hundred species of carnivorous plants known to exist on our planet. When one considers the many subspecies, forms, hybrids, and cultivars of carnivorous plants in cultivation, the numbers move up into the many thousands.

There is a second surprise in store. Many folks assume that such weird vegetation certainly must come from some far-off, exotic and tropical country, necessitating a hot and steamy greenhouse in which to grow them. In truth, while some of the most popular carnivorous plants do indeed come from tropical places, most carnivorous plants grow in temperate climates, and there is at least one newly discovered species growing on glacial ice! The Venus flytrap, for instance, is native to the coasts of North and South Carolina, and the North American continent has the widest variety of ornamental carnivorous plant genera in the world. By comparison, tropical Africa and South America have only a few.

When the uninformed see well-grown plants for the first time, a third surprise is in store for them. Many carnivorous plants are truly beautiful to behold, but that beauty often masks the underlying savageness of the natural world.

The purpose of this book is simple: how to grow carnivorous plants. If you are a hobbyist with a growing collection of plants or a beginner without a clue, I hope you'll find this book helpful and informative. This book will be a guide not only for the collector, but for the teacher who may want a terrarium of carnivorous plants in the classroom or children's museum; for the horticulturist at a public botanical garden whose specialty may lie elsewhere; for the nursery manager who throws out more carnivorous plants than she sells; or for a young person whose mom just bought him a flytrap—at half price!

I first began to grow carnivorous plants when I was around eleven years old. Now, over three decades later, I have witnessed a gradual change in public opinion: what began as an "eccentric" interest of the very few has become a rewarding hobby for many. Unfortunately, finding good horticultural information on the plants has changed only slightly over the years. Books on carnivorous plants have come and gone and are often hard to find once they go out of print. Journals on the subject grow out-of-date, and researching old back issues can be tiresome for beginners. And even when some colorful and fascinating new book does appear, I still have found myself sighing in frustration and asking, "But how do I grow it?"

This book will tell you how.

ACKNOWLEDGMENTS

THIS BOOK IS THE RESULT OF the support and enthusiasm of many kind people. Early on, there was Russell Driscoll, Glenn Fischer, and Carolyn Bevis. Bill Barnett of San Francisco played a key role in my all-consuming interest in these wonderful plants.

As friends and untiring editors of the Carnivorous Plant Newsletter, I am deeply indebted to Dr. Donald Schnell; Leo Song at Cal State University, Fullerton; Dr. Larry Mellichamp of the University of North Carolina, Charlotte; and special thanks to Joe Mazrimas of Livermore, California. Thanks also goes to Barry Meyers-Rice, Steve Baker, and Jan Schlauer.

Among hobbyists and collectors it is hard to find nicer people than: Chuck Powell, Tom Kahl, Scott Hootman, Stephanie Changaris, Hawkeye Rondeau, Cindy Slezak, Joe Miller, Larry Logoteta, Rick Walker, Mike Ross, Carl Wong, and many other members of the San Francisco Bay Area Carnivorous Plant Society, most particularly Geoff Wong, whose beautifully grown carnivorous plants have caused many a person to faint.

Special thanks go to Joan and Bob Ellis, the Associated Vintage Group, and the staff at Mark West Vineyards, Forestville, CA.

It was Barbara Stevens of the San Francisco Landscape and Garden Show who urged me to display some of my collection in 1989, and the response was overwhelming. The result was California Carnivores. Jacqui Giuffre of the Sonoma County Fair was always a delight to work with, and Betsy Fischer of Sonoma County Farm Trails offered complete enthusiasm and many a good laugh. Judy Boyce of the Russian River Chamber of Commerce was a tremendous source of help as well.

California Carnivores would not exist were it not for the help of many people: Eve Kahn, James Benét, and Anne Raver, of the *New York Times*, Simone Wilson of *Sonoma Business Magazine*, Peter Fish of *Sunset Magazine*, Jerry Graham of *Bay Area Back Roads*, Victoria Coviello of the *San Francisco Examiner*, Christopher Reeve and Ali MacGraw, and the folks at Martha Stewart Living and CNN. Tireless volunteers Cheryl, Christopher and Catherine Ishida, Ann, Aaron, and Joshua Haiman, and Charmaine Rable, are much appreciated. And we are deeply grateful to Vic Fujii, Marie Baumgartl, Bill Baumgartl, Jim Mitchell, Lisa Adams, Joel Stern, Michael Fantus, Sean Samia, Jeff Shafer, Bob Hanrahan, Cliff Dodd, Ron and Isabell Groll, Ray Triplett, Craig Gardner, Rob Gardner of the North Carolina Botanical Garden, Ron Determan of the Atlanta Botanical Garden, Lori Sarosi, John Rizzi, Jeff Graham, Allan Merryman, Lee and Angelo D'Amato, Margaret Erickson, Hal Kowenski, Frank Valdez, Helene Milman, George Marcopulos of the Conservatory of Golden Gate Park, Lionel Gazeau, Bobbi Morgan, Alan Hindle, Randi Covin, Liz Brown, Bob Newton, Barbara Barton of "Gardening by Mail," and Victoria Baken.

In the preparation of this book, the help and slavery of the following people were invaluable: Judith Finn of the University of California at Berkeley's Botanical Garden, Ron Gagliardo of Atlanta Botanical Garden, Chuck and Cindy Ratzke, Scott Bennett, and Sharon Bergeron. At Ten Speed Press my sincere thanks to Tom Southern, Phil Wood, Jonathan Chester, Donna Latte, Catherine Jacobes, Toni Tajima and Mariah Bear, all of whom never said no to anything.

INTRODUCTION:
WHAT ARE CARNIVOROUS PLANTS?

*"The Venus flytrap, a devouring organism,
aptly named for the goddess of love."*

—TENNESSEE WILLIAMS,
Suddenly Last Summer

I WAS A KID GROWING UP in the sixties when I had my first love affair with a Venus flytrap.

It was an advertisement in *Famous Monsters* magazine that first seduced me. The ad shouted something about the plant eating hamburger, and next to it was a fuzzy picture of Charles Darwin. As I already had pet turtles and a South American alligator trained to eat hamburger from a spoon, I convinced my mother that we could afford another mouth to feed and promptly had her write out a check.

The plants finally arrived in a Styrofoam pot wrapped in plastic. The pot was filled with dry peat moss and three or four "bulbs" with all of their leaves cut off. I followed the directions but nothing spectacular occurred. A few semideveloped leaves came up but soon all of the plants turned black.

It was my first experience with unrequited love. It never crossed my mind that the dim corner of my bedroom next to the heater in the month of December had anything to do with the plants' demise. Venus flytraps, I thought, must come from some dark, steamy, tropical jungle—didn't they?

I was surprised when the following spring a friend and fellow student whispered to me, "I know where Venus flycatchers grow." I had just raised my hand in science class and volunteered to do a report on the Venus flytrap. As love springs eternal, I figured doing a school report was one way my mom would write out another check and I could give Venus flytraps a second try. Since we lived on the seashore of southern New Jersey, I found my friend's statement rather hard to believe.

He took me to the boggy edge of a small lake right in the middle of town. The ground was covered in billowy, spongy green moss that my friend called sphagnum. The moss hugged the bases of southern white cedars that grew in the shallow, tea-colored water. It was a beautiful sight.

"There they are," my friend said, pointing. I looked in awe at the strangest plants I had ever seen. Half buried in the moss were rosetted clumps of deeply purple hollow leaves, with spiny collars and strange reddish flowers rising from the center. "These aren't Venus flytraps," I said, but I was hardly disappointed.

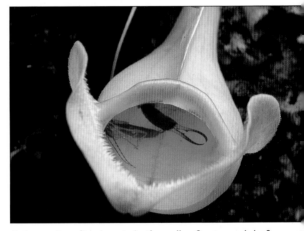

When my friend assured me they still ate bugs, I peered into one of the hollow, leathery leaves, and sure enough I saw insects struggling in the wells of water that each leaf held.

"Look at this," my friend said. He plucked something from the moss and held it up in his fingers. It was an im-

"...I saw struggling insects in the wells of water each leaf held."

age that would forever be imprinted upon my brain. A ray of sunlight broke through the cedars, shining directly on what he held in his hand. It was a small, circular green leaf covered with hundreds of red tentacles like a pincushion, each ending in a tiny drop of dew. Every drop caught the light of the sun, and they sparkled and glittered like jewels. These small plants were dotted with numerous dead and struggling insects, their circular leaves sometimes clenched like tight fists, with wings and antennae sticking out and twitching. I looked around in awe, for it was an unforgettable image: tea-colored water, grayish trunks of cedars, and spongy mounds of reddish green islands with strange plants that looked like they came from outer space!

"It was an image that would forever be imprinted upon my brain."

My friend and I dug up some of the weird plants and took them to school the following week. Even our teachers were mystified. But soon I was led to the library and found several books that satisfied my curiosity. What we had found growing on the swampy edge of the lake were purple pitcher plants and sundews—carnivorous plants not unlike the famous Venus flytrap! I was also surprised to learn that the pine barrens of southern New Jersey were practically teeming with flesh-eating plants, and that the flytrap was native only to the Carolinas, a mere day's drive south of where I lived. I was almost dumbfounded to discover that North America has probably the widest variety of carnivorous plants in the world: pitcher plants, sundews, butterworts, cobra plants, bladderworts, and Venus flytraps all grow here! I wouldn't have to fly to Madagascar after all.

For me, it was the beginning of a mind-boggling adventure that would change my life.

Our general impression is that plants are fairly passive forms of life. Insects and animals eat them. We chop down trees to build houses, shred cabbage for coleslaw, and decorate our homes with their sex organs, which we call flowers. We eat their fruit, pull "weeds," and make medicine out of their sap. We bleed trees for maple syrup and burn them in fireplaces. We bake them, boil them, and sauté or stir-fry them. We even smoke them.

Plants can't scream and run away, but some of them do fight back to an extent. Mushrooms can kill you and poison ivy can make you itch. Many plants defend themselves with needles and toxins or bitter tastes and bad smells.

Typically we are not afraid of plants, but humans love to project their own fears onto other life-forms. That we can do this with plants, seemingly the most passive and unfrightening of life-forms on earth, is obvious by just examining some of our more popular horror movies. *The Thing* featured an alien humanoid plant that fed on human blood. In *Day of the Triffids,* walking plants were stinging humans to death in their effort to take over the world. *Invasion of the Body Snatchers* had plant "pods" duplicating human beings and taking over their minds and bodies. In *Little Shop of Horrors,* a talking plant with a sense of humor swallows people whole. That these four famous horror movies were made—and remade—reflects the unconscious fear that we all have of pretty, pulpy, passive plants. Perhaps deep within our brains, tiny neurons still fire off flashbacks of ancient, inherited memories, horrible memories of the days when our ancestors had good reason to fear plants!

You might smirk and shake your head, but this primal fear may not be quite as far-fetched as you think. Just last year at the carnivorous plant nursery I own, where we have on public display over 500 varieties of flesh-eating plants, a well-to-do couple came in and were marveling at our collection of tropical pitcher plants, the *Nepenthes.* They told me with glee how they had recently returned from Malaysia, where they saw magnificent *Nepenthes* at a botanical garden. "We arrived early," the wife told me, "and we waited in line at the front gate. I peered through the fence, and saw these huge pitcher plants hanging in the trees. To my shock, an attendant was pulling tiny baby monkeys out of the traps! Most were alive, and scampered away. The dead ones he dropped in a pail." Her husband added that when they later caught up with the attendant and asked him about what he was doing, the embarrassed attendant explained that dead monkeys in the pitcher plants were upsetting to the tourists. While I have never been able to document this story, and suspect the prey were more akin to rodents, such tales have persisted for a very long time, a mythology that may have a basis in fact.

Thus, the following equation is not necessarily true: Plant eats monkey. Monkeys are primates. Humans are primates. Plant eats humans.

But surprisingly there was a brief time when some people truly believed in the Man-Eating Tree of Madagascar. It was in 1860 that Carle Liche wrote an article claiming he had witnessed a sacrifice of a young maiden to such a tree by natives of the island. Since he offered grisly details and was published in scientific and popular magazines, the report was widely believed to be true. It was not.

During the same period Charles Darwin, among many others, studied and reported on the amazing carnivorous habits of many plants both familiar to them and being newly discovered around the world. Science was exploding in popularity during the nineteenth century, and explorations were uncovering many strange and exotic forms of life. Even plants long familiar to Europeans, like the sundews and butterworts common to local bogs and moors, were suddenly suspect.

This suspicion over which plants are or are not carnivorous is a matter that is not quite settled even at the close of the twentieth century. "Carnivorous" means "flesh-eating." An older term, used by Darwin and sometimes referred to even today, was "insectivorous," or insect-eating. The latter term is not quite accurate and is rather limiting, for even though the vast majority of prey eaten by carnivorous plants are insects, this group of plants also consumes spiders, sow bugs, worms, tadpoles, frogs, lizards, and even rats, although admittedly the capture of larger animals such as mammals is a very rare event.

A typical "normal" plant works in the following way: the roots in the soil absorb water, including minerals. The leaves in the air absorb carbon dioxide. Through the complex process of photosynthesis, chlorophyll in the leaves uses the energy of sunlight to transform the carbon dioxide and minerals into carbohydrates and other organic compounds, which give the plant energy to grow.

But what if the soil a plant lives in is low in minerals, particularly nitrogen, phosphorous, or potassium, which are vital to the plant's health?

Most carnivorous plants grow in mineral-deficient soils. More often than not, these soils are very wet. The water moving through the ground carries away most of the much-needed minerals. Even nitrogen, returned to the soil by the slow decay of older, dying leaves, does not remain for long. A plant living in such an environment might be able to survive year after year, but wouldn't be able to manufacture the energy needed to produce flowers, seed, or offshoots.

Carnivorous plants have an answer to that survival dilemma. All around them are little, moving packets of minerals and nutrients, like

Small ants getting drunk on *Nepenthes ventricosa*

vitamin pills with legs and wings. We call them animals. All the plant has to do is catch them and somehow absorb through their leaves what they would normally take up through their roots. The development of leaves for such a purpose is what makes carnivorous plants so bizarre and beautiful.

Even "normal" plants can absorb minerals through their leaves. You can spray your rosebush with a watery solution of Miracle Grow and watch it take off. If you made a fertilizer solution for your rose bush by pulverizing dried crickets, mixing them in water, and spraying the solution on your plants, would you have a carnivorous rose? In fact, root fertilizers for plants such as palms do often have ground-up crickets, oyster, and crab shells in them. Do you then have an insectivorous or seafoodivrous or—God forbid—shellfishivorous palm tree? Maybe…maybe not.

The confusion over which plants are or are not carnivorous stems from how we define the term. It has been generally assumed that to be called carnivorous a plant needed to do several things: lure prey, somehow catch it, kill it, and then digest it, usually through the production of enzymes and acids used to dissolve the victim into palatable form. It's this "digesting" that's the controversial part.

Some plants are included under the heading of "carnivorous" even though they don't produce actual

Pinguicula esseriana snacking on fungus gnats

digestive enzymes. *Darlingtonia* and *Heliamphora* are two examples of pitcher plants that apparently rely on bacterial action to dissolve their prey. This "digestion by proxy" can make the discussion of carnivores a rather complicated thing. If we simply defined a carnivorous plant as one that possibly benefited from the absorption of minerals obtained from captured and killed animals, instead of several hundred species, we might be talking about many thousands!

Petunias catch and kill insects. So do potato plants, tobacco, rhododendrons, and teasels. But they do so, it is believed, for defensive purposes. Plants like petunias are covered with sticky hairs, which make life difficult for insects like aphids who wish to eat them. Many insects become caught in these hairs and die. Potato plants also are covered with hairs. If an aphid breaks one of these hairs, a glue is secreted that cements the aphid to the spot. The common teasel has leaves that form "cups" where they join the stem. Rainwater collects in the cups, insects fall in, drown, and eventually dissolve. All of these plants, at one time or another, were viewed with suspicion by scientists studying carnivores. All of these plants probably absorb some nitrogen or other trace minerals through their leaves as the insects decompose. The rest of the minerals are possibly taken up through their root systems after rain. But they are not considered carnivorous because they lack the process of digestion.

Perhaps our definitions should be revamped. Many plants might fall under the category of "semicarnivorous." Take for example the long-standing problem of *Roridula*. The two species of this genus grow in South Africa. They look and behave so much like sundews they were originally included under the genus *Drosera*. Their leaves are covered with sticky glands that catch enormous amounts of insects. But earlier in this century *Roridula* was excluded from the carnivores because it did not produce digestive enzymes. And so it stood until the 1990s, when two surprising discoveries were made. The first was by Steve Williams. Through DNA research, he discovered that *Roridula* was more closely related to *Sarracenia,* the pitcher plants on the other side of the Atlantic, than they were to *Drosera*. He jokingly suggested that *Roridula* be included in the family Sarraceniacea and that its carnivorous nature be re-explored. It was, which led to the second surprise. It has been long known that *Roridula* plays host to a curious insect called the assassin bug. These bugs live on the plant, and for reasons still unknown can traverse the sticky glands with no problem at all. When other insects become caught, the assassin bugs close in, stab their needle-like mouths into the struggling prey, and suck out the juices. Alan Ellis and Jeremy Midgely discovered the amazing reason for this cooperative venture. Assassin bugs, after sucking dry *Roridula's* prey, secret a nutritious substance onto the plant that the leaves then absorb—true carnivore by proxy! *Roridula* plays host to assassin bugs who act as a "surrogate gut."

This discovery led Oxford carnivorous plant specialist Barry Juniper to comment on petunias, potatoes, and tobacco: "They're all killing machines. I wouldn't be surprised if they absorb decayed products from their prey."

How have such plants evolved? Definite theories on the evolution of carnivorous plants are few; the almost complete lack of fossil evidence coupled with the current shifting of ideology among evolutionists may make theorizing an exercise in futility. Uniformitarianism, or gradualism, as popularized by Darwin, Wallace, and other nineteenth century scientists, holds that evolutionary change in both biology and geology is a very slow progression of events that occurs even as we speak. Darwin's theory of the origin of species by natural selection

Roridula gorgonius covered with prey—but is it carnivorous?

relied on rare and random mutation giving rise to new traits that, if beneficial to the species, allowed it to compete better among its peers and pass those traits down to its offspring. Darwin's dream that the fossil evidence for such transitional forms were simply missing from the evolutionary record has turned out to be mere wish fulfillment, for most scientists today agree that there are no transitional forms.

Thus, under gradualism, Darwinists imagined how a basic oval leaf slowly evolved, step by step, into the simple, rolled up, funnel shape of something like a *Heliamphora* leaf; then through random, accidental mutations over aeons of time, added genes to eventually produce the drug coniine in *Sarracenia flava* or the light windows of *Darlingtonia* or the symbiotic relationship of *Roridula* and assassin bugs…well okay, maybe it's not so easy to imagine! Or, in the words of Francis Lloyd, who in his 1942 book, *The Carnivorous Plants,* mused on how the complex trap of *Utricularia* could have possibly evolved under gradualism: "Since we cannot answer these questions, it is perhaps as well to say no more."

Currently, beliefs in gradualism are eroding. Scientists are realizing that for long periods of time species of life on earth are stabilized, with little or no evolutionary progress. Then periodically and very suddenly, geological and biological changes take place. Older species suddenly vanish, while new ones appear quickly with no transitional forms. Others remain unchanged. While research in areas such as DNA may lead to conclusions concerning relationships between species, including carnivorous plants, how those species actually evolved is still the deepest of mysteries. The answers may come over the next century—maybe through the theories of punctuated equilibrium, but more likely through cosmic catastrophism; possibly through the studies of DNA or population genetics, or perhaps through some new theory no one has thought about yet.

The invention of the greenhouse in the early 1800s and its growing popularity during the Victorian age among Europe's upper classes allowed for the first time exotic plants from around the world to be successfully grown under controlled conditions. Commercial nurseries were developed to cater to the demand for exotic plants. Some of these firms, such as the famous Vietch and Sons in England, financed expeditions to far-off lands around the world to collect unusual plant life. Their fanciful catalogues in the late 1800s boasted palms, orchids, hoyas, succulents, and carnivores. Among the most popular insect-eating plants offered were the *Nepenthes,* but such firms also sold *Sarrace-*

Tropical pitcher plants, such as this *Nepenthes sanguinea*, were popular greenhouse specimens in Victorian England.

nia, Drosera, Dionaea, and *Cephalotus.* Breeding programs developed showy hybrids that competed—along with roses and orchids—for prestigious awards at the Chelsea Flower Show. Magazines like the *Gardener's Chronicle* popularized the plants and offered cultural techniques. Usually, exotic plants were very expensive and during the 1800s were affordable only to the very rich. But hardly a greenhouse existed on the estates of the wealthy that didn't have *Nepenthes* hanging from the rafters along with the palms and the orchids.

But World War I changed all of that. The shortage of fuels to heat the greenhouses caused the sudden death of vast botanical collections. Many prized cultivars and species disappeared forever. Only here and there, hidden away in public botanical gardens and universities, did some of the plants survive.

It wasn't until after World War II that the hobby of growing carnivorous plants began to make a modest comeback. During the war Francis Lloyd published his scientific work *The Carnivorous Plants* in America, the first such work since Darwin's 1860 *Insectivorous Plants.* In Japan, where the love of cultivating exotic plants (such as dwarf rhapis palms and bonsai) suffered heavily during the world war, the first carnivorous plant society was begun in 1948. It still thrives.

During the fifties and sixties, the cultivation of ornamental plants steadily increased with the booming economies worldwide. But except for a handful of interested individuals, carnivorous plants remained obscure to the general public. Venus flytraps, dug up out of their native North Carolina habitat and sold as an occasional novelty, were the only insect-eating plant available on the mass market. No popular literature on the plants appeared except for occasional articles in magazines such as *National Geographic.*

The modern carnivorous plant hobby began in earnest during the seventies. Two hobbyists, Joe Mazrimas in California and Don Schnell in North Carolina, began to communicate with other collectors around the world. This developed into the International Carnivorous Plant Society (ICPS) and its publication: *The Carnivorous Plant Newsletter.* For the first time, enthusiasts had an organized format to exchange cultural information as well as seed and plant material from around the world.

The seventies and eighties also saw the publication of several books on the subject, as well as a few nurseries and collectors that began to take the ecology of carnivorous plants seriously. Instead of removing plants from their rapidly diminishing native habitat, they began to propagate them. Three nurserymen who helped distribute hundreds of rare, sought-after carnivores were Adrian Slack in England, Marcel Lecoufle in France, and Bob Hanrahan in the United States. Plants that many hobbyists never dreamed they would see in their lifetimes were suddenly becoming available.

The nineties have seen a steady increase in the popularity of carnivorous plants. Smaller local societies, usually associated with the ICPS, have sprung up in various parts of the United States, Europe, and Australia. Tissue culture propagation has made many once rare plants common and affordable. Numerous nature programs on cable television are making carnivorous plants more visible to the general public. The plants are beginning to appear more often at flower shows and public botanical gardens. General nurseries are retailing a wider variety than just the familiar Venus flytrap.

So how does one use this book?

I have written *The Savage Garden* as a practical guide to growing carnivorous plants (which, for the sake of brevity, I will refer to as "CPs" throughout the rest of the book). It is divided into three main parts: Part 1 covers the primary points of cultivation, including hard goods. Part 2 outlines the various places you can grow CPs, from greenhouses to bog gardens. Part 3 introduces all the popular genera of insect-eating plants, as well as their history, habitats, and habits, including their specific cultivation requirements. This is followed by a brief section on resources.

❧ PART ONE ❧
THE BASICS OF
CULTIVATION

Sarracenia flava "red tube form" with *Drosera filiformis* ssp. *tracyi* and *Pinguicula* species in an open, wet, sunny habitat in the Florida panhandle.

Dr. LARRY MELLICHAMP of the University of North Carolina once told me, "Whenever I have seen carnivorous plants in the wild, whether it was in South Africa, the Florida panhandle, or Northern California, the habitats were often strikingly similar." Broadly speaking, this is a rather true statement, although of course some CP habitats are vastly different from others. I have been struck by the similarity of pygmy forest bogs in Mendocino County, California, to those I had explored as a youngster clear across the continent in the pine barrens of New Jersey. If someone were to show me photos of each, they would be virtually indistinguishable. In fact, in a small boggy area of the pygmy forests near Fort Bragg on the Northern California coast, many carnivorous plants from around the world have been introduced, much to the annoyance of ecological purists. Once privately owned, this bog is now managed by the Nature Conservancy. Although the only native carnivorous species is *Drosera rotundifolia,* plants that have been introduced and have been growing well for many years include Venus flytraps from North Carolina, many *Drosera* species from South Africa, Australia, and Asia; *Sarracenia* from the southeast of North America; *Pinguicula* from Europe; and *Darlingtonia,* whose native habitat is found a few hundred miles to the north of Fort Bragg. Even *Heliamphora,* from Venezuela, survived—until the plants were stolen!

The above example illustrates that many CPs grow in habitats so similar to one another that cultivating the plants is simplified by an understanding of a few general facts. Carnivorous plants typically inhabit wet, low-nutrient soils through which water may be slowly moving. This moving water usually carries away what minerals there are in the soil, which explains why it tends to be low in nutrients. The soil is often sandy, with a ground cover of patchy mosses such as sphagnum, which turns into peat as it ages. The habitat is often sunny, and the few trees are commonly stunted due to the infertile soil. Pines or other evergreens, whose needle-droppings may further add to the soil's acidity, are most common in such habitats. Grasses are also common. In short, a wet, low-nutrient, sunny environment is preferred by most CPs. The only major difference between habitats, usually, is the climate.

SOILS

Specific soil recipes will be offered in the section on genus cultivation. Here I will discuss the individual ingredients used in most artificial soil mediums for carnivorous plants.

Peat Moss

Peat moss is probably the most important soil ingredient for most CPs. It must always be sphagnum peat moss; the word "sphagnum" must always appear on the moss' packaging. Peat moss is usually sold in packages ranging from small bags to large, dried, bricklike bales. It is commonly of Canadian, Irish, or German origin. It is a fibrous moss, with

Soils

TOP: Soil ingredients for carnivorous plants. *Left to right, top:* Pumice, lava rock, perlite. *Bottom:* Peat moss, sand, vermiculite.

LEFT: Dried long-fibered sphagnum moss is on the left. On the right is decorative green moss—lethal to carnivorous plants.

a consistency close to a fine sawdust, and from light to dark brown in color. It is available in most general nurseries, usually as an additive for garden soils. It is what many carnivorous plants grow in naturally. Sphagnum peat is very acidic, usually with a pH between 3 and 5. (On a scale of 1 to 14, a pH of 7 is neutral.) It can hold as much as ten times its own weight in water.

Peat moss should be broken up until it is similar to sawdust before it's used, with all lumps and clods gone. It should then be mixed with water until it resembles a soft, wet mud. Then it is ready for use. Avoid sedge peat or Michigan peat, which are entirely different substances. If the package doesn't say "sphagnum," don't use it!

Long-Fibered Sphagnum Moss

This is a problematic soil ingredient for two reasons. The first is that what is sold in most nurseries is often not sphagnum moss at all, but decorative green moss or "Oregon sheet moss." "Sphagnum moss" has unfortunately become the generic term used for any dried, fibrous moss used in horticulture. Decorative moss is often used as a basket liner or topdressing for potted plants, as is true sphagnum. Worse, I have seen packages of decorative green moss actually for sale as sphagnum moss. I have seen many CPs killed because decorative green moss was mistaken for true sphagnum.

Further complicating the situation is the confusion between long-fibered sphagnum and sphagnum peat. Sphagnum moss, usually greenish or reddish in color, grows along the surface of the moss bed in a typical bog. It grows in long, ropy strands, with the growing head of the strand at the bed's surface. These strands can be rather lengthy, extending deep below the surface of the growing tips. Only the first few inches at the surface are colorful and alive. Underground, the moss turns brown and a couple of feet below decomposes into sphagnum peat moss. The peat may extend quite a way underground and may be hundreds of years old. Testifying to the sterile conditions of the moss is the fact that centuries-old, virtually unspoiled human bodies have been found deep within peat bogs in Europe.

Long-fibered sphagnum usually refers to the dried, ropy strands collected from the moss bed's surface. Sphagnum peat is the decomposed moss harvested from deep underground. In soil recipes for most carnivorous plants, it is the more reliably labeled peat moss that is the preferred ingredient. For the few plants preferring long-fibered sphagnum moss, be sure you obtain your moss from a knowledgeable dealer. When in doubt, use the peat.

There is another item, available less frequently in specialty nurseries, known as New Zealand moss or New Zealand sphagnum. It is most often available through orchid dealers, as this moss is a recent favorite of orchid growers. New Zealand moss is a true, long-fibered, high grade sphagnum from the alpine bogs of that country. It is cleaned and sterilized before export, and is an excellent medium for plants that prefer long-fibered sphagnum. It is pale yellow in color, and is resistant to decomposition. Unfortunately, it is also very expensive. I have found that domestic long-fibered sphagnum, often sold uncleaned with twigs and leaves interspersed, works just as well and is much more affordable.

Live Sphagnum Moss

Living sphagnum is a beautiful moss...lush, billowy, and colorful when well grown. Many carnivorous plant growers love the sight of bright green or red sphagnum covering the soil surface of a potted CP, even if it isn't used throughout the whole pot. Live sphagnum can be induced to grow as a topdressing to peaty, wet soils, although sometimes with difficulty.

The drawbacks to live sphagnum are many. First, it is difficult to obtain commercially. Second, it grows slowly. Third, when it does grow, it will easily cover up small plants like Venus flytraps, causing them to rot. Fourth, it is difficult to maintain. Hot sun will burn the growing tips and the lightest application of fertilizers or minerals can cause algae growth and death to the moss.

Among my own plants I have found that the only reliable place live sphagnum will grow for the long term is as a topdressing in pots of highland *Nepenthes* or similar genera that receive frequent overhead sprinkling with purified water. Live sphagnum will not survive for more than a year in hothouses, as the moss usually grows in cool alpine climates or climates with cold winters.

Live sphagnum will also usually grow well outdoors in climates that are humid and receive lots of rain. It will succeed in very wet bog gardens and, for instance, undrained tubs of tall Sarracenia. Since this is a live "soil" that grows, trimming will be needed to keep it from crowding smaller plants.

Dried, unsterilized long-fibered sphagnum can be encouraged to grow if you follow the above suggestions. Dormant spores in the moss will germinate if the moss is kept cool and very wet. Place some well-soaked, long-fibered sphagnum in an airtight plastic bag or in a seed tray covered with a clear plastic dome lid. Place it in a cool, bright area, and after many weeks the moss should start to grow.

Milled Sphagnum

This is dried, long-fibered sphagnum moss that is shredded to the consistency of fluffy, coarse sawdust. Usually sold as a medium on which to germinate seed, and resistant to the dreaded damp-off fungus that attacks seedlings in damp environments, it would be excellent as a peat substitute were it not so expensive.

Peat Pellets

These are condensed beads of sphagnum peat moss, most often used to filter the water of acid-loving fish in aquariums. It can serve as a medium for some CPs rather successfully.

Sand

All sand used in soil recipes for carnivorous plants should be sand that has been well washed. Nurseries and garden centers usually have washed silica or other sands available for use with potted plants. Washed "play sand" meant for use in children's sandboxes is also good, and is often sold in plant nurseries. Avoid self-collected beach sands or river sands, which are often contaminated with mineral salts.

Perlite

Perlite is a mineral rock that is heated until it expands, creating a light-weight, granulated soil additive that will hold both water and air. Usually white in color, it is available at garden centers. Fine and medium grades are preferred for most CPs. As it is sterile, it adds no minerals to the soil.

Pumice

Another lightweight, airy, sterile rock used in horticulture. It's usually gray in color.

Lava Rock

This volcanic rock is sterile, reddish brown in color, and available at most garden and landscape centers.

Vermiculite

This is a mica, processed similarly to perlite and serving a similar purpose. It is usually a golden-brown color. Since most vermiculites contain some minerals (such as magnesium and potassium), it is used less often for most CPs but is excellent for a few varieties that grow in slightly richer soils, such as Mexican butterworts and *Nepenthes*.

Orchid Bark

Available at most garden centers, this is usually the bark of evergreen trees. Popular for orchids, it is helpful in soils for *Nepenthes,* among other CPs, and makes a decorative topdressing on peaty soils used for plants such as *Sarracenia.* A fine-grade bark is preferred by CPs.

Shredded Bark

Similar to orchid bark, this is shredded to the consistency of confetti.

Osmunda or Tree Fern Fiber

This natural material is usually blackish brown in color and has a consistency not unlike broken toothpicks. It is used to aerate soils.

Charcoal

Only charcoal meant for horticultural purposes should be used. Charcoal is rarely needed for most CPs, but it is helpful to aerate soils enjoyed by plants such as *Nepenthes.* It is also sometimes used in soils for terrariums. Charcoal is known to neutralize chlorine and is found in CP habitats that commonly burn in the wild.

Rock Wool

This interesting substance is sometimes used for plant propagation, especially in cases where stem cuttings are used. Rock is liquefied and spun into lightweight fibers, then usually molded into small bricks. Difficult to find in the general nursery, it can sometimes be obtained through specialty houses. Bricks of rock wool retain moisture, and stem cuttings of *Nepenthes* root well in it. The entire brick is later planted in soil.

WATER

This is probably the single most important issue concerning the cultivation of carnivorous plants. Generally speaking, CPs require water that is low in dissolved mineral salts, and they usually need lots of it. Dissolved minerals are usually indicated upon analysis as p.p.m., or parts per million. Water used for the cultivation of carnivorous plants is safest for the plants when it is below one hundred p.p.m. of dissolved solids, and the lower the better. It is the use of hard, mineral-laden water that most often causes carnivorous plants to decline in cultivation. Since the majority of CPs are grown in basically undrained conditions, constant use of hard water continually adds minerals to the soil. Since CPs are adapted to grow in low-mineral soils, roots will begin to rot and the overall health of the plant will suffer when dissolved minerals are left behind as water evaporates or is absorbed by the plant. The more you water, the more minerals you add to the soil.

Some public water systems supply water that is naturally low in minerals, depending of course on where you live and where your water comes from. Your water company can supply you with an analyses of your tap water, or you can have it analyzed at a farm-supply business or pharmacy. Some folks mistakenly believe that boiling water or allowing it to sit out in an unsealed container for a day or two will allow the minerals to magically disappear. This is not true. The only thing that will vanish from the water with such treatments is the dissolved chlorine gas that is added to water to kill bacteria. The minerals, unfortunately, are left behind.

A reverse-osmosis water purifier

If you have hard tap water, the best water to use for carnivorous plants is collected rainwater or water that has been demineralized or purified. If you live in an area of frequent rainfall on a year-round basis, you can collect this water for use with CPs. Be sure, however, if you collect rainwater from the gutters on the roof of your house, that your roof has not recently been treated with fire retardant or other chemicals. In other situations, it is best to buy purified water or purify it yourself. For a small selection of plants, such as those in a terrarium under grow lights, water demand may not be high and you can purchase purified water from a grocery store or water machine.

Commercially bottled water has become a big business (in the United States, at least) as consumers have become wary of public water being contaminated and unsafe to drink. But this does not mean that any bottled drinking water you buy in a store is safe for carnivorous plants! Often, bottled drinking water is purified and salt is added to improve the taste. (Purified or distilled water can taste rather flat.) So if you buy prebottled water, make sure the water is distilled or specifically states that it is low in sodium. Do not use mineral water, mountain water, or spring water, unless the label states it has been purified or is low in sodium.

If you purchase your water from a water machine, make sure you are buying low-sodium water. Some water machines offer a choice of salted drinking water or purified, low-sodium water. Always choose the latter. If you have bottled water delivered to your home or business, again, this is most often water that has been purified and has then had salt added to improve the taste. You can often request low-sodium water from the vendor who supplies your prebottled drinking water.

If your water use exceeds more than a couple of gallons a week, the only answer is to purify your own. Distilleries are impractical for home use, as much fuel is needed to boil water to evaporation and recondense it as distilled water. Much more practical is a reverse-osmosis unit to produce your own purified water. Reverse-osmosis (R.O.) systems used to be expensive and hard to find, but in recent years prices have gone down dramatically and under-the-sink units are available in most large home-supply and hardware stores, or at some specialty plant nurseries.

Most under-the-sink units run tap water through particulate canister filters, then through the R.O. membrane, which "squeezes" the water through a fine micron filter, separating the good, purified water from the bad, mineralized water. The former is collected in a tank under the sink, while the latter goes down the drain. The collected purified water, about 99 percent free of dissolved solids, is usually accessible through a separate faucet on the sink. A typical system of this sort will produce between three to five gallons a day of pure water. The wastewater can be as much as five to ten times the amount of pure water collected.

No-frills R.O. systems can be purchased through nurseries or magazines catering to people who need pure water for plants, such as orchid and CP growers. These units are hooked up to hose bibs in the garage or a protected place outdoors. With these simplified units, the user collects the purified water in his or her own bottles, water tanks, or clean plastic waste cans. The wastewater is either allowed to go down a sink drain or run out via a tubing for use in the general garden. (Most garden plants are unaffected by the concentrated minerals, and rain will leach them away.)

R.O. units of either type should have their particulate prefilters changed every three to six months. The R.O. membrane itself will need to be replaced every two to four years, and is usually available through the supplier. If your water is chlorinated, you might prefer that at least one of the prefilters be charcoal-based to neutralize the dissolved chlorine gas in the water. Otherwise, let the purified water sit in an open container for a day or two and the chlorine will dissipate on its own.

The life of an R.O. membrane can be extended if your tap water first goes through a conventional water softener. However, the water softener adds salt, so using softened water directly will kill your plants rather quickly. Once water from a softener goes through the R.O. unit, all of the added salt will be removed.

Since water purified through reverse-osmosis is good not only for plants but for people too, I should add a cautionary note. Never let R.O. water meant for drinking sit out unrefrigerated for more than two days or so. Airborne bacteria, harmless to plants, may contaminate the water and make you ill. Always refrigerate R.O. water intended for human consumption.

THE WATER TRAY METHOD

Since most carnivorous plants need to grow in soils that are permanently wet, the easiest way to accommodate them is to grow the plants in pots that have drainage holes at the bottom, and set the pot in a saucer or tray that always has some water in it. The majority of CPs are happy when approximately one inch or so of water is maintained in the saucer at all times.

There is a wide variety of containers that can be used as a water tray, and unless you are around your plants all the time, or have a dependable person to water your plants when you are away, I recommend you search for rather large saucers to accommodate your plants.

In the greenhouse, most collectors use large, undrained seed flats that can hold several pots and are around two inches in depth. For single pots, regular saucers may be used but should be one or two sizes larger than normal so it will hold as much water as possible. There are plastic saucers available that are extra deep, often as deep as the pot, and these are excellent for most CPs. Extra deep saucers are often used for houseplants whose pots sit in decorative baskets. They make great containers for pots of CPs because water can be flooded to the top of the pot and allowed to gradually evaporate before you add more. Not only will you have to add water less frequently, but this technique mimics the habitats of those carnivorous plants that live in soil waterlogged after heavy rains. As the water table drops, oxygen will permeate the still-wet soil.

So-called self-watering pots, sometimes used for plants such as African violets, are generally unsuitable for CPs. These pots work with wicks set into a water tray. They will keep the soil lightly dampish, which is fine for most houseplants but not wet enough for most CPs.

Avoid using clay saucers, unless they are glazed and therefore waterproof. Plastic water troughs can be decorative and large enough to hide the pots themselves. Busboy and dish tubs may not be attractive, but can serve the same purpose. The same goes for clean kitty litter trays.

POTTERY AND CONTAINERS

Generally speaking, plastic pots are usually best for carnivorous plants, but as we will later see in the section on genus cultivation, there are exceptions to this rule. Terra-cotta clay pots are usually avoided for several reasons. Evaporation will be high through the porous material, and clay can absorb harmful mineral salts that may accumulate in the soil. Also, since the soil is usually kept rather wet, unsightly and slippery algae and mosses may grow on the pot's surface. However, you will see in Part Three, on individual varieties of CPs, that there are a few plants that will actually prefer terra-cotta clay pots.

On the other hand, clay pottery that has been glazed makes very attractive and suitable containers in which to grow CPs. Glazed pots may be of the type with holes in the bottom, which can then be set into a saucer of water. But some CPs, such as *Sarracenia* and most *Drosera, Utricularia,* and *Pinguicula,* will also thrive in undrained pottery that has been glazed.

Although the tray system is the most common method used to grow carnivorous plants, it certainly is not necessary if you grow the plants

Pottery and Containers

LEFT: Containers for carnivores. *Clockwise from upper left: Sarracenia minor* in a plastic pot and saucer; *Darlingtonia* in a glazed ceramic pot and saucer; *Nepenthes villosa* in a wooden box; an undrained, glazed ceramic with *Drosera intermedia, D. filiformis* ssp. *filiformis* and *Utricularia gibba; Pinguicula moranensis* in an undrained ceramic teacup. ABOVE: *Sarracenia minor* "Okee Giant" in an undrained glazed ceramic bowl.

in undrained containers. These containers should be waterproof and made of materials such as plastic, glazed clay, or glass. Containers that are wooden may be lined with a durable sheet plastic, thus making them both undrained and waterproof. When CPs are grown in an undrained container, the soil should remain wet at all times. The water table should be allowed to fluctuate somewhat, from waterlogged to damp, so that air may be allowed to enter the soil.

Undrained containers are certainly not suitable for all carnivorous plants. *Nepenthes,* for instance, always requires wet but well-drained soil, and Venus flytraps and the West Australian pitcher plant generally despise undrained containers unless they are particularly deep. In short, while almost all CPs grow in wet soils, the degree of that wetness may vary from genus to genus.

NATURAL LIGHT

Only rarely will you find carnivorous plants growing in the wild in deep, dense shade. Although a few tropical pitcher plants may grow in the shade of a forest canopy, and several butterworts may be protected from sun by growing in shaded grottos of dripping, wet rock, the vast majority of CPs are found in open, sunny habitats. The occasional pine tree or tall grasses may offer partial shading in some instances, but for the most part sunlight is as important to many carnivorous plants as wet, acidic soil.

Let me be clear about what I mean when I use the terms "sunny," "partly sunny," and "bright shade" throughout this book. By "sunny," I mean that the plant will do well outdoors in full sun for most of the day. On a windowsill, sun should shine directly onto the plants for at least a few hours. A greenhouse should be in full sun most of the day, even when shadecloth is applied. "Partly sunny" conditions means that direct sun should bathe the plant for at least two to four hours, the rest of the time being spent in bright shade. "Bright shade" means intense light, but direct sun should not hit the plant for more than an hour or so each day.

How much sun your plants should receive may be influenced by where you live and how you grow them. In the northern hemisphere, east-facing windowsills receiving morning sun are generally less hot and burning than a west-facing window receiving afternoon sun. Some plants will look lush and beautiful at the former location, yet may burn at the tips and suffer low humidity at the latter. A trumpet plant outdoors in full sun in a humid state like Georgia may be lush and green, but a grower in California may find that the low humidity dries out the plants in the afternoon sun. The Californian will have healthier plants when they are exposed to sun only in the morning, or protected by a canopy of shade cloth in the afternoon.

Photoperiod (the length of time a plant is in the light) is an important part of natural lighting. This light does not necessarily mean direct sun. Along the equator, the daylight/darkness period is more or less evenly divided, with roughly twelve hours of daylight and twelve hours of darkness. In a temperate zone, the daylight/darkness ratio changes season to season as the earth spins along its axis of rotation, so a *Nepenthes* from the tropics may receive an evenly divided day and night period through much of the year, while a Venus flytrap from North America may receive fifteen hours of light in summer and only nine hours of light in winter. This is very important when a grower is considering the dormancy or rest period of temperate carnivorous plants. Some people may think that cold weather is what makes a temperate species hibernate, but that is only half of the story. The length of the daylight period is the story's other half. Photoperiod also influences other things in the life cycle of plants, such as flowering times and the formation of reproductive brood bodies, as in the pygmy sundews.

DORMANCY

Dormancy in plants is rather similar to hibernation in animals. Many carnivorous plants go dormant during adverse seasonal conditions. Most temperate plants that grow in climates with cold winters and short daylight periods lose their leaves and stop actively growing during this time. As the weather warms up in spring and the photoperiod gets longer, the plant resumes its growth.

Dormancy can also take place for other reasons. As we will see with plants such as tuberous sundews from western Australia, almost the

opposite occurs. Some plants actively grow during the cool, wet winters, and then go dormant as the days get longer, heat increases, and the winter-wet soils dry out.

Dormancy in carnivorous plants that require it must be respected and permitted to occur. Otherwise, the plant may die. A temperate Venus flytrap, for example, grown in tropical-like conditions such as a

Dormancy is crucial to many carnivorous plants. *Left to right: Sarracenia oreophila* showing characteristic phyllodia, *Drosera filiformis, Dionaea m., Sarracenia rubra* ssp. *alabamensis.*

warm terrarium with grow-lights operating permanently on a sixteen-hour photoperiod will eventually get sickly and die.

Winter dormancy in temperate carnivorous plants generally requires two things: a shortening of the photoperiod and a cooling of the temperature. For plants requiring a summer dormancy, usually a drying out of the soil is crucial. Other varieties, like most Mexican butterworts, change from a carnivorous habit during wet, hot summers, to a noncarnivorous stage of succulent-like growth during the cooler and drier winter months, when most of the subtropical zone experiences a drought.

For the most part, if left alone and if grown in the proper environment, carnivorous plants will go dormant on their own. Allow them to do so; you should never force a carnivorous plant into growth during a season when it should be resting.

People who live in tropical places often wonder if they can grow temperate plants there. The answer is yes, sometimes, if some extra effort is made to accommodate a plant's cool rest period. An American pitcher plant, for instance, grown outdoors in a warm, subtropical place like Hawaii, may need to be uprooted, put into a plastic bag, and refrigerated during the winter. If the Hawaiian gardener lives in the cooler highlands, the temperature drop and shorter daylight period in winter may be sufficient to carry his or her plant through its winter rest period. Cool basement windowsills may offer a similar environment.

ARTIFICIAL LIGHT

You live in a fifth-floor apartment in, let's say, Quebec, Canada, and all of your windows face north and are sunless. You have no patio to summer-grow your plants, and the fire escape is in permanent shade. Can you still grow carnivorous plants? Yes. In fact, even if you live in a dark basement or a densely shaded house in a redwood forest, carnivorous plants can thrive even in the darkest of corners. The solution is to grow them under artificial light, which can be done with or without a terrarium.

There is no doubt that the easiest and most affordable way to artificially light carnivorous plants indoors is to use fluorescent grow-lights. Equally good, but more expensive, are the Halide and sodium incandescent bulbs specifically meant for growing plants. These high intensity lights are more suitable for growing taller plants in a larger area.

Bulbs can be purchased of such high wattage that an entire room can be turned into a jungle, although you may have to sell the rest of your house to keep up with your electrical bills!

If you wish to use fluorescent lights, the most convenient size are the 40-watt, 48-inch-long tubes that will fit into 4-foot-long "shop-light" fixtures. These fixtures will sit comfortably on top of a 55-gallon "long" aquarium, or may be supported by other means if you don't wish to use a tank. Smaller size tubes are also available. You may use brands such as Vita-Light, Gro-Lux, or GE Plant and Aquarium Lights for a good spectrum for plant growth. Use a minimum of four bulbs for a 55-gallon tank. Two bulbs can be used over 20-gallon tanks. It is a good idea to surround most of the growing area with reflectors such as mirrors, Mylar, white cardboard, or other material that will reflect otherwise lost light back onto the plants. More will be said about this under the section on terrariums (page 41).

There is a common misconception about how far below the fluorescent lights the plants should be. The lights should generally be no further than ten to twelve inches above the pots, and even closer is better. Naturally, this means that tall plants such as mature *Sarracenia* are usually unsuitable for fluorescent grow-lights.

Halide and sodium lights, on the other hand, typically begin with a wattage of 175, and can be suspended about 24 inches above the pots. One 175-watt bulb will give you a growing area of about 6 square feet. Higher wattage bulbs will, of course, give you more growing space.

High intensity bulbs, because of their brilliance, are not the type of lights you would use, say, in a living room, unless you enjoy sitting next to a supernova! Usually growers will suspend these lights over tables in basements or large closets, as the light will be rather distracting elsewhere.

One form of grow-lights I cannot recommend for carnivorous plants are GE Grow and Show light bulbs, which are funnel-shaped, blue-tinted incandescent bulbs used for houseplants. The heat produced by these lights is too strong and the plants need to be too close to them for good growth. Plants such as sundews will dry out and be burned by them.

If the humidity in your home usually remains above 50 percent, many carnivores, such as Venus flytraps, Mexican butterworts, sundews, and most pitcher plants, will do fine out in the open and will not need a tank or aquarium. However, most CPs appreciate the higher humidity provided by such enclosures, especially the tropicals. We will discuss this further under the section on terrariums, beginning on page 41.

fEEDiNG YOUR PLANTS

> *"I gotta find food for Master. Food I gotta find for Master. For Master I gotta find food."*

—SEYMORE KRELBORN, *Little Shop of Horrors,* 1960

In horticulture, feeding one's plants usually means the application of fertilizers. With carnivorous plants, of course, we are speaking literally!

If you are growing your plants outdoors, feeding them certainly won't be necessary. CPs will lure, catch, and eat numerous insects outdoors on their own. Flies, ants, gnats, moths, beetles—the different plant species will attract and feed on prey similar to those they lure in their natural habitats. Flying insects usually are the most common victims. But even ants won't necessarily be saved by the water trays that surround the pots. Older trumpet leaves may lean over and touch the ground, providing a bridge for ants to cross. Some folks I know purposely put twigs or sticks across water barriers to entice crawling insects to visit their potted plants—a visit the insect may later regret.

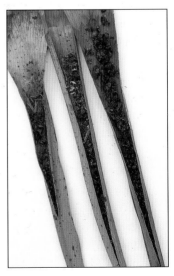

Be warned, however, that bridges to pots set in water trays will also allow certain pests access to your plants, and a slug may eventually be caught in a flytrap only after having munched a few holes in a tender and newly emerging *Sarracenia* leaf.

Outdoors, some carnivores will catch such large quantities of insects that the result can be startling. A sundew's leaves may be black with gnats, every flytrap leaf may be shut tight upon flies, and American pitcher plant trumpets may topple from the weight of

An autopsy on *Sarracenia* proves they are gluttonous pigs.

hundreds, if not thousands, of prey. Sometimes the pitiful buzzing of trapped yellow jackets or flies may be unsettling to some people. The sensitive should never peer down the tube of a trumpet plant that is infested with ants and flies. The ants, quite insane by their predicament, will be merciless toward the helpless housefly who tumbles into their madhouse prison. At times, I have been so disturbed by their suffering I have freed ladybugs and even yellow jackets from an agonizing death.

And speaking of ants, I have a warning: Ants in a greenhouse will not only provide ample food for American or tropical pitcher plants, they will also sometimes begin to cultivate some of their own food, namely scale insects and aphids, from which the ants extract honeydew. This may be a revenge tactic of the ants: plant eats ants, ants farm scale on plant, scale sucks juices from plant, ants feed on scale honeydew. Nature works in funny ways.

Ants in the greenhouse are often of the nomadic sort. A queen may set up a nest in a potted *Nepenthes,* wondering where all her workers are disappearing to. (I have never found ant nests to do any particular damage to the roots of a potted CP.) When the pot is watered, the whole nest swarms in a panic, carrying eggs and pupae out of the deluge. They promptly move the nest to another pot, or return when the water drains.

If you have ant nests in your potted greenhouse plants, keep an eye on them. At the first sign of scale, you will have to use an insecticide, or you may want to discourage the ants by laying a few flea collars around the infested pots to keep the ants away. You'll find more about this under the section on pest control, beginning on page 25.

For plants grown in insect-free areas, you will have several possibilities of how to go about feeding them. One method is to simply hand-feed them. Usually, forceps or tweezers are helpful: if you catch a fly yourself, it is usually much easier to apply the doomed insect by means of forceps into the maws of a Venus flytrap, because you will have to stimulate the trigger hairs within the trap; you cannot simply drop the fly in. Often the fly escapes just as the trap closes, which is as cruel to the plant as stealing candy from a baby. Be sure to wash your hands after handling germ-ridden flies, and urge children to do likewise...or feed plants cleaner food such as sow or pill bugs.

Many CPs eat tiny insects. You can gather small ants from an ant trail on a sidewalk with a damp paper towel and drop them into a paper cup. Your neighbors may think you strange, but if they know you grow carnivorous plants, they probably think you're strange anyway! You will have to separate the ants from the grains of sand and other debris. Then the ants can be sprinkled on plants such as sundews or butterworts.

Alternatively, some windowsill plants may be placed outdoors temporar-

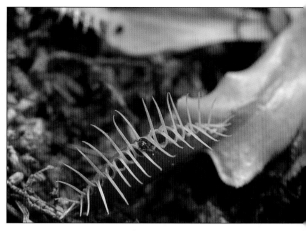

The unhappy face of an earwig as it is digested alive

ily to catch their own food. Be careful not to place them in an area hotter or sunnier than their normal environment, or the plant may burn or go into shock. Shade is best for a windowsill plant placed outdoors for "the hunt."

Aquatic bladderworts typically feed on minute swimming things such as daphnia (water fleas). You can collect these in almost any pond or lake with a paper cup, then add the contents to the water bowl where you grow your *Utricularia.*

Perhaps the easiest way to feed most carnivorous plants grown in an insect-free environment is to visit your local pet shop. Here you will usually find a great assortment of insect food, particularly if the shop caters to reptile and amphibian fanciers. Live crickets, from pinhead-sized newborns to adults, can be used to feed various plants from Venus flytraps to pitcher plants. Wingless fruit flies can be fed to sundews, butterworts, rainbow, and other sticky plants. Mealworms will drown quickly when dropped into various pitcher plants, but make sure they don't escape or they may infest your soil.

You can also freeze these insects for future use, whether you purchase them or catch them yourself. If feeding your plants live insects makes you feel ill or guilty, there is also an assortment of dried insect food available at good pet shops, which most carnivorous plants readily accept. Some are even vitamin fortified! Dried flies, musca larvae, and ant eggs will save you much fuss and bother. Even plants like sundews, which normally require some moving stimuli to activate the feeding process, will soon curl around and drool over a dried insect applied to the leaf.

Carnivorous plants will also sometimes eat human food. (I am not suggesting you feed your plants humans, since this is highly illegal....) Some CPs will accept and even drool over tiny bits of raw hamburger, cheese, powdered milk, and even chocolate (female plants). But these food products may be harmful to your plant, especially if they are overfed. A sundew leaf may curl around a bit of Hershey's chocolate, soon secreting digestive juices and making a pig out of itself. But a few days later, mold or fungus may set in, so it is best to avoid such food as a regular part of the diet.

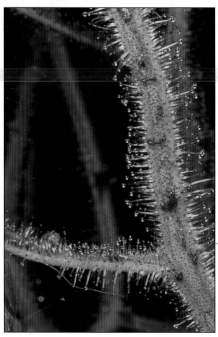

This staghorn sundew is a graveyard of insects.

Do carnivorous plants really need to eat insects for their health and well-being? The answer, in my opinion, is more of a yes than a no. Insect food is highly beneficial to most CPs in that it provides them with the extra nutrients they need to flower, set seed, and grow larger each year. When deprived of such nutrients and minerals, a gradual decline in the plant's health will occur over time. They may not flower or set seed. The following year the plant may grow weaker, and the year after that weaker still.

On the other hand, a *Sarracenia,* for instance, when going dormant in autumn, sends all of those minerals from the thousands of insects it has caught in its leaves down into its rhizome for winter. The rhizome swells, more offshoots develop, and more flowers are sent up in spring. The stored energy has to go somewhere!

This does not mean you have to feed your plants on a daily basis during the growing season. A once-a-month feeding schedule from spring through autumn will usually do the trick. A few houseflies for your flytrap or a dozen or so crickets for your pitcher plants will usually provide the plants with the minerals they need for good growth.

But you will probably notice that your healthiest plants are the ones that have eaten the most!

FERTILIZING CARNIVORES

The basic rule of green thumb concerning the application of artificial fertilizers on carnivorous plants is: Strongly dilute the fertilizer and apply it as a foliar feed. That most noncarnivorous plants can absorb minerals through their leaves is well known in horticulture; spraying the foliage of plants with a fertilizer can be as effective as feeding through the roots. This is of course also true with carnivorous plants. Since most of their leaves are especially adapted to absorbing minerals through specialized digestive glands, artificial fertilizers can be as readily absorbed as insect prey. By applying fertilizers on the leaves and avoiding drenching the soils, you won't have to worry about changing the low-mineral content of the plant's preferred nutrient-poor medium.

I will offer specific fertilization recipes in Part Three of this book; here I will only suggest some guidelines. First, if your plants are receiving a steady diet of insects, it is probably not necessary to feed them. But you may want to supplement their diet in the hope of growing even more vigorous plants. Or, you may be using a terrarium and do not want to hassle with obtaining insect food. Or perhaps you wish to display a plant at an upcoming flower show, and would prefer to present a beautiful but "clean" specimen, without the carcasses of digested insects distracting from the beauty of the leaves. There are some varieties of carnivorous plants that certainly seem to benefit from a regular fertilization program. Others, however, seem to detest it.

There are many fertilizers on the market that have been developed for a wide variety of plants and purposes, and different products are available in different countries, but nowhere has a fertilizer ever been developed specifically for carnivorous plants. Therefore, we must select and experiment from the general forms of fertilizers available.

Fertilizers for Acid-Loving Plants

These are readily available in most general nurseries. They are used for plants that prefer an acidic soil, such as pines, firs, rhododendrons, and so on. Since many CPs grow in acidic soils, this form of fertilizer is useful. I have used it successfully on all *Sarracenia* species, *Darlingtonia,* most but not all *Drosera,* temperate, acid-loving *Pinguicula,* most *Utricularia,* and *Dionaea.* Avoid it on tropical *Pinguicula* and most *Nepenthes.*

Orchid 30-10-10

This form of plant food is used to promote foliage growth, as opposed to bloom growth. I have used various brands on *Nepenthes, Heliamphora,* tropical *Pinguicula,* and most terrestrial *Utricularia,* and I believe it can be used successfully on most of the plants enjoying acidic conditions, as well.

Epiphytic Fertilizers

You may have to hunt for these in your nursery, as they are specifically developed for epiphytes such as *Tillandsias* and other Bromeliads. Many of these plants do not live in soils, and like carnivores absorb much of the nutritional requirements through their leaves, often in the form of leaf debris. These fertilizers were developed particularly to enhance mineral absorption through the leaves, and therefore can be quite beneficial to carnivorous plants. I have used brands such as Epiphytes Delight on virtually all carnivorous species, except those few that I will mention a bit later, which seem to dislike any fertilization regardless of the brand.

Generally speaking, fertilizers for carnivorous plants are usually best used when diluted to one fourth or one half of the manufacturer's directions. It can then be sprayed on the leaves of the plant until the foliage is wet. It is usually necessary to do this only once or twice monthly during the active growing season. (Do not fertilize dormant plants!) You can also apply fertilizer to the soil of some plants if they have good drainage and are watered frequently from overhead with purified water. Plants grown this way, such as *Nepenthes* in a greenhouse, will have excess minerals leached out of the soil every time the plants are watered. This avoids the much-feared mineral buildup. Otherwise, I would not apply fertilizers to the soil, especially in undrained containers such as bog gardens. Over time, the excess minerals will build up in the medium and possibly cause harm to the plants.

Some growers prefer to fertilize their plants more frequently using a more heavily diluted ratio. For instance, a 10 percent solution applied weekly to varieties such as *Sarracenia* can work well.

Be warned that by misting or spraying CPs with fertilizers, some will fall upon the soil surface and will subsequently encourage algae growth. The same is true of water trays, so it is wise to clean these periodically. Algae growth on soil can be scraped away with a spoon when the buildup becomes substantial, and fresh soil can be laid out to replace it. Mosses will often utilize the small amounts of fertilizers that fall upon it from mists or sprays. However, live sphagnum moss dislikes fertilizer buildup and usually only succeeds in pots that are frequently leached from overhead with pure water.

It is not wise or necessary to apply fertilizers directly into pitcher leaves. This can upset the delicate chemical balance of its digestive juices, and will often produce algae. Simply misting the foliage will benefit the plant enough.

Vitamin B-1 is a supplement for plants commonly available in nurseries, and found in the popular American brand Superthrive, which adds other vitamins and ingredients to its solution. These are not fertilizers as commonly supposed, and their use is often controversial among carnivorous plant enthusiasts. Some growers greatly applaud their use, while others find their benefits dubious. Personally, I have found products such as Superthrive quite good for carnivorous plants when one follows the manufacturer's instructions. Vitamin B-1 has long been used as a root-growth-promoting ingredient, primarily for general garden and houseplants. It is most often used when transplanting bare-rooted plants, and helps them overcome shock by encouraging root growth. Bare-rooted plants are usually soaked in a solution of ten drops per gallon of water for half an hour or so before they are put into soil. For general plant care, manufacturers of products such as Superthrive recommend a one-drop-per-gallon application with each regular watering. I have noticed that bare-root soaking of carnivorous plants in Superthrive or vitamin B-1 during the process of transplanting them can reduce losses due to shock. It is particularly helpful when moving tissue-cultured CPs from flask into soil. In my experience, losses due to shock were reduced considerably, if all other conditions were good. Keep in mind that a general application of such products in high doses will increase the growth of algae even more dramatically than is caused by the application of fertilizers. I would therefore not recommend high doses applied directly to soil.

CARNIVOROUS PLANTS AS PEST CONTROLLERS

I am often asked if insect-eating plants are suitable as pest controllers. Sometimes, yes, but more often…no.

Carnivorous plants are not the answer to problem insects in the home and garden. They will not zap mosquitoes around your patio, nor devour slugs and snails among vegetables. They are useless in combating aphids, mealybugs, or scale insects, and in fact are themselves often attacked by such pests.

But in a few limited circumstances, carnivorous plants may be somewhat helpful in controlling bothersome pests. In some situations where

Yellow Trumpets love houseflies.

African violets, orchids, and other exotics are grown, a few sticky plants such as sundews or Mexican butterworts may be helpful in reducing fungus gnats, a bothersome insect when in its larval stage. Fungus gnats lay eggs on damp soil, which develop into tiny worms that may damage the roots of seedling plants. The gnats are very common among most plants, including cultivated carnivores, but usually are not harmful unless the plants are young and the infestation great. CPs will catch the tiny flying adults in large numbers, providing food for the plant. Terrestrial bladderworts also feed on the larva underground, sucking up the minute worms in their pinhead-sized suction traps. Mexican butterworts and some larger sundews have been known since the Victorian age to be grown in greenhouses as a gnat controller.

Whitefly can be greatly reduced in enclosed places like small greenhouses where a couple of large sundews in hanging pots are grown. An excellent species is *Drosera dichotoma* 'Giant', whose pale, yellowish green leaves attract whitefly.

One hobbyist told me she had great luck catching fleas in her house by using some windowsill- and terrarium-grown CPs. At night she would place large butterworts and cape sundews in saucers on the carpet of the infested rooms. She would place a desk lamp or similar light close above the plants. The heat and light attracted the fleas, and the sticky plants would catch them. I tried this myself one bad flea season and was surprised at the positive result, although it is probably more beneficial to the plant than to any cat or dog!

Probably the most effective use for insect pest control are American pitcher plants. The trumpet varieties catch many houseflies and wasps, both of which find the *Sarracenia* irresistible. A trumpet plant on a deck, patio, or a sunny windowsill will catch a surprising number of such pests.

Restaurants with outdoor seating might benefit by having a pot of *Sarracenia* on each table instead of the usual cut flowers. The trumpet varieties can be a very ornamental conversation piece, and the plants will certainly lure and catch many flies. Good species to try would be *S. flava, S. rubra, S. alata,* and *S. leucophylla,* as well as hybrids of these.

PESTS AND DISEASES

Even though carnivorous plants eat insects, there are insect pests that, will, unfortunately, eat carnivorous plants. There are also diseases that can attack CPs. To add further to one's anxiety, larger pests such as raccoons, squirrels, blue jays, and small children can wreak havoc on outdoor collections.

Do not despair. First of all, insect pests rarely kill CPs completely. Usually the infestation makes itself known to the collector fairly rapidly. Since the plants are so hypnotically beautiful, we barely can keep our eyes off our precious plants for more than a day! Secondly, despite our fears of chemicals, most are safe if one carefully follows the manufacturer's instructions. I strongly recommend isolating treated plants in large, airtight plastic bags or small tanks to make them even safer. I repeat: follow the manufacturer's instructions.

Let me also state something that is quite obvious to the most experienced and confident grower: sometimes plants die. Plants are not immortal. Most can be propagated and passed on generation after generation, but even redwood trees eventually die, even if it takes over two thousand years! A few carnivorous plants are annuals, meaning they only live a year at most. Many will offer decades of pleasure (I have one

Sarracenia purpurea that has been in my care for almost thirty years). Lastly, even if your cultivation techniques are meticulous, sometimes, for reasons inexplicably mysterious, a plant may kick the bucket for no apparent reason at all. But that is rare. The causes are usually obvious.

That said, let me mention a couple of points. The first is that whenever you obtain a new plant for your collection, inspect it thoroughly—even if you purchased it from a reputable nursery. Try as they might, no nursery is infallible. Secondly, if possible, propagate the plant immediately by taking some leaf or root cuttings. On rare occasions, plants may go into shock and decline in health when moved from one environment to another. Typically they come back with vigor after an adjustment period. For example, I have taken cape sundews and *Nepenthes* from my greenhouse nursery to a windowsill in my home. Occasionally the existing growing point on the plant stopped developing and went into suspended animation. After many weeks, after adjusting to the lower humidity and light levels, new shoots appeared at the base of the stems and grew beautifully. I then trimmed off the older tops.

Finally, I must admit that when compared to other plants, there is something a little odd about growing CPs. Because so many of them seem almost animal-like—they can appear to have faces and mouths, and most can be hand-fed—for many folks they become more like pets than mere plants! We project our own self-consciousness onto these plants and become emotionally attached to them. I have seen children weep over the demise of a beloved Venus flytrap whom they affectionately named Chuck or Cynthia. (Note that "whom" seems to fit better than "that" in the previous sentence!)

The Pests

Aphids

These are tiny, sap-sucking insects barely the size of a pinhead. They attack the newly developing leaves, and are the most common pests of CPs. Since females are born pregnant, they can spread faster than rabbits. Aphids can be green, brown, or even black. They are slow-moving and occasionally they fly. Ants like to farm them for their honeydew. Symptoms of an aphid attack are twisted, deformed leaves and sometimes whitish flecks of skin castings around the crown of the plant. They most frequently attack Venus flytraps, sundews, and American pitcher plants, among others.

Pests

CLOCKWISE FROM TOP: Aphid damage on a Venus flytrap. Mealybug on *Sarracenia*. Thrip damage on *Sarracenia*.

Fungus gnat

These tiny gnats provide a good food source for plants like butterworts and sundews, and their minute, wormlike larvae are eaten by terrestrial bladderworts. I rarely consider them a pest, as they live in almost any damp soil, but a bad infestation of the larvae in a pot may negatively affect the roots of plants. A spiderlike webbing may be seen on the soil surface, especially after misting.

Mealybug

Related to scale, this bothersome pest is the most difficult to eradicate when infestations are bad. Repeated applications of systemic insecticides are usually necessary to eliminate it completely. Mealybugs are slow-moving, soft-bodied, fuzzy little bugs that enjoy attacking pitcher plant rhizomes and leaves. Symptoms of a mealybug infestation are fluffy dabs of cottony tufts among the growing points and older leaves of the plant. An excess of sooty mold (see page 31) is also a symptom.

Raccoons, opossums, squirrels, and blue jays

These can be an occasional hassle for outdoor plants. These critters enjoy playing with your water trays, carelessly tossing pots around, or digging in bog gardens in search of snails or winter storage caches. Jays love to collect shiny things like jewelry and sundews, and can also peck at *Sarracenia* to steal its bugs. I have no solutions to these problems, besides waiting for gene-splicing experiments to produce plants large enough to eat them!

Sarracenia root-borer and exyra moths

These two pests are found only in the southeastern United States, where they are a natural (and exclusive) pest of *Sarracenia*. The root-borer eats rhizomes of the pitcher plant, and is easy to spot due to the reddish orange piles of debris that appear above the rhizome. The moth attacks the pitcher leaves by sealing them up with a webbing at the mouth until the leaf crumples and withers. Both are easily controlled with insecticides.

Scale

Small, sucking insects that live under tiny, protective brown or tan oval shells barely larger than a pinhead. These clamlike shells won't move when you tease them, and are also farmed by ants. They can be scraped off the leaf, and those killed by insecticides leave their shells intact. They most often attack pitcher plants.

Slugs and snails

They occasionally chew a hole or two in newly developing pitcher plant leaves, but after ruining the leaf they seldom eat further, probably due to the taste. They can, however, ruin the appearance of butterworts and sundews, and love the bromeliad *Catopsis*.

Spider mite

The nightmare of plant lovers, this pest is only a problem in drier climates where humidity and rainfall are low. This minute pest appears as tiny red dots on the leaf, with a faint webbing not unlike that of spiders. I have only seen them on both *Sarracenia* and Venus flytraps in California during the dry summer months. Symptoms of a mite outbreak are vaguely similar to those of thripes (below), with a slight discoloration in leaf color and slow decline of the plant. Systemic insecticides are best.

Thrips

These pests attack pitcher plants, most commonly *Nepenthes, Sarracenia,* and *Darlingtonia.* These are very small, thin, black insects that move slowly while eating the surface cells of leaves. Symptoms are a silvery, "scraped" look on the leaf, with small peppery dots of their droppings. Easy to control with good pesticides, this irritating pest is damaging but not necessarily lethal.

The Controls

Many insecticides are harmless to carnivorous plants, but others can be rather damaging. Never use soap insecticides, such as Safers' Soap or Schultz Instant, as these products are alkaline and can severely harm your plants. Never use any insecticide from an aerosol spray can, as I have found the propellants to be rather harmful.

Listed below are some popular and easy-to-find insecticides that generally do CPs little or no harm. Occasionally, leaves of plants such as sundews may be damaged by prepared insecticides containing petroleum wetting agents, but the plants recover. Whenever possible, go for wettable powders, as these are mixed with water using no oils. Wettable powders are most often sold through agricultural supply companies.

Diazinon

Very good, particularly in wettable powder, but liquid brands with wetting agents (see above paragraph) such as Lily Miller appear fairly harmless.

Flea collars

Flea collars are a useful insecticide when placed in close proximity (such as in a small tank) to an infected plant. Don't let the collar come in contact with water saucers or soils.

Malathion

Another good insecticide, particularly in wettable powder form, but it may need reapplication, as it is not systemic. Good for all insect pests.

Orthene

This is the best insecticide to use, as it is systemic and absorbed by the plant, slowly poisoning the insects for many months. Excellent for mealybug, scale, thrips, aphids, and mites.

Sevin

Another good pesticide, best in wettable powder form.

Slug and snail poison

These powders and pellets are effective in keeping these pests under control. Avoid placing them on soils. Water trays and saucers provide good moats to prevent access of these pests. A slug captured by forceps makes a vengeful snack for Venus flytraps. Slightly crushed snails will provide ample vitamins for *Nepenthes*. Yum.

Some people wonder about natural controls, such as ladybugs (to eat aphids) or mealybug destroyers (beetles that eat, as you might guess, mealybugs). During an aphid outbreak one spring in my greenhouse nursery, we released ten thousand ladybugs to see what would happen. What happened was we found out that ladybugs make an excellent food for carnivorous plants, as all were eaten in about two days. Ladybugs were so drunk on the nectar of pitcher plants, we watched them stepping over aphids as they followed the nectar trails to their death. Members of a gardening group came by (timid growers of African violets, I believe) and, horrified at the wholesale massacre, promptly fled our facilities. The same result occurred when we tried the rather expensive mealybug destroyers.

Diseases

Diseases of carnivorous plants are thankfully few.

Black spot

This is similar to (or the same as; we're not sure) the disease fungus that attacks plants such as apple trees and roses. I have only seen it occur on Venus flytraps. As its name suggests, black spots appear on the leaves, gradually spreading until all the leaves rot away.

Rust spot

This fungi can cause reddish-orange spotting on *Nepenthes*. It rarely kills the plant, but can be unsightly.

Botrytis

This fungus is also known as damp-off disease. Fungus will most often attack newly sprouted seedlings and some rosetted sundews, among other plants. This most often occurs in terrariums that are overly humid, with poor air circulation and low light levels. It can also occur in greenhouses, mostly in winter, when days are cool and overcast. Botrytis appears as a gray, fuzzy growth that usually attacks the crown of a plant. I have even seen it in the wild, killing sundews during dank winters. It loves the seeds of *Sarracenia* in late winter, just as they begin to germinate.

Fungicides to control the above diseases

Benomyl was a great control, but it was removed from the market in the early nineties. Check your nursery for Benomyl replacements. In the meantime, I have had excellent results with Captan. Captan is usually sold as a powder. Follow the manufacturer's directions to make a paste of this, which can then be dissolved in water and sprayed on the afflicted plant. Two other fungicides work well, particularly on black and rust spot diseases: Domain and 3336 Cleary. A distributor of these fungicides is V-J Growers Supply in Apopka, Florida. You can call them at (800) 327-5422.

Slime mold

This delightfully named pest is, I think, actually an algae and can grow in green, oozy puddles along soil surfaces. It is usually harmless to carnivorous plants, but is rather gross-looking and liable to lose you the blue ribbon at the county fair. Fertilizers and hard water encourage its growth. Scrape it off with a spoon and replace with fresh soil.

Sooty mold

This unsightly pest is actually harmless to CPs, and most often occurs on pitcher plants, where it feeds on nectar. True to its name, it looks like black soot. It can easily be wiped off with a wet towel. However, if sooty mold is produced in excess on *Sarracenia* or *Nepenthes,* it may be also feeding on the honeydew of scale insects and mealybugs, which is a warning sign that you may need to check for these pests.

Now a word about small children. If the pitter-patter of little feet is something you hear as you stare hypnotically at your carnivorous plants, make sure your CP growing area is child-safe. I will never forget the numbness in a friend's voice when he told me his toddler had pulled the plug on his greenhouse heater the night before a big freeze!

❧ PART TWO ❧

WHERE TO GROW CARNIVOROUS PLANTS

A S WE HAVE SEEN, most carnivorous plants come from rather similar habitats. The most pronounced differences are the climates from which the individual species originate. Some varieties may require extremes of heat and cold, wetness or dryness, higher or lower humidity, photoperiod fluctuation, and so on. Therefore, there is no ideal situation in which one can grow all carnivorous plants all of the time. But there are several artificial environments in which a rather large variety can be grown. Some plants, on the other hand, may require rather specialized treatment.

But certainly gone forever are the myths that carnivorous plants can only be grown in humid terrariums or hot, steamy stove houses. Thanks to the years of experimentation by growers around the world, one can find CPs not only in greenhouses and indoor tanks, but on windowsills, decks and patios, corporate offices, outdoor bog gardens, and even in basements.

Following is a list of some of the many diverse places you can grow these unusual plants.

GREENHOUSE CONDITIONS

The controlled environment of a greenhouse is no doubt the most ideal place to grow beautiful carnivorous plants. Here is a listing of the most basic greenhouse conditions, but for more detail I suggest you also consult one of the many good books that are available at libraries, bookstores, and home-supply businesses. What follows is a listing of the main concerns for a good and functional greenhouse.

Heating

There are certainly some carnivorous plants that can be grown in unheated greenhouses, even if you live in a climate with cold winters. But most people will find it necessary to heat their greenhouses if they wish to grow a wide variety of CPs. It is always best to have the heat mechanically controlled with thermostats, and fans are helpful to circulate the air while the heat is on. Small greenhouses can often make do with space heaters designed for this specific use, and many larger heating systems are available from greenhouse specialists.

Shading

This is a requirement for most houses, and is very helpful to cut down on heat buildup from the sun, known as greenhouse effect. The two most common shading methods are shade cloth and whitewash. Usually a 50 percent shade cloth is ideal for CPs. Any denser cloth, such as 70 percent, will be too darkening for the health of most CPs. Whitewash is usually gypsum mixed with water, which is then "painted" on to the roof and sides of the house. However, whitewash frequently has to be replaced, as rain will gradually wash it away. Be warned that gypsum, being alkaline, is lethal to most CPs if it is applied by accident to their soil or water. Therefore shade cloth is often the safest product to use.

Fans

Exhaust fans in the greenhouse are another requirement, and should be set by a thermostat to turn on when heat reaches a certain temperature, usually between seventy and eighty degrees Farenheit. Automatic vents on the opposite end of the house will allow cooler outside air to enter.

Swamp or Evaporative Coolers

This is an often necessary method to cool and humidify most greenhouses. As temperature goes up, humidity goes down, and simple exhaust fans on a very hot and dry day will simply draw in hot and dry air through the house. There are many types of swamp coolers available on the market. The general systems have water dripping through pads, which is recirculated from a water reservoir. Fans are necessary to produce the effect. In small, free-standing units that look like air conditioners, a built-in fan blows air through the pads, cooling and moistening the air through an "evaporative" method. These are often called "personal coolers" in department stores. The method is the same for larger units, but typically a wall on one end of the greenhouse contains the large, water-moist pads, while the fans are usually exhaust fans located on the opposite wall of the house. When the fans are engaged, hot, dry air from the outside is drawn in through the pads by the fan's effect, cooling the temperature of that air by ten to twenty degrees while adding humidity by evaporating water.

Misting Systems

These cooling systems operate by atomizing water into a cooling mist, and can be quite effective for many greenhouses, especially where low humidity is a concern. But be warned that the water source should be purified or of a low-mineral content. Otherwise, the mist nozzles will become clogged by mineral salts and CPs will be harmed by the minerals deposited upon their leaves and soil. (And they will look unsightly when these dissolved salts dry up on their foliage.) Some plants, such as sundews, will not appreciate having their leaves frequently wetted by mist, but others, such as *Nepenthes,* thrive in such conditions.

Humidifiers

Small room humidifiers can be purchased through greenhouse suppliers, as well as home-supply businesses and drugstores. These small units are inexpensive and helpful when added humidity is needed in small greenhouses. Typically, humidifiers have small reservoirs to hold water, which is then heated and released as a vapor. These units can also be helpful for larger propagation chambers.

Air Conditioners

If you live in a climate that has extended periods of warm summer nights, yet wish to grow carnivorous plants adapted to chilly night temperatures, you may consider installing an air conditioner in your greenhouse. Some varieties of CPs require a substantial drop in night temperatures for good growth, among them highland *Nepenthes, Darlingtonia, Heliamphora,* and *Drosophyllum.* Temperatures where these species grow often drop into the fifties at night.

Types of Greenhouses

Here I will slightly amend the general information on greenhouse types and simplify their descriptions to suit the cultivation of carnivorous plants.

The Cold Frame

This type of greenhouse is unheated, except through solar radiation (the sun). This means its usefulness is dependent primarily on the climate you live in. In areas that experience cold winters, where temperatures are often below freezing, you can thus only grow carnivorous plants that come from similar climates. Generally these species have long, sustained winter dormancy. Some suitable species are *Pinguicula* from the northern latitudes, such as *P. vulgaris, P. macroceras, P. longifolia,* and *P. grandiflora; Sarracenia purpurea ssp. purpurea; Drosera rotundifolia, D. anglica* and *D. intermedia* from the northern latitudes; and those species of *Utricularia* that are from cold temperate climates.

Alternatively, if you live in a warm-temperate climate where cold winter temperatures only occasionally drop below freezing, a wider selection is available for cold frames. An unheated greenhouse in the southeastern U.S. coastal plain, much of California, the Mediterranean countries, or the subtropical coastal areas of Australia, for example, can be home to a wide range of CPs. All

A large commercial warmhouse with a hothouse in the background.

Sarracenia would be suitable, as would *Dionaea.* Temperate to hardy subtropical sundews, butterworts, and bladderworts would also do well, as would the dewy pine and cobra plant, among others.

The Cold House

This type of greenhouse would be heated when temperatures drop below thirty degrees. Suitable plants for this environment are: all *Sarracenia, Dionaea, Darlingtonia, Drosophyllum,* temperate and subtropical *Drosera, Pinguicula, Utricularia,* and *Aldrovanda.* At some risk would be the pygmy and tuberous sundews from western Australia, if the foliage were allowed to freeze.

The Cool House

Heated at forty degrees, this would be a safer environment for the plants mentioned in the preceding paragraph. But you would also be able to grow some Mexican butterworts, *Cephalotus,* and at least one *Nepenthes* species: *N. khasiana.* A few of the more cold-hardy highland *Nepenthes* species and hybrids may stop growing in winter but otherwise should survive. *Heliamphora* would do well also.

The Warm House

Heated at around fifty degrees, this type of greenhouse is ideally suited for growing a wide variety of carnivorous plants. Although a low of fifty degrees is considerably warmer than many CPs would experience in the wild during their winter dormancy, the naturally shortened photoperiod of winter would keep them dormant for a suitable enough time, unless you live in the tropics. However, the warm house would not be the best

Highland *Nepenthes* in a warm house

for plants from a northern latitude such as *Pinguicula vulgaris* or *Drosera rotundifolia,* which may do better in winter if they're placed under benches where cooler temperatures might be maintained. It is also not wise to allow the greenhouse to get too hot on sunny winter afternoons; exhaust fans should be set to cool the greenhouse at around sixty degrees.

Varieties suitable for the warm house are *Sarracenia; Dionaea;* most temperate to subtropical *Drosera,* including the pygmies and winter-growing species; all subtropical and Mexican *Pinguicula; Darlingtonia; Heliamphora; Roridula;* temperate, subtropical, and epiphytic *Utricularia; Drosophyllum; Byblis; Cephalotus; Aldrovanda; Ibicella;* the carnivorous bromeliads; and the highland *Nepenthes.*

In short, the only unsuitable varieties for the warm house would be the species from the most northern latitudes and the lowland tropicals, particularly lowland Nepenthes.

The Hot House

The heat goes on in the hot house when the temperature drops below sixty degrees. This is a good environment only for those plants considered tropical. Highland *Nepenthes* do well here, particularly if daytime temperatures don't exceed eighty-five degrees. However, much more suitable are the lowland *Nepenthes,* although a few of these might slow their growth in winter. Tropical sundews, *Genlisea, Byblis liniflora, Ibicella,* and Mexican butterworts thrive in hot-house conditions. Humidity should be high at all times.

The Stove House

Temperatures are maintained above seventy degrees, with hot days in the eighties and nineties. Only true lowland tropical species should be grown here, such as the lowland *Nepenthes, Genlisea,* tropical *Byblis,* and *Drosera.* High humidity is also essential.

Remember that if your greenhouse is large enough, you can always build a small enclosure within it and heat this section separately from the main growing area. An example of this would be heating the main section at fifty degrees (warm-house conditions) while heating the enclosure at, let's say, sixty-five degrees (somewhere between hot and stove house requirements). You can then grow lowland tropicals in this smaller space while more temperate or highland tropicals are maintained in the main house. The heating can be accomplished with small space heaters set on a separate thermostat. Heating pads used for propagation are also suitable for the warmer enclosure. Set at seventy degrees, a heating pad (there are many types available) will keep the pots warm while the air may be somewhat cooler.

Likewise, smaller enclosures within the greenhouse can be cooled separately with an air conditioner or small swamp coolers, should this be necessary in your area to grow the plants requiring cooler climates.

WINDOWSILL GROWING

A *Nepenthes* in your living room? Sundews over your kitchen sink? Butterworts in your bathroom?

Twenty years ago many carnivorous plant enthusiasts would have raised eyebrows over such possibilities, assuming that to grow a CP indoors, terrariums would be a requirement. Not necessarily so. From London to New York to San Francisco to Melbourne, many carnivores are finding happy homes in people's houses and offices, requiring minimal care while offering maximum pleasure.

This does not mean you can grow a Venus flytrap wherever you grow a parlor palm. Most houseplants are cultivated for their low light tolerance, and in fact may dislike or be burned by direct sun. CPs in general are sun lovers, and this is perhaps the most important fact to consider when choosing carnivores to grow indoors.

I use the term "windowsill" to stress the point. Most carnivorous plants, to be successful indoors, usually need to be as close to a window as possible. A windowsill or tabletop right next to the glass is the brightest place in a room, and this is what CPs would typically require.

Nepenthes khasiana, Drosera copensis "alba," and Pinguicula moranensis growing in the author's living room

Furthermore, since most carnivores are sun lovers, direct sunshine streaming through the window for at least part of the day is also a necessity, although there are a few exceptions. Direct sun should hit most CPs a minimum of two to five hours during the growing season. Bearing in mind that the sun moves about in the sky from season to season, there are few windows that receive the same amount of sun throughout the year. Many people in the northern hemi-sphere assume south-facing windows are the sunniest, but this may only be true in the winter when the sun is low in the southern sky. Come summer (the primary growing season for most plants) when the sun moves directly overhead, a southern-exposed window may receive no direct sun at all, especially if your house has a roof overhang.

Most growers have found that east- or southeast-facing windows that, in the northern hemisphere, receive cooler morning sun, are prob-ably the best indoor location for CPs. West- and southwest-facing win-dows are also quite good, but if the afternoon sun is too hot in your house, screening or sheer curtains may be needed to make the sunlight less harsh and keep the plants from burning.

There are several things to consider when growing carnivorous plants indoors. If you wish to grow temperate plants, such as the Venus flytrap or American pitcher plants, you will have to take strong heed of their dormancy requirements. It will be the shortening of the daylight period that will trigger the plant's rest period. Dormancy also requires cooler temperatures. Your plants won't necessarily require temperatures as cold as in their native habitat, but dormant plants should certainly be protected from hot sun and warm temperatures indoors.

It is therefore wise to move such dormant plants outdoors, if your climate can sustain them, or perhaps to the coolest north-facing win-dowsill in a room that is not overly heated, especially at night. Base-ment and garage windowsills can fill this requirement, as can enclosed porches that get chilly in the winter.

Some folks who have no such environment to place dormant plants may instead remove the plant from its soil late in the season and store the rhizome in an airtight plastic bag after trimming whatever leaves may be remaining on the plant. A few strands of damp, long-fibered sphagnum moss or a handful of moist peat moss can be added to the bag, and the bag may then be refrigerated over winter. Come late win-ter, the rhizome is repotted and the plant returned to the windowsill.

Minimum dormancy for temperate plants should be around three months. In the United States, I like to remind people that plants should enter a rest period sometime between Halloween and Thanksgiving and can be brought out of dormancy as early as Valentine's Day but no later than Easter. By March, and the approach of spring, the well-rested plants will begin the season's growth.

Of course, many subtropical and warm-temperate CPs will continue to grow through winter and won't require a cold rest period, although they may slow down their growth. These plants, like *Cephalotus,* Cape sundews, or the Mexican butterworts, will be happy year round on the windowsill. You may want to grow such plants on a sunny, south-facing window in winter, and by spring, move the plants to an east- or west-facing window for the summer.

Alternatively, you may grow plants outdoors in the summer and then move them to a sunny windowsill for winter, to protect them from unsuitably cold weather. In a city like Boston, you might grow Mexican butterworts or Cape sundews outdoors for the summer, then move them to a windowsill before the first frosts. Remember, if you do this with a Venus flytrap or yellow trumpet plant (perhaps because your winters are too cold to leave them outdoors) be sure you respect their rest period and keep them in a cool and sunless window.

Success with windowsill growing may depend on where and how you live. Humidity is certainly important for carnivorous plants indoors, but not as important as good light. If you live near a coastline, indoor humidity is often suitable for CPs. If you live in a desert community, air conditioning or evaporative coolers will often help plants grown on windowsills. In winter, heating your house may drop humidity drastically, especially with energy sources such as woodstoves. You may want to keep a kettle on your woodstove to replenish water vapor.

Misting indoor CPs can be quite beneficial, and I recommend you keep a spray bottle of purified water near your plants if your house is on the dry side. Wetting the foliage in the morning and evening would be appropriate if your humidity is low.

The following are all suitable for the windowsill, if conditions are appropriate: Venus flytraps; most Mexican butterworts; *Sarracenia* species and hybrids, although all will require much direct sun; most terrestrial and epiphytic bladderworts that are subtropical to tropical in origin, such as *Utricularia livida, U. sandersonii, U. reinformis,* and *U. humboltii; Aquatics* such as *U. gibba; Cephalotus; Byblis* species; Sundews such as rosetted subtropicals, Cape sundews, *Drosera regia, D. binata; Darlingtonia* will do well if your house is cool; highland *Nepenthes* such as *N. khasiana, N. x rokko, N. alata,* and *N. ventricosa,* including hybrids. Some lowland hybrids can also do surprisingly well, such as the beautiful *N. x dyeriana,* which has some highland ancestry.

TERRARIUMS AND TANKS

The method of growing carnivorous plants in tanks is still one of the most popular and enjoyable ways to raise carnivores. Not only can a well-presented tank of flesh-eating plants rival a commonplace aquarium for decorative beauty, but the maintenance can be but a couple hours a month or less, and, unlike fish hobbyists, you won't have to feed your plants every day! Also, tanks and terrariums can be kept almost anywhere in the home, school, or office. I strongly suggest you consider cultivating the plants under grow-lights, as recommended on page 15.

There are several ways of growing CPs in tanks. Although the traditional terrarium may be the first to come to mind, this old-fashioned, soil-at-the-bottom-of-an-aquarium style may not necessarily be the best. One drawback is that variety may be limited, since some plants may require a dormancy while others do not. Another problem is that some plants may spread through root or seed growth and become a weedy mess. Still further, setting up and redoing a terrarium can be a sloppy ordeal, and if one plant succumbs to disease or pests, the whole terrarium may soon follow suit. Finally, some of the plants you may wish to grow in your terrarium may require somewhat different cultivating techniques than others. A Mexican butterwort, for example, needs a somewhat drier winter and different soil than *Cephalotus*.

The next section deals with a few basic terrarium styles, moving from the easiest to the most difficult to maintain.

Greenhouse-Style Terrarium

This is my favorite method of growing CPs in tanks. Basically, you take an empty aquarium, sit fluorescent grow-lights along its glass-covered top, and grow the plants in pots that sit in individual water saucers.

There are several reasons why this method is superior. The first is variety. Kept in individual pots and saucers, you can grow *Nepenthes* in their preferred soil mix, while rainbow plants grow alongside in a completely different medium. You can grow temperate plants with the tropicals most of the year, but can easily remove a Venus fly trap or purple pitcher plant during the winter and place it elsewhere for its dormancy. Should aphids suddenly appear on a sundew recently added to the tank, it can be promptly removed and treated before the pest spreads to other plants.

A greenhouse-style terrarium at the author's home. *Left to right, back row: Nepenthes carunculata, Pinguicula moranensis x ehlersiae, Nepenthes tentaculata, Heliamphora nutans, Nepenthes macfarlandi, Drosera extrema, Nepenthes spathulata. Front row: Byblis liniflora, Drosera adelae, Drosera capensis "alba," Drosera aliciae, Utricularia livida, Pinguicula agnata and Drosera capensis "red."*

Keeping the potted plants in individual saucers allows you to maintain the wetter/drier cycle some plants may require, such as Mexican butterworts. Also, species such as *Byblis liniflora, Cephalotus,* and the *Nepenthes* would not appreciate water-logged conditions all of the time.

Probably the biggest relief comes at cleaning time. Large and heavy tanks can be an ordeal to clean when the algae and splashed soil particles become unsightly. Using the saucer method will make cleaning the tank much easier.

The third benefit of the saucer method for the greenhouse terrarium is that lower-growing plants like rosetted sundews can be raised closer to the lights by placing the pot and saucer on an empty, upside-down pot, or some other pedestal. Further, plants with larger drooping or pendulous leaves, such as forked sundews or *Nepenthes,* will be shown to a better advantage with the pedestal method. Your basic square or circular green plastic pots work well here, or you may choose an opposite approach and grow the plants in a variety of ceramic, glazed pottery.

A SUBTROPICAL GREENHOUSE-STYLE TANK

Plants should be kept in individual pots; on a twelve- to sixteen-hour photoperiod; minimum temperature 45–55 degrees; maximum temperature 75–85 degrees. The following plants do well:

Highland *Nepenthes* varieties, Cape sundews, rosetted subtropical sundews, such as *Drosera aliciae, D. spatulata, hamiltonii, venusta,* and *anglica* "Hawaii". Tropical sundews such as *D. adelae, D. schizandra, prolifera,* and *D. intermedia* "Tropical Form". Forked sundews like *D. extrema* and *D. x marston dragon*. Most pygmy sundews. All Mexican, subtropical, and warm-temperate butterworts. *Byblis liniflora. Heliamphora* species and hybrids. *Cephalotus*. Subtropical terrestrial bladderworts, such as *Utricularia sandersonii, U. livida,* and *U. calycifida*. Tropical bladderworts such as *U. longifolia, U. alpina,* and *U. reniformis*.

The above-mentioned plants do not require cold dormancies and most will generally be attractive year round. It is best to reduce the photoperiod to twelve hours in winter, gradually increasing the period to between fourteen and sixteen hours in summer. This will usually keep flowering times on schedule and also trigger winter rosettes in the Mexican butterworts and gemmae production in pygmy sundews.

HEATED, GREENHOUSE-STYLE TROPICAL TANKS

When warmed to a minimum of 60–70 degrees, the following plants do well. Photoperiod should be twelve to sixteen hours. Lowland *Nepenthes* varieties, Mexican butterworts, *Genlisea, Byblis liniflora,* Tropical sundews such as *Drosera adelae, D. schizandra, D. prolifera, D. petiolaris,* and *D. indica* varieties. Tropical bladderworts such as *Utricularia longifolia, U. alpina, U. reniformis, U. pubescens* and *U. calycifida*.

The Potted-Landscaped Terrarium

This method is rather similar to the above except that the space between the pots are filled with fine orchid bark, lava rock, perlite, pumice, or mosses to give the appearance that the plants are planted in soil. Long-fibered sphagnum makes a good medium to use for this method, and live sphagnum growing along the surface can be rather attractive. Trimming the live moss will be necessary to prevent it from overgrowing some of the shorter potted plants. One can also use orchid bark, pumice, lava rock, or perlite as a base to hide the pots, with sphagnum as a top-dressing, although the whiteness of perlite may be distracting. You can still keep the plants in individual saucers, but it is easier to set them on a base of moss, pumice, lava rock, or bark, and then raise or lower the base as would suit the plant's wetness or dryness requirements. The water table would be visible through the glass.

It can be fun to decorate a tank with this method. Raised pots of *Nepenthes* can be hidden with Spanish or sphagnum moss draped along its exterior. Potted bog grass, orchids, or ferns can make the tank more natural-looking. I like to set mossy branches, rocks, and *Tillandsia* air plants along the soil surface of such a tank, giving the appearance of a tropical jungle even if the plants are not native to such an environment. Although lethal as a growing medium, decorative or green sheet mosses can be used as a soil dressing as well.

When the plants are kept in individual pots, you have the advantage of moving them around, as with the greenhouse-style tank. Cleaning out and redoing the whole tank would be necessary—usually every one or two years.

There are four things to consider if you wish to make your terrarium more attractive and easier to maintain. One is to attach your grow-lights to a timer, so they will go on and off without your having to be around. The second is to keep your tank ventilated. This means having an air gap of one to two inches along the top of the tank to allow good air circulation. A constantly steamed-up tank with an overabundance of humidity and stagnant air is a sure invitation to mold and fungus. A third important suggestion is to line the back and sides of the tank with a reflective material such as Mylar, white cardboard, or mirrors. This will greatly enhance the strength of light upon the plants and color them up beautifully. Some growers place a removable reflector on the front of the tank, removing it when they are home or wish to view the plants. This will cause the light to bounce around the tank, and the vivid colors of the plants—even some distance from the grow-lights— will take your breath away. Finally, I like to keep a spray bottle of purified water near the tank. Giving the terrarium a heavy mist in the morning and evening will increase humidity and circulate the air.

The Classic Terrarium

Despite its limitations, the classic terrarium, where plants are grown in soil at the bottom of an aquarium, is still a feasible way of growing some CPs. The most important thing to remember is that your selection of plants should be of a variety that share a similar soil and climate in their wild habitat. In other words, don't mix temperate Venus flytraps and tropical pitcher plants, since not only do they come from differing climate zones, but their soil requirements are rather different as well.

A habitat terrarium is a fun idea. In this type of tank you would choose plants that grow in the wild together, such as a southeastern U.S. savanna. Typically, this is easy to set up: on the bottom of the terrarium, lay two or three inches of horticultural sand, pumice, lava rock, or charcoal. This will allow good drainage and a visible water table. On top of this, place a layer of premixed and wetted peat moss and sand; about a fifty-fifty ratio is good. Sloping the medium is a wise idea, so the water-loving plants can be placed in the lower portions and better-drained plants in the upper or higher grade of the medium. Usually, three to six inches of soil is good for most plants.

In a temperate terrarium such as this, when grown under artificial light, remember to fluctuate the photoperiod between winter and summer as discussed on pages 13–14. Also, dormancy will be critical in winter (see page 14); the tank should be moved to a cooler room, outdoors to a covered porch or patio, or to a garage window.

Permanent indoor terrariums, grown under artificial lights on a twelve- to fourteen-hour photoperiod, are more suitable to subtropical CPs. In a similar peat/sand soil, you can grow Cape and rosetted sundews, *Cephalotus,* some Mexican butterworts, and rainbow plants, although the latter three varieties will need good drainage. You could also scoop out some of the peat and sand, replacing it with a pocket of *Nepenthes* soil for better drainage, and try tropical pitcher plants there.

Some *Nepenthes,* such as *N. mirabilis,* often tolerate swampy conditions in the wild.

A word of warning, however. Some plants in a classic terrarium may run wild if left unchecked. *Drosera capensis* will produce so much seed that if the flower stalks are not removed, cape sundews will come up in the hundreds within a year. Some terrestrial bladderworts, like *Utricularia livida,* will spread in months throughout the whole tank until it is a mass of lovely flowers—but you may not see much else in your terrarium! Trimming the flowers will do these plants no harm.

TEMPERATE CLASSICAL TERRARIUM

Use a soil base of half peat to half sand. Photoperiod should be reduced to eight hours in winter, with cool temperatures: 40–60 degrees. By summer, increase the photoperiod to sixteen hours with temperatures of 60–90 degrees. The following plants do well:

Venus flytraps, low-growing American pitcher plants such as *Sarracenia purpurea, S. psittacina, S. rubra,* and the smaller hybrids. Warm temperate butterworts such as *Pinguicula caerulea, P. pumila, P. lusitanicum, P. primuliflora, P. lutea.* Terrestrial bladderworts such as *Utricularia subulata* and *U. cornuta.* Temperate sundews such as *Drosera rotundifolia, D. intermedia, D. capillaris, D. filiformis.*

As mentioned, this type of terrarium is difficult to maintain due to the often chilly to cold temperatures the plants require during their winter dormancy or rest period. Many subtropical plants will also succeed in such a tank if temperatures do not drop below freezing.

Heating a Terrarium

Should you desire to grow lowland tropical CPs in a tank, it is best to supply a heat source so the minimum temperature is maintained at roughly sixty to seventy degrees. To accomplish this, visit your pet shop. A simple way to heat a terrarium is to place an aquarium heater in a large jar of water and set this in the tank (the jar can be disguised with decorative mosses). Set the thermostat between eighty and ninety degrees. The warm water will also provide additional humidity.

Alternatively, various heating pads and "hot rocks" can be used to warm a greenhouse-style terrarium, particularly those designed for reptile habitats. The pads can be placed under the tank. The thermostat should be set at around seventy degrees minimum.

GROWING CARNIVOROUS PLANTS OUTDOORS

Since carnivorous plants are so exotic looking, many people assume they are all tropical in nature, which of course is far from the truth. Since there is a wide variety of CPs from various different climates of the world, chances are you live in an area where some, if not many, can be grown outdoors. Furthermore, some CPs, such as the popular Venus flytrap, can often grow better outside than inside, even if you live in a climate with cold winters. It is startling to realize that you would probably have better luck growing the flytrap outdoors year round in New York City than you would if you lived in Key West, Florida.

In Part Three of this book, we will explore the specifics of which species will grow where. Here I will give a basic overview of what carnivorous plant enthusiasts have discovered over the years. This information is, of course, quite general, and most of it from the United States. The terms I use for climate zones are defined on page 59.

Unless you live in a swamp, carnivorous plants grown outside will always be container plants. See the sections on the tray system and pottery and containers (pages 11–13) for

Many carnivores thrive on decks and patios as container plants grown on the water tray method. *Upper rear, left to right: Sarracenia flava "coppertop," Drosera binata, Sarracenia oreophila. Lower front: A garden bowl of Sarracenia flava, Sarracenia (purpurea x flava) x flava.*

more detailed information. Growing CPs outdoors is not much different than growing the plants elsewhere. The simple rule is that once you have a plant in its proper location, all you have to do is keep it watered well, and occasionally weed and trim it.

Direct sun is important to most carnivorous plants. How much direct sun will depend on the plant and where you live. As a rule, if you live in an area of high humidity, full sun will cause most CPs to become colorful and robust. Outdoors in a place like humid North Carolina, American pitcher plants, Venus flytraps, and warm temperate sundews and butterworts (all native to the southeastern United States) thrive in sunny conditions, as witnessed by the attractive bog garden displays at the North Carolina Botanical Gardens in Chapel Hill (see photo on page 52).

But if you live in California, where hot summer days often reduce the humidity to 50 percent, 40 percent, 30 percent, and even lower, some protection may be needed to keep up the appearance of your outdoor plants. Morning sun is less harsh than that in the afternoon, and screening on a porch or a cover of shade cloth will also soften the often burning afternoon rays. Strong sun combined with low humidity will cause nectar burn along the edges of trumpet plants, and may evaporate the gluey drops of a sundew. Also, water evaporation from trays and saucers can be startling. In short, if you live in a hot and dry area, CPs will benefit from morning as opposed to afternoon sun, possible protection by screening or shade cloth, and a lot of water. On hot days you may have to fill a deep water bowl up to the surface of a pot and replenish this in a day or two, as the lower humidity will evaporate the water very rapidly.

This may not be the case if you live on the coastline of a Mediterranean-like climate. California, with its numerous microclimates, can be sixty-two degrees and foggy near the beach, yet just fifteen miles inland, east of the coastal range, temperatures can be in the nineties and hot and dry. Consider your own climate when deciding where you can grow your plants outdoors.

Certainly the opposite should also be a consideration. A white trumpet plant, *Sarracenia leucophylla,* is adapted to the warm and humid summers of the Gulf coast, where it is native. If you live in Seattle or right against the Pacific Northwest coastline, *S. leucophylla* may not do very well, as the summers are often cool, foggy, and overcast. You may want to choose a sun-trap area outdoors, such as a courtyard or against a sunny exterior wall. Or better yet, build a small cold frame to house your plants, to allow the greenhouse effect to warm them.

Indoors/Outdoors

Let's say you live in Germany or Wisconsin. You want to have a nice pot of Venus flytraps, Cape sundews, or hooded pitcher plants on your sunny patio table. But your winters are too cold to grow them outdoors year round. No problem.

Venus flytraps and American pitcher plants are dormant and rather unattractive for a few months in winter anyway. They need a chilly winter, but not as cold as Wisconsin's or Germany's. Cape sundews, native to South Africa, can survive a light frost but don't require a dormancy. You can still grow these plants outdoors much of the year simply by moving them indoors for winter. Cape sundews, or other subtropicals that grow year round without a rest period, can be moved indoors to a sunny, south-facing window when the first frosts threaten in early autumn. Warm temperate plants such as flytraps can be moved indoors before the first severe freezes begin. Just remember that a Venus flytrap requires a cool dormancy. Don't place this plant on a warm, sunny windowsill in winter—you will force it into growth out of season, which will eventually exhaust and may kill it. Instead, choose a cool room, garage windowsill, or porch, out of excessive winter sun, and keep the plant there for its dormancy. Minimum dormancy should be around three months.

The Cold-Hardiness of Warm-Temperate Plants

More experimentation is needed to find out just how cold-hardy some CPs really are. But as hopeful examples, let me mention some extremes I have heard about as a nurseryman and long-time CP grower.

Venus flytraps are native only to the Carolina coastline, yet plants have been introduced and have succeeded for many decades in bogs 500 miles to the north, in New Jersey.

American pitcher plants such as *Sarracenia flava* and *S. rubra* have been successfully introduced near Vancouver, Canada, as well as eastern Pennsylvania. Published accounts indicate that outdoor bog gardens in Vermont, planted with CPs native to the southeastern United States, have survived for twenty years, with mulching for protection in winter.

A customer of my nursery once told me that in Ohio for many years he had an outdoor bog garden planted with southern CPs. Every winter, despite a heavy mulch of hay, the soil of his garden rose out of its container like a block of ice, yet all *Sarracenia* and *Dionaea* survived. In such northerly climes, the plants may not grow as fast or produce as many offshoots as in areas of longer summers, but still can grow surprisingly well.

A woman in Dallas kept her plants in pots outdoors on a patio. One winter the temperature briefly hit ten degrees. Her Venus flytraps and American pitcher plants survived, and her cape sundews returned in spring as a result of their thick roots, but she did lose a pot of Australian forked sundews *(Drosera binata)*. Even her South African bladderwort *(Utricularia livida)* survived.

Atlanta Botanical Gardens has outdoor bog gardens of CPs native to areas somewhat warmer than northern Georgia. Brief lows near zero degrees left flytraps, pitcher plants, and other warm-temperate species unharmed.

Remember that the duration of deep freezes can be a deciding factor on the cold-hardiness of CPs. Brief drops near zero degrees may not kill a Venus flytrap if temperatures quickly rise, but many weeks below freezing may lead to a plant's demise. Also, plants in a bog garden survive freezes better than in exposed pots.

Drosera capensis "alba" two months after a 24°F freeze. New plants are emerging from the older dead stem.

In Part Three on genus cultivation, I will offer more information on the cold-hardiness and heat tolerance of different species of CPs.

Tropical CPs Outdoors

If you live in a tropical climate, you can certainly grow CPs native to similar areas as outdoor container plants. Most growers report that plants such as *Nepenthes* thrive in sunny areas, but do best when protected with shade cloth from the hot tropical sun.

Altitude plays an important part in the temperature range of tropical climates. You will have better luck growing lowland *Nepenthes* outdoors if you live in a low-lying tropical region. However, if you live on a mountain above three or four thousand feet, where night temperatures can cool considerably, highland *Nepenthes* will be a better choice than the lowland varieties.

Growing warm temperate plants in highland tropical climates is also possible. People living in Hawaii, on the edge of the tropical zone, can often succeed with Venus flytraps and *Sarracenia* outdoors if they live in a cooler, high-altitude region. Folks in the lowlands may have to bare-root such plants and store them over winter in the refrigerator.

Subtropical climates, such as Miami, and warm temperate Mediterranean-like ones, such as San Diego, rarely see frost. Yet the climates are rather different in another way. The latter city will experience cool nights year round, even when summer days are warm. Highland *Nepenthes* thrive in such weather and can be successful outdoors, but only near the humid coast. Yet only lowlanders would survive the hot summer nights of Miami. In both places, it is wise to bring the plants indoors when a cold snap is predicted. Tropical *Nepenthes* may slow down or stop growing during the cooler winter months, but usually become vigorous as the weather warms up.

There are a few *Nepenthes* that have been found to be surprisingly cold hardy. I have found that *N. khasiana,* one of the most cold-tolerant tropical pitcher plants known, can tolerate brief temperature drops into the twenties without damage, when protected overhead from frost. Large *N. khasiana* returned to health after a freeze of fifteen degrees.

Some tropical sundews are also frost hardy. *Drosera adelae* has been known to return from its roots after light freezes in the San Francisco area.

Savage Gardens

Carnivorous plant bog gardens can be a center point of drama and intrigue as well as beauty. Artificial bogs can be large or small. They can be placed in the ground, so as to appear natural, or constructed in a container as a dish garden for the deck or patio. Even greenhouses can be the home of such a savage garden. Provided you have enough pure water to keep the bog wet, its maintenance can be simple for many years, requiring only basic weeding and trimming.

The plants you can grow in an outdoor bog garden will be primarily the same as the plants your climate allows you to grow outdoors year round. Greenhouse bogs will naturally offer protection in harsher weather, and smaller containers or minibogs can be moved about should protection be needed. Even in cold-temperate climates, larger bogs that are in the ground can be protected from extreme temperatures by mulching during winter dormancy, allowing plants to be grown far from their native habitats. There is even a method of growing individual carnivores in a mixed, noncarnivorous garden setting, as in a rock garden or one consisting primarily of cacti and succulents.

The Outdoor Bog Garden

Setting up a bog garden outdoors is not unlike, but much simpler than, constructing a small pond. Instead of water, the container is filled with a wet mixture of peat and sand. There are two methods of construction. The first is to dig a hole conforming to the dimensions you wish your bog to be. Its depth should be a minimum of about ten to twelve inches. Deeper bogs will hold more water, so may require less watering in drier climates. Its width should be of a size so that the center is easily accessible from the bog's edge. Very wide bogs can be later garnished with stepping stones to make access to the center easier. Remember, you won't be able to walk in your bog to weed or trim plants later.

This shallow hole is then lined with sheet plastic. It is best to use actual pool or pond liners meant to hold water. They are much more durable than greenhouse sheet plastic. If the ground soil is very rocky, you may want to

Raised bog gardens beautifully display the collection at North Carolina Botanical Garden, Chapel Hill.

place a thin layer of sand or dried peat along the dimensions of the hole, so that small, sharp rocks or pebbles won't pierce the liner when it is weighted down with the bog's soil. Liners that overlap the bog's edge can be trimmed and later covered and decorated with rocks.

You should not construct a bog in depressed areas of your property where there is a risk of flooding during heavy rains. Also, I like to put several holes in the liner around its periphery, around two to three inches below the surface of the bog's soil. This will allow drainage of excess water after heavy rains, so plants won't be permanently waterlogged.

The second method for setting up a bog garden is somewhat simpler. Instead of a pool liner, one can use a prefabricated container such as a children's wading pool or a molded plastic pool designed for a small pond or water garden. Water gardens have become so popular in recent years there are many intriguing shapes, sizes, and designs available at nurseries and garden centers. Simply excavate a hole

Bogs and mini-bogs border a pond at Atlanta Botanical Gardens.

to accommodate the molded pool and set it into the ground. Again, I recommend drilling a few drainage holes into the sides.

The peat and sand should be of equal parts, and premixed with water before you add it to the bog container. Be sure to pack it firmly. I also like to vary the depth of the surface, so that you have well-drained mounds and wetter low areas to better suit the individual species' preference. It is often fun to have a shallow depression in the bog, where water will be permanent, so as to grow aquatic bladderworts or *Aldrovanda* there. In very large bogs, you may want to have a shallow moat of water encircling the whole garden, to bar access of certain crawling pests such as slugs and snails. Aquatic carnivores or other water plants can then be grown in the moat.

Once the soil is in the garden and packed firmly, planting can begin. If you use potted plants, a bog garden can be planted at any time of the

Another view of the stunning and savage gardens at Atlanta Botanical Gardens.

year. If you obtain bare-root plants for your bog, it is best to set this up in the late winter or early spring as the plants are coming out of their dormancy.

Designing the layout of your bog will take foresight. If your garden is to be viewed from all sides, it is best to group taller plants toward the center, such as trumpet plants. Smaller varieties, such as Venus flytraps, parrot pitcher plants, and sundews are best along the outer edges. If you place your bog so it is viewed primarily from one side, such as against a fence, taller plants would naturally look best toward the back, gradually terracing the smaller varieties towards the front. Keep in mind the species' growing habits. A single crown of a sweet trumpet plant, *Sarracenia rubra,* can spread into a large dense mass in a few years. *Drosera binata,* likewise, can spread through its root system. You might consider growing such plants in a porous container within the bog, such as peat pots or cloth bags, but these in time will deteriorate anyway, and most people prefer their plants to spread.

The species of plants you can grow in a bog garden of this type will naturally be the same as those found naturally in a peat-based soil. You could not grow *Drosophyllum* in such a bog, for example. Most enthusiasts enjoy growing a wide variety of carnivorous plants in such a garden, such as *Sarracenia, Dionaea, Drosera, Pinguicula, Cephalotus, Byblis,* and *Utricularia.* But equally stunning are theme bogs, such as a garden of all trumpet plants, either all one species or mixed, including hybrids. Alternatively, a low-growing bog can be just as impressive, using species such as *Sarracenia purpurea* and *S. psittacina, Dionaea,* rosetted *Drosera,* and temperate *Pinguicula.*

If you live in Connecticut, yet want to grow warm-temperate species from the Florida panhandle or elsewhere, you can protect the bog in winter. The fact that it is set in the ground will automatically offer some protection, but you should take further precautions: After the autumn equinox, as the plants go dormant and the first hard frosts occur, trim off their old leaves so that most of the taller foliage is removed. Then scatter several inches of a mulch that is later easily removed, such as pine needles or hay. Now cover the bog with a large sheet of plastic or burlap. You can secure this with stone or, if your winters are particularly severe, cover the plastic with

Bog pockets along an artificial stream in a mixed garden in northern California

a mound of mulch around twelve inches deep. A blanket of snow will insulate the bog even further.

After winter, when the last of the severe frost dangers are over, the coverings can be removed. Some plants that do not form true winter resting buds, such as the short-lived *Drosera capillaris* or *Pinguicula lusitanica,* will probably have died off. Such varieties usually return from, or can be reintroduced by, seed from the previous season.

NONCARNIVOROUS ADDITIONS

Noncarnivorous plants can make attractive additions to the savage garden. You can check with your local nursery or water garden specialist for wet-tolerant plants to add to your bog. Ornamental grasses, in particular, make handsome contrasts. Below are some suggestions. Most of these plants are native to the damp pinelands of the southeastern United States.

Yellow-eyed grass *(Xyris baldwiniana)*
Pipewort *(Eriocaulon compressum)*
Shoe button *(Syngonanthus flavidulus)*
Bog buttons *(Lachnocaulon anceps)*
Grass pink *(Calopogon tuberosus)*
Rose pogonia *(Pogonia ophioglossoides)*

Yellow star grass *(Hypoxis hirsuta)*
Coneflower *(Rudbeckia graminifolia)*
Comfort root *(Hibiscus aculeatus)*
Bay blue-flag *(Iris tridenta)*
Japanese blood grass *(Imperata cylindrica 'Rubra')*
Teena turner grass *(Isolepis cernuus)*
Disa orchids from South Africa

Carnivores in a Mixed Garden

Carnivorous plants growing among cacti and succulents, ornamental grasses, or in a rock garden can be rather startling. Yet this is easily accomplished if you grow carnivorous plants in undrained containers that are set into the ground. I like to use large plastic pots that have no drainage holes, such as the ones that floral shops use to store cut flowers. Plant your carnivore in such a pot with its preferred soil mix, then dig a hole in your garden to accommodate the container and set it into the ground. The rim can be disguised with rocks or mosses. Be sure you water the CPs frequently and separately from your other garden plants. Avoid using sprinklers on the CPs if your tap water is hard, or protect them by covering them with small patches of sheet plastic when you water.

Long, rectangular containers set in the ground along a sidewalk can be planted with rows of *Sarracenia* trumpets for an unusual and effective border. Circular plastic garden bowls planted with a mass of cape sundews, Venus flytraps, or flowering terrestrial bladderworts can be the center point of a mixed "alpine" rock garden. If your climate permits, a drained container of climbing *Nepenthes* can be set in the ground among small palms and ferns for an unusual tropical effect.

The Minibog

Miniature carnivorous plant bog gardens are one of the most popular and simple ways to grow CPs. These are set up in the same way as larger, in-the-ground artificial bogs. The only difference is that you'll use smaller, freestanding containers. These can be grown on sunny decks, patios, or balconies. If you live in a climate with harsh winters, the containers can be moved to bright garage windows or basement windows for the winter to accommodate the bog's dormancy, if needed, or into a sunroom if the plants grow year round.

Containers for minibogs? You can use a wide variety of plastic garden bowls for this purpose, or even wine barrels or wooden planter boxes that are lined with sheet plastic under the soil (remember, the container needs to be undrained). Wooden window boxes lined with plastic and planted with forked sundews or pitcher plants certainly draw more attention than geraniums, and snares houseflies before they come through the window!

A visit to your local weekend flea market can often be a source of fabulous and unusual minibog containers. Undrained, glazed ceramic flower pots, urns, bonsai dishes, salad bowls, large ashtrays, water basins, and cut flower vases are just some of the possible containers in which to grow a minibog. The smaller containers can be ideal for tiny bogs of miniature plants: pygmy and rosetted sundews, short-rooted butterworts, terrestrial bladderworts—all do well in shallow containers. Larger and deeper containers can be planted with a similar variety of CPs as a sizable in-the-ground bog garden, but on a smaller scale.

Jana Olson Drobinsky's intriguing mini-bog in an antique tub

For many years, I grew the following in a fourteen-inch, plastic garden bowl: *Sarracenia rubra* ssp. *wherryi, S. flava,* and *S. psittacina; Drosera capensis, D. spatulata, D. filiformis ssp. tracyi,* and *D. nitidula* x *occidentalis; Utricularia livida;* plus a clump of yellow-eyed grass.

An interesting variation on the minibog is the miniature island bog. In this setup, I use a plastic garden bowl with a removable plug, which I discard. I cover the hole with a handful of long-fibered sphagnum to prevent the leakage of soil. Then I fill the container with a peat-and-sand mix, and plant it as I would any other minibog. I then set this container

An inexpensive plastic urn is the perfect home for *Sarracenia x readii*, *Sarracenia purpurea* "red form", *Drosera capensis* and ornamental grasses.

into a similar but much larger garden bowl, leaving the plug intact. This larger container then acts as the water tray, and I keep the water fairly deep most of the time. Not only will this method allow for less watering stress, but the moat around the minibog will act as a barrier to slugs and snails. Further, the moat becomes the ideal place to grow aquatic carnivores such as *Utricularia gibba* or *U. purpurea,* or the waterwheel plant, *Aldrovanda.*

Bog Gardens in the Greenhouse

Although the most common way to grow CPs in the greenhouse is to set potted plants into water trays or saucers, a bog garden is certainly an option. You could, if you wish, put a bog garden into the ground of your greenhouse as you would outdoors. But it is much easier to construct a tableau or boxed bog garden right on the benches or staging of the greenhouse.

You could use a prefabricated plastic container such as a wading pool and set this upon your greenhouse bench, but it is often cheaper to construct your own. A simple way is to make a rectangular wooden frame out of 8 X 2-inch boards. I like to use a sheet of plywood as the base. This box is then lined with a sturdy, 6 mm sheet plastic, stapled along the interior. Simply fill the box with your soil mix of pre-wetted peat moss and sand, and landscape as you would any outdoor bog garden. Depending upon the size of your boxed container, features such as *Utricularia* puddles or moats can also be added, just as with outdoor gardens.

GROWING CPs OUTDOORS

The following terms referring to climate zones will be found throughout this book. Temperatures are given in Fahrenheit.

Cold-temperate: Warm summers, with very cold and long winters, with temperatures below freezing lasting for many days at a time.

Temperate: Warm summers, with winters having many cold snaps, usually of brief duration and not below 22 degrees, although colder temperatures may rarely occur.

Warm-temperate: Warm summers, with occasional winter cold snaps of short duration usually not below 28 degrees, although colder temperatures may rarely occur.

Subtropical: Warm summers with mild winters. Occasional cold snaps, but rarely below freezing, or 32 degrees.

Tropical: Few temperature extremes, but no freezing temperatures expected.

Highland tropical means warm days and cool nights. Lowland tropical means hot days and warm nights.

Mediterranean-like: Warm, dry summers and cool, wet winters. May be temperate, warm temperate, or subtropical. Cool Mediterranean-like climates have cool but dry summers.

❧ PART THREE ❧
THE PLANTS AND HOW TO GROW THEM

Nepenthes villosa

— 1 —
THC UCNUS FLYTRAP
(*DIONAEA MUSCIPULA*)

The Venus flytrap

AWE INSPIRING WHEN FIRST SEEN in action, the Venus flytrap is without doubt the most famous of all carnivorous plants. In 1763, then governor of North Carolina Arthur Dobbs brought public attention to the plant for the first time, calling it the "Fly Trap Sensitive." A few years later, specimens were sent to England, where it was the first plant ever suspected of being carnivorous. Carolus Linnaeus, the Swedish botanist, remained unconvinced and named the plant after Diana, the Greek goddess of love and beauty.

Venus flytraps are native only to the coastal plain of southeastern North Carolina and extreme northeastern South Carolina, in roughly a hundred-mile radius from Wilmington. Once very abundant, the species is now rather threatened, due primarily to habitat destruction and to a lesser extent collection for the retail nursery trade. This latter practice is changing, thanks to a growing reliance on nursery tissue culture.

Unfortunately, the loss of habitat is occurring at an alarming rate, due to a rapidly growing population and the drainage of wetlands for lumber, agriculture, and residential development. Native populations also decline due to the prevention of naturally occurring brushfires, usually caused by frequent lightning strikes. Flytraps are choked out by thick scrub that would otherwise be burned back by these fires. Although the Venus flytrap has been introduced with some success in states such as New Jersey and California, it has been naturalized in great abundance in only a small area of the Florida panhandle.

A pot of Venus flytraps grown on the author's screened-in porch

In their native Carolina habitats, Venus flytraps grow primarily in sandy, peaty soils in damp areas on the edges of swamps, fens, and pocosins. Typically they are found in open, sunny, wet savannas or grasslands amid sparsely scattered pines. Their climate is warm-temperate and humid. In the summer, the days are hot and nights are warm. Winters are chilly, with occasional periods of frost, but only rarely does it snow.

Venus flytraps are perennial plants. Grown from seed, they usually take about four to five years to reach maturity and can live for two to three decades.

Mature plants produce a rosette of leaves averaging four to eight inches in diameter. The leaves consist of two parts: the petiole (actually an expanded leaf base) and the trap, which is the true leaf. Adult plants usually have traps averaging one to two inches long. The leaves come up from a short, thick rhizome or underground stem. The few thick, black roots are several inches long.

In late winter or spring, at the start of their growth for the season, the plants produce a small rosette of leaves with wide, heart-shaped petioles that usually hug the ground, and small traps.

The plants usually bloom in spring, sending up a wiry stem eight to twelve inches tall. Each of the several white flowers are about one inch across. Flowering can have an exhausting effect on plants in cultivation, so unless you want seed, the flower stalk is best clipped off when it's two or three inches high.

After flowering, as summer approaches, larger traps are produced. There are two forms of Venus flytraps that appear to be genetically induced. Some plants have traps that hug the ground on short petioles year round. Others send their traps several inches into the air on long, narrow petioles during

The flowers of the Venus flytrap. Now that you've seen them, cut them off!

the summer months. The interior color of the traps is also a genetic quality enhanced by sunlight. Some traps are deep red in color, others pink, and a third variety lacks any color and always remains green. This latter form is often called "heterodoxa." Deep red, ground-hugging traps are sometimes called "red rosetted." There are a few cultivated varieties, or cultivars, in which the whole plant is a lovely deep red or maroon color.

The plants continue to produce leaves throughout summer. Older leaves, several weeks old, turn black and die. These should be trimmed off. As autumn arrives in late September, all of the summer leaves die away and are replaced by smaller, low-growing traps. In mild winters some of these traps remain, but they react indifferently to the capture of insects. During hard frosts, all of the leaves may disappear.

The trapping mechanism of the Venus flytrap is amazing, and prompted Charles Darwin to call *Dionaea* "one of the most wonderful plants in the world." It was he who ultimately offered proof of its carnivorous nature. In his book *Insectivorous Plants,* Darwin performed many experiments upon the flytrap, including some strange ones: he found he could paralyze the trap by making certain incisions upon it, and that the traps could be anesthetized with ether.

The exact mechanism of the trap is still a mystery that is hotly debated. The general principle is as follows: The trap consists of two halves not unlike a clam shell. The outer margins are lined with teeth, or cilia. When the trap is open, the two halves or lobes are actually concave or dished inward. Each lobe has three or four tiny trigger hairs set near the center.

A sweet nectar is produced by glands found along the inner base of the teeth that rim the trap. Insects, most often ants or flies, are lured by this nectar to enter the trap. As the insect moves about, drinking the nectar, it needs to touch or bend two of the tiny trigger hairs or one hair twice within twenty seconds to spring the trap. What occurs next is startling.

A mild electrical current runs through the trap. The cells on the outer walls of the lobes suddenly lengthen, doubling their size in less than a second. This quick growth causes the concave dished shape of the lobe to rapidly reverse itself. The trap snaps shut, causing the teeth to intermesh—imprisoning the insect in a cage.

The trap does not close tightly right away. Darwin surmised this allowed small insects to escape through the intermeshed teeth, so the plant wouldn't waste time and energy eating an insignificant meal. But if a larger insect is caught, its struggling will stimulate the trigger hairs even further. In a few hours, the lobes are pressed tightly together and the trap seals itself. Glands on the inner surface of the lobes begin to secret digestive juices. Shortly the insect drowns in this fluid.

It takes a flytrap from four to ten days to digest its prey. The soft parts of the insect are dissolved and this resulting fluid is then absorbed by the plant. When the trap reopens, only the dried, shriveled exoskeleton of the insect remains. Rain may wash the carcass out of the trap. More often, spiders are lured by the crusty shell and become a second meal. In the wild, large ants and spiders are the most frequent prey.

If a trap is closed empty, as a result of a falling leaf or rude finger,

The Venus Flytrap

A ladybug seconds from doom

Gotchya!

The trap seals while digesting

it will usually reopen within one or two days. Each trap can catch one to three meals, after which the trap and petiole die and turn black. Depending on the age of the leaf or the size of its prey, a trap may turn black after one meal. This is normal. Remember to trim all dead traps off the plant.

Forms and Varieties

Although there is only one species of *Dionaea muscipula,* making it a monotypic genus, several forms and cultivars exist. Some of these may represent natural varieties found in the wild, and a few are artificially bred-and-named cultivars or are mutations that occurred in tissue-cultured plants.

"Clumping Cultivar"

Although to my knowledge never actually published as a cultivar, these plants produce clumps of rosetted growing points, which result in a mound of densely packed leaves.

Dionaea m. 'Red Dragon' growing in peat and sand with a top dressing of live sphagnum

'Dente' and 'Dentata'

Both are tissue-cultured mutations. The teeth are numerous, short, and jagged, like a beartrap.

"Fused Tooth"

A tissue-cultured mutation. The teeth are few and fused together by "webbing."

"Heterodoxa"

The whole plant is green, usually with rosetted leaves year round.

'Red Dragon'

An all-red cultivar, selected by Atlanta Botanical Gardens from breeding done by Ron Gagliardo. Full sun is required to maintain its stunning purplish color.

"Red Rosetted"

The leaves are rosetted all year, with deep red interior traps.

'Royal Red'

An Australian cultivar of a tissue-cultured mutation, with reddish peti-oles and traps. The patent on this plant caused much con-troversy among the nursery trade, primarily in Australia.

"Sawtooth"

A handsome mutation similar to dentata, often with deep red interior traps.

"Typical"

These plants are rosetted most of the year except in summer, when traps are held erect on narrow petioles. The color of the trap interior is most often pinkish red.

Dionaea muscipula "Sawtooth"

CULTIVATION *(See Parts One and Two for further information)*

Soil recipe	Flytraps thrive in a mix of one part sand to one part peat.
Containers	Best in plastic pots or glazed ceramics. Four- to five-inch pots for single, mature plants. Several plants look good in six- to eight-inch pots. They do well in deeper minibogs and bog gardens.
Watering	Use the tray method, keeping the soil damp to wet year round. Flytraps do not appreciate persistent waterlogged conditions, and do best with a lower water table.
Light	Full to part sun.
Climate	Warm-temperate plants, flytraps need warm summers and chilly winters. Tolerant of light frost and brief freezes.
Greenhouses	They do well in cold houses, cool houses, and warm houses, and in cold frames in warm-temperate climates.
Outdoors	They do very well in temperate, warm-temperate, and Mediterranean-like climates.
Terrarium	Seasonal candidates for the greenhouse-style tank, best removed in winter. Good for the classic, temperate terrarium.

Windowsills	Good candidates for sunny windowsills. Best kept cooler for winter dormancy.
Bog gardens	Do very well in temperate, warm-temperate, and Mediterranean-like climates. Mulch in colder zones.
Feeding	Readily accepts houseflies, large ants, spiders, sow bugs, or pill bugs. Moistened dried insects are also accepted.
Fertilizers	Do best without it, but can sometimes benefit from a light misting of an acid fertilizer.
Transplanting	Potted flytraps are invigorated when transplanted into fresh medium every one to two years, best done in late winter.

PROPAGATION

Division

Occasionally, Venus flytraps will produce offshoots and develop into a clumping plant. These are best divided in late winter to early summer. Be sure that each crown of leaves has a separate root system before you divide them.

Leaf cuttings

In spring or early summer, peel leaves off the rhizome with a downward tug,

being sure the whitish base of the leaf is intact. Lay the whole leaf right-side up on a peat/sand mix, or long-fibered or milled sphagnum. Lightly cover the base of the leaf with a pinch of soil. Keep humid and damp in bright light. Clear plastic bags or seed propagation trays work well to insure high humidity. In a few weeks plantlets will appear at the leaf base or on the leaf

A baby Venus flytrap of about two years old

margins. In a few months, when plantlets have several leaves and roots, they can be potted up individually. Leaf cuttings can produce mature plants in about two years.

Seed

The individual flowers open for a few days. The anthers release the pollen immediately. The stigma is receptive in two or three days when it appears fuzzy. Transfer the yellow pollen grains from anthers to a receptive stigma. Rubbing open flowers together will usually pollinate them. Numerous small, black shiny seed are produced in about six weeks.

The seed can be sown immediately or refrigerated for later use. Scatter the seed on a peat/sand mix. Keep humid and in bright light. Germination occurs in a few weeks. Transplant the seedlings when they are about one year old.

Tissue culture

Flytraps can be propagated in vitro through seed, newly emerging leaves, and flower buds.

Pests and diseases

Aphids are the most common pest, and result in twisted and deformed new leaves. They are effectively controlled by insecticides such as Orthene, Diazinon, and Malathion. Flea collars placed very close to the plant or in an enclosed plastic bag or terrarium work well also.

In hot and dry climates, spider mites can attack flytraps. Orthene is the best control.

Black spot fungus can appear on plants in an overly wet and humid environment. Use a fungicide for control.

— 2 —
THE AMERICAN PITCHER PLANTS
(SARRACENIA)

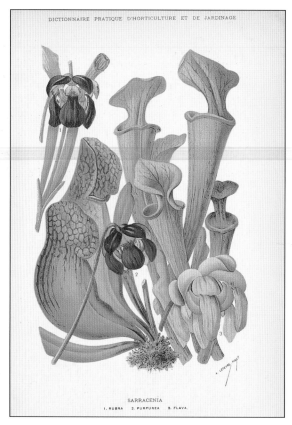

French print of Sarracenia

BEAUTIFUL AND EASY TO GROW, American pitcher plants may be the most ravenous and underappreciated plants in horticulture. The bizarre and often handsome leaves can sometimes catch thousands of nasty insects such as ants, flies, and wasps. Their flowers are showy, brilliant, and very unusual—a wonderful bonus to an already handsome class of foliage plants. Yet of the few varieties sometimes available on the mass market, tens of thousands die needlessly due to poor handling in countless nurseries, where the plants often go down the dismal path to the compost heap, like millions of Venus flytraps before them. What a shame! The *Sarracenia* are one of the simplest carnivorous plants to grow, and certainly among the most fun and rewarding.

There are currently assumed to be eight species, all of which are confined to the southeastern United States with the exception of one species extending north along the seaboard into the upper midwest and much of Canada. For such unusual and once-common plants, they were slow to be recognized by the early European settlers. The first published illustration was of *S. minor* from Florida in 1576. In 1700, Tournefort described *S. purpurea* from plants sent to him by Dr. M. S. Sarrazin of Quebec, and Linnaeus followed his lead, naming the genus *Sarracenia* in 1731. William Bartram, in a 1793 book about his travels in the southern United States, first mentioned the vast quantity of insects caught in the pitcher leaves but doubted that the plants could benefit from them.

Darwin suspected their carnivorous nature but did not study them. It was in 1887 that Dr. Joseph H. Mellichamp's research ultimately proved *Sarracenia* eats insects. The general knowledge of the plants was greatly extended by the field and laboratory studies of Dr. Edgar Wherry in the 1930s, and more recently by Drs. Donald Schnell and Frederick Case. There is still some controversy over

A wet meadow of white trumpets in the Florida panhandle. Scenes like this were once abundantly common.

the natural species and subspecies status of the genus. Here I will follow the general conclusions of Schnell.

The typical habitat of American pitcher plants is found on the southeastern coastal plain of North America. Scattered individuals or dense colonies are most frequently found in permanently wet, open, grassy savannas, fens, swamps, and similar wetlands. The soils are a sandy peat, often derived from sphagnum moss. Stands of long-leaf pine or other trees may populate the area, but the pitcher plants will prefer the sunniest areas and avoid the dense shade of trees. In its natural state, these wetlands were frequently the targets of lightning strikes, and the ensuing brush fires kept scrub, bushes, and tree seedling in check, keeping the habitat grassy and open. In the past, Native Americans started fires for a similar purpose, primarily to maintain open fields for the ease of hunting deer. The pitcher plants thrived in such areas.

At lease one species (*S. oreophila*) and a subspecies (*S. rubra* ssp. *jonesii*) are severely endangered plants in mountain or foothill remnant wetlands above the coastal plain, in places such as northern Alabama and the North and South Carolina piedmont foothills of the Appalachian Mountains. The northern purple pitcher plant, *S. purpurea* ssp. *purpurea,* is the only species found north of Virginia. Its habitat is primarily wet, acidic sphagnum bogs found in scattered areas of northeastern North America and throughout much of Canada. Ironically, in the Great Lakes area, this plant is also found in wet, marly, alkaline wetlands.

The climate of the southeastern coastal plain is considered warmtemperate. Rain falls throughout much of the year, and summers are warm and humid. Winters are cool and often frosty at night. Occasional brief deep freezes and rarer light snowfall also occur. In its northern range, *S. purpurea* ssp. *purpurea* experiences extremely frigid winter conditions, often with a lot of snow.

The seeds of *Sarracenia* are usually dispersed in autumn. In late winter and spring of the following year, they begin to germinate as the weather warms. By the end of the first year's growth the seedlings will have tiny pitcher leaves one or two inches long. A typical plant takes around five to eight years to reach maturity. Over the years, individual plants develop a thick, branching underground rhizome, from which several growing points emerge.

The annual growth cycle of mature plants begins after winter dormancy. Most plants start the season by flowering. Each growing point will send up one bloom on a one-to-three-foot-high stalk. The first pitcher leaves appear from the rhizome soon after the developing flower bud, but the plant flowers first, before any pitchers open. They wouldn't want to eat their pollinators!

The flowers are showy, and depending upon the species may be from one to over four inches in diameter. The flowers hang upside down from the tall stem. The five petals, from one to several inches in length, hang pendulously from the bloom. Four of the eight species have yellowish petals; the other four have various shades of red petals. The flowers are rather unusual and beautiful, and most are in bloom from one

The flower of *Sarracenia purpurea* ssp. *venosa*

to two weeks. Bees are the primary pollinators. Each species flowers at slightly different times between late February and May. In areas where two or more species grow together, this usually eliminates cross pollination of species. However, quite often two or more species may flower at similar times, often resulting in swarms of hybrids. Hybrids of *Sarracenia* species occur fairly frequently in the wild. At the turn of the century, many commonly found hybrids were thought to be species.

Almost all of the species have flowers that are scented. The aroma may be strong or mild, sweet to musty. As the petals drop off, the ovary and style remain all summer as the seed develops for autumn release. The fruit or seed pods are so often attractive in their own right that many people assume them to be flowers even though they have lost their colorful petals.

It is after petal-drop that the first pitcher leaves of the season open for business. The difference in the structure and trapping mechanism of the various species is rather dramatic and will be described later. But generally speaking, insects are lured to the leaves by a combination of nectar and color. It is generally assumed that a drug in the nectar strongly assists in the trapping of prey. A drug called coniine has been isolated from the nectar of *S. flava*. This narcotic causes paralysis and eventually death to those insects drinking enough of it. While most American pitcher plants catch insects in a pitfall method, where the prey fall into tubular leaves from which they cannot escape, at least one, *S. psittacina,* catches victims with a one-way trap, while another, *S. purpurea,* drowns its prey.

A pitcher of *Sarracenia flava* opening for business.

Pitcher leaves are produced from spring until late summer or early autumn. Some species produce leaves more or less on a continuing basis throughout the growing season. Others will send up their leaves in crops: spring, early summer, and late summer. The individual leaves are in prime condition for a period of time ranging from several weeks to a couple of months. After this period they begin to deteriorate, often filled with insects. After the autumn equinox most species stop leaf production and by winter are in a dormant state. Usually all leaves brown and decompose over winter, although some species may hold on to some of their leaves during this time, only to lose them rapidly when spring growth resumes, as with *S. purpurea.*

Insects that encounter the purple pitcher plant, *S. purpurea,* drown in collected rainwater, where they slowly decompose by bacterial action and weak enzymes. All of the other species trap their prey in tubular leaves, near the bottom of which digestive acids and enzymes are produced and secreted more heavily as more insects are caught. Microorganisms also play a part in digestion. The soft parts of the insects break down, and the plant slowly absorbs this nutritious soup, gaining nitrogen, potassium, phosphorous, and other trace elements that are lacking in the plant's soils. Research indicates these minerals play heavily on the plant's ability to flower and set seed.

Authorities estimate that less than 5 percent of the original *Sarracenia* stands remain in the southeast.

THE PURPLE PITCHER PLANT
(*SARRACENIA PURPUREA*)

Sarracenia purpurea has the widest range of any American pitcher plant, and is divided into two subspecies, one variety, and several forms.

In all of the plants the pitchers are decumbent, more or less sitting on the ground in a rosette fashion. The length of the leaves can be from a few inches to over a foot in length. The hollow leaves resemble colorful, flared cornucopias. A large, often undulating collar is open to the sky, allowing rainwater to be collected by the leaf, unlike the leaves of other *Sarracenia*. This collar is also covered in bristly, downward-pointing hairs. Insects often cling to and slip from these hairs, which are wet with nectar. The prey tumble into the water below, where they drown.

The subspecies known as *S. purpurea* ssp. *purpurea* is sometimes called the northern pitcher plant. Its range is throughout much of Canada, the Great Lakes region, and the eastern seaboard from Newfoundland south to New Jersey, where it meets its southern subspecies. It has also been introduced and naturalized in some regions of Europe. The pitchers are narrower than those of its plumper sister to the south, and are often more numerous and more densely packed. They frequently last through the most frigid winters.

Normally a denizen of acid sphagnum bogs, the form ruplicola is found in alkaline fens around the Great Lakes, where the smaller pitchers take on a more brittle consistency. These plants revert to normal when moved to acid conditions. The flowers have red to purplish petals, and the plants may bloom in midsummer in its most northerly range. The form heterophylla is an uncommon strain in which the all-red color is absent—instead, the pitchers and flowers are entirely yellowish green.

S. purpurea ssp. *venosa* is the southern subspecies of the plant, and the one most commonly found in cul-

Sarracenia purpurea ssp. venosa "red form"

tivation. Its range begins in the New Jersey Pine Barrens, where intermediates between it and *S. purpurea* ssp. *purpurea* occur. From New Jersey, the plants grow south along the coastal plain to Georgia. There they continue west (with a gap in central Georgia) across Alabama, the Florida panhandle, Mississippi, and into Louisiana.

The southern purple pitcher plant produces leaves much more robust than its northern cousin, appearing fatter and broader and often with fewer leaves. The pitchers are usually green with red venation, but there have recently been found all-green plants much like in the far north, which are also called form heterophylla. Throughout its range, a common genetic variant produces solid maroon or red leaves, which is very popular in cultivation. While the flowers of *S. purpurea* ssp. *venosa* are typically red, the plants along the Gulf Coast consistently have oval pinkish petals, sometimes variegated with white, and a pale green to white umbrella style. For many decades these forms were nicknamed "Louis Burke" after a horticulturist who once grew them. Dr. Donald Schnell has given this race the varietal name 'burkei', as it is a true genetic form quite distinct from the Carolina plants.

The flower of *Sarracenia purpurea* ssp. *venosa* var. *burkei*

The purple pitcher plant is often the first Sarracenia species the hobbyist encounters. Although a poor insect catcher compared to other species in its genus, its beauty and compact size make it a popular mass-market plant, second only to the Venus flytrap. The species is so variable, many collectors hunt out exceptional forms. To my knowledge, the only cultivar in existence is *S. purpurea* ssp. *venosa* 'Red Ruffles'. This plant produces short, squat, maroon leaves that are almost held upright by the leaf petiole, and have a highly undulating collar. 'Red Ruffles' is also known to produce numerous offshoots over time, developing dense clumps of pitchers. It is my own selection from a plant given to me by Don Agnostinelli of California State University in Sacramento. See the photograph in the section below on "cultivars."

THE YELLOW TRUMPET PLANT
(*SARRACENIA FLAVA*)

Sarracenia flava is another highly variable pitcher plant, and is second in popularity after *S. purpurea*. Named for its large tall flowers with long, pendulous, bright yellow petals, it occurs from southern Virginia, where it is almost extinct, south along the coastal plain to extreme northern Florida, and then east to Mobile Bay, Alabama. Plants have been introduced into areas such as eastern Pennsylvania with some success.

S. *flava* produces erect, tall pitchers from around twenty inches to thirty-six inches, and occasionally taller. The species is often one of the first to flower, sometimes as early as late February in its southernmost range. The best pitchers are usually grown in spring and summer, although some varieties continue pitcher production until early autumn. This species is one that produces secondary leaves known as phyllodia, which look similar to flat, straight iris leaves. Phyllodia usually appear in late summer and can remain on the plant through winter, long after the pitchers have deteriorated.

The pitchers themselves are rather handsome. They appear as elongated, narrow funnels with a flared mouth and rather broad lip, or peristome, and a narrow neck that holds erect the large, almost horizontal lid. Unlike *S. purpurea*'s collar, this lid effectively keeps out most rain, and acts as a landing platform for flying insects. Crawling insects follow nectar trails up the pitcher's length, particularly along the reduced ala at the leaf's front seam. Various color patterns lead the prey to the most treacherous parts of the leaf. Insects appear quite intoxi-

Sarracenia flava "veined form"

cated by the time they are in the vicinity of the wide mouth, under the lid, or at the neck where the foothold is rather slippery. Drunk insects fall down the narrowing tube. The beating of wings may cause a vacuum in the pitcher, sucking it down further.

The interior is so waxy smooth the insects rarely can maintain foothold. Downward-pointing, needle-like hairs are found at its deepest point. Digestive juices are secreted by the plant in the lowest portions of the trap, and the level of this liquid rises as more insects are caught. The first victims typically drown in this fluid, which dissolves them down to their exoskeletons. Yellow trumpets may catch such enormous quantities of insects, the pitchers may topple from the weight. Flies, ants, wasps, beetles, and moths are the most common prey.

Although no subspecies have been named, there are several naturally occurring varieties known to exist, plus an assortment of forms grown by hobbyists who often bestow nicknames upon them. The taxonomy of these plants is in much confusion. Names used by collectors for years have been shown to be incorrect, and similar plants may be known by different names in different countries. Add to this many artificially produced hybrids between the forms, and the confusion becomes rather acute. Below is a small attempt at sorting all this out.

Sarracenia flava, a red tube form

"Typical form"

Found naturally throughout its range, the pitchers are primarily green with a large red splotch at the throat. Incorrectly known as 'Rugelli' and 'Maxima'. Commonly called "cut throat" or "red blotch."

"Veined form"

The pitchers are green with red veins over much of the leaf, and a concentration of red color at the throat. Veining is variable, from light to heavy. Naturally occurring in the Carolinas. The "Heavy Veined" forms are most desirable. One form is called "Ornata."

"Coppertop"

is the common name of this Carolina variety, in which the lid and upper pitcher have a coppery red coloration with heavy red veins throughout.

"All Green form"

This tall form from the Carolinas lacks any red pigment in the pitchers, although the phyllodia may have faint tints of red. This is the true 'Maxima' named in the late 1800s.

"Red Tube form"

This popular variety comes from the Florida panhandle. The exterior tube is richly red in color, while the lip, throat, and lid are green with red veins. Sometimes much of the lid is reddish as well. The color temporarily fades when the plant is moved, or may fade late in the season. Commonly called "Burgundy," in England, by Adrian Slack, and "Atropurpurea" in the United States.

"All Red form"

Another rare Carolina plant, in which the whole pitcher is a stunning deep red. Unfortunately, this maroon color is difficult to maintain in cultivation, and plants often end up looking like a reddish "Coppertop."

Adrian Slack, a British nurseryman and author, mentions a few varieties grown primarily in England. 'Claret', which he introduced into cultivation, he describes as being tinted maroon with heavier red veins. I grow his handsome but incorrectly named cultivar 'Maxima', an unusual lightly veined plant notable for a bluish gray tint in the phyllodia and lower pitcher. 'Marston Dwarf', a cultivar chosen by Slack, produces clumps of heavily veined pitchers not more than twelve inches high. If anyone is still growing this latter plant, please contact me, and name your price!

THE SWEET TRUMPET

SARRACENIA RUBRA

Sarracenia rubra is a species with a long and controversial history that is still debated today. Currently the plants are divided into five subspecies. Some botanists argue that a few of these are species in themselves, while others point out that the similar flowers of all tend to indi-

Left to right: Sarracenia rubra ssp. rubra, S. rubra ssp. gulfensis, S. rubra ssp. jonesii, S. rubra ssp. wherryi, S. rubra ssp. alabamensis, and Sarracenia alata.

cate one rather variable group. There are also plants that are clearly S. *rubra* but don't seem to fall under any yet defined group.

As a whole, the plants are generally clump-producing trumpets that are comparatively smaller in stature than some of their cousins. S. *rubras* are notable for their small, bright red to dark red flowers—some of which are fragrant to variable degrees, hence the common name. The scent of some is reminiscent of roses or, as some collectors have noted, cherry-flavored Kool Aid. Since the rhizomes commonly branch into multiple growing points, not only are masses of pitcher leaves produced, but the multiple flowers in spring, added with their perfume, can make a showy spectacle.

All of the subspecies produce two types of pitchers. In the spring, the pitchers are generally small, somewhat floppy, and snakelike, looking remarkably similar among the different forms. The summer pitchers are much more erect and robust, and all are highly veined in fine red venation.

The insect-catching mechanism is rather similar to the other upright trumpet species. The prey are lured by color and nectar to the area of the mouth, where the insects fall down the lanky, narrow tubes.

S. rubra ssp. rubra

This most popular subspecies has highly fragrant flowers. The summer pitchers are narrow, highly veined, with a short pointed lid, and reach a height of twelve to eighteen inches. From eastern North Carolina and South Carolina.

S. rubra ssp. jonesii

This very endangered species is virtually extinct in its mountainous habitat of North and South Carolina. Notable for its handsome pitchers, which are rather similar to ssp. *rubra* but with a noticeable bulge in their upper parts. The flowers are particularly sweet smelling and are a very bright red color. The pitchers can be over twenty-four inches tall. This variety is especially cold hardy.

S. rubra ssp. gulfensis

A plant from the Florida panhandle, the pitchers are tall and superficially resemble ssp. *jonesii,* but can be more variable. The large lid undulates slightly. The flowers have a weak scent.

S. rubra ssp. alabamensis

Also known as *S. alabamensis,* this plant is endangered and only found in a small area north of Montgomery, Alabama. The pitchers are robust and stocky, with a large lid that has very wavy margins. Up to twenty inches tall.

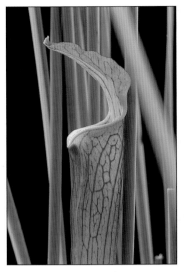

Sarracenia rubra ssp. *wherry*

S. rubra ssp. wherry

Rather similar in appearance to ssp. *alabamensis,* this plant is limited to southern Alabama. The undulating lid may be tinted red. The flowers are very fragrant.

THE PALE TRUMPET
(SARRACENIA ALATA)

Sarracenia alata occurs naturally in a somewhat broken range from southern Alabama west along the Gulf Coast into eastern Texas. Its unique flowers are the palest of yellow to almost pure white, hence its common name.

The upright trumpets are generally green with much red venation, and can be thirty inches tall. The pointed lids are not as flared as in *S. flava,* but are held more closely to the mouth with a wider column or neck, rather similar to *S. rubra* ssp. *rubra.*

There is some strong variability in this species, with the most colorful forms fur-

The pale trumpet, *Sarracenia alata*

ther west in its range. Near Mobile Bay, some of the populations have stockier pitchers that are covered with a soft, fuzzy hair, and are often referred to as "pubescent." Further west, in Mississippi, the plants often have a reddish bronze coloration in the upper pitchers. But it is in Texas that the most stunning variants occur. "Nigrapurpurea" is a form in which the throat and underside of the lid can become such a dark red color, it nearly approaches black.

THE WHITE TRUMPET
(SARRACENIA LEUCOPHYLLA)

Considered by many to be the most beautiful of the American pitcher plants, *S. leucophylla* grows from southwestern Georgia to southern Mississippi, being most abundant in the Florida panhandle and southernmost Alabama.

The flowers are large and red. The pitchers are green in their lower parts, while the upper pitcher, mouth, and lid are a pure, bright white, heavily laced with a network of veins. Pitchers can top thirty-six inches.

The plants are rather variable. In some populations the veining can be rather coarse, while in others it appears as a thin netting. There are color differences as well in the veins—from green to the darkest burgundy. Hence plants may be given nicknames to describe them, from "Green and White" to "Typical" to "Red and White." One green-and-white variety is a true genetic form lacking any red-colored genes, as the flowers are yellow. It has been called "Schnell's Ghost" by hobbyists.

White Trumpets

S. leucophylla generally sends up two crops of pitchers. The spring set, with thinner pitchers, is the weaker of the two. In early summer a few phyllodia are grown. But the species is truly at its best in late summer and early autumn. It is then that robust pitchers appear, being in prime condition until the first frosts occur, often as late as early December.

White trumpets are most attractive to their insect prey, and when the pitchers open they are often filled to the brim much faster than other *Sarracenia*. The highly decorative pitchers, with their hair-lined ruffled lids, are often sold as cut flowers for floral arrangements. This practice is controversial, as the leaves are often removed en masse from the rapidly disappearing wild populations.

A green-and-white form of *Sarracenia leucophylla*

THE MOUNTAIN TRUMPET
(SARRACENIA OREOPHILA)

On the verge of extinction, *Sarracenia oreophila* manages to survive in only a handful of populations in central and northeastern Alabama, and in the mountainous areas where Georgia, North Carolina, and South Carolina meet. It was once more populous but always considered rare, and may soon disappear from the wild.

The plant is unusual in that the pitchers are primarily produced in spring and early summer. By midsummer its natural habitats often become somewhat drier, and the pitchers wither and are replaced by strongly curved phyllodia. This carries over in cultivation even when the plants are kept very wet.

The flowers are yellow. The pitchers, vaguely similar to *S. flava* except for the more broadly opened mouth, wider neck, and somewhat dome-shaped lid, grow to

Sarracenia oreophila 'Don Schnell,' a cultivar named by the author

about twenty-four inches tall. Typically the plants are green with light red venation, but some varieties, particularly from the Sand Mountain

The hooded pitcher plant

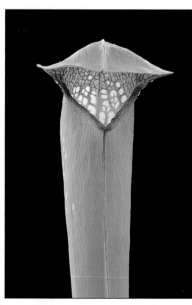

The drooling nectar of *Sarracenia minor* lures insects to the edge of doom, while the light windows offer a false hope of escape.

plateau in Alabama, are so richly colored and veined they are much sought after by hobbyists.

Two points are notable with this rare species. One is its cold hardiness, as its mountain habitat will see snowfall more regularly than will other *Sarracenia* on the warmer coastal plain. Temperatures briefly down to zero degrees are not unheard of. The second is the plant's capacity to add vigor to offspring when hybridized with other species of *Sarracenia*. Hybrids with *S. oreophila* can attain stunning coloration and spectacular size.

THC HOODCD PiTCHCR PLANT
(*SARRACENIA MINOR*)

S. minor is a curious-looking and widespread pitcher plant. Its range is along the coastal plain from southeastern North Carolina south into much of the Florida panhandle and all of the northern half of Florida. Recently, populations have been found as far south as Okeechobee County, making it the most southern-growing member of its genus.

The unusual pitchers of *S. minor* have an almost grinning, monkish appearance. In most of its range the leaves average around twelve inches in height. The tubes are smooth with a wide ala at the front seam. The lid of the pitcher forms a domed canopy over

84

the mouth. On the upper portion of the back side of the pitcher are many opaque light windows. The pitchers are generally green with a coppery red coloration along the upper parts when grown in full sun.

Trapping of prey is rather unique. When insects are lead to the lip of the mouth by nectar trails, they find themselves in a rather darkened position, due to the overhanging hood. Crawling insects are encouraged to enter the trap where it is much brighter, due to sunlight shining through the windows. Flying insects are fooled into believing the windows are escape hatches. The crawling prey find no foothold on the waxy interior of the hood, while the flying ones slam into the windows for a stunned surprise. Either will tumble helplessly down the narrowing tube and into digestive juices below. In the wild, hooded pitcher plants seem most attractive to ants, although a large buffet of flying insects are lured and eaten, too.

The flowers are medium-sized and of a pleasant, buttery yellow. Unique among *Sarracenia,* the spring flowers often open simultaneously with the first leaves of the season.

Hooded pitcher plants are mildly variable over their range. Some populations have thinner, stiffer pitchers, while others may be plump and soft. The exception are plants from the Okefenokee Swamp in southern Georgia. Here, often growing on floating mats of sphagnum moss, the plants can attain a startling size of three or four feet in height. In cultivation, *S. minor* "Okee Giant," as it is called, more commonly reaches a still impressive height of thirty to thirty-six inches.

THE PARROT PITCHER PLANT
(SARRACENIA PSITTACINA)

Unlike any other plant in its genus, *Sarracenia psittacina* seems to have more in common with its distant Pacific coast relative *Darlingtonia* than with a typical trumpet plant.

Parrot pitcher plants have an affinity for wetter, low-lying areas of swampy savannas, and are often flooded by heavy rains. The species grows along the coastal plain throughout southern Georgia, the Florida panhandle, and west into southern Mississippi.

The pitcher leaves are decumbent, lying in a rosetted pattern pressed along the ground. The elongated tubes have a large, wavy ala, and end in a hollow, puffed hood that is rather beaked, hence its com-

The entrance of a beaked leaf of the parrot pitcher plant. Upon entering this doorway, an insect is assured a painful death.

mon name. Under the beak, where the nectar-baited ala ends, is a small circular opening. Inside of the inflated hood, this opening is surrounded by a collar, making it not unlike a minnow trap or lobster pot. The back side of the hood and upper part of the narrow tube is laced with numerous light windows, similar to those of *S. minor and Darlingtonia*. The interior of the tube is lined with extra-long, intermeshed, needle-like hairs, all pointing towards the base of the leaf.

Prey caught by this plant suffer a hideous death. Once inside the hood, the exit is difficult to find due to the puckered collar. Insects thus enter the brighter tube lighted by the windows. However, there is no retreat, for to back out means to be painfully pierced by the numerous needle-like hairs. The victim has no choice but to proceed into the digestive acids in the lower part of the pitcher.

That the parrot pitcher plant catches aquatic animals when underwater is known by the numerous tadpoles and other swimming creatures found in the leaves after a flood. When the water recedes, the plant resumes catching ants, slugs, and other crawling things. Flooding the plant in cultivation is not necessary for good growth.

The small flowers are red and have a mild, sweet aroma. The plants are variable in nature, mostly in color and leaf size. Some leaves are mottled in green, red, and white, while other forms may have extra large hoods of predominantly red and white coloration. Typically, a pitcher is five to eight inches in length, but within some populations, as in Mississippi and the Okefenokee Swamp, the leaves can be over twelve inches long with particularly globose hoods. There is also an all-green form with yellow flowers, as there are with most other *Sarracenia* species.

SARRACENIA HYBRIDS

American pitcher plants are unusual in the plant world because the species can be readily hybridized, and these offspring are not sterile, as with most other plants, but are capable of being self-pollinated or hybridized even further.

This situation can be vexing to the field botanist, as it was in the last century, when many natural hybrids were thought to be species, and in fact were given Latin names. But to the horticulturist the ease of hybridizing *Sarracenia* is both fun and exciting, as the results are often beautiful. Further, when one takes into account the already intriguing forms of some of the more complex crosses already existing and projects into the future the additional possibilities as hybridization programs become more serious and popular, the results will probably be utterly fantastic. As with orchids and roses and African violets, there is no end to the possibilities. Carnivorous vegetable gargoyles may be the future of *Sarracenia,* with carefully selected breeding.

In the wild, where two or more species are found growing together, the differing flowering times usually keep hybrids in check. But now and then the flowers of different species coincide, and the result may be scattered hybrid offspring or the occasional hybrid swarm. Add to this future backcrossing, and the result in some stands may be pitcher plants of very confused ancestry.

Because some of the common natural hybrids were once given Latin names, as if they were a separate species, these names have remained in use. These are names of convenience, and most modern growers will also know them by their correct species name. Thus *S. leucophylla* x *rubra* is also called *S.* x *readii.* (See the sidebar on page 89.)

For many decades, very few people were hybridizing *Sarracenia* and horticultural crosses rarely went much

Sarracenia hybrids provide an explosion of color.

beyond simple liaisons. Also, when a cross was done, it was usually known by its parentage. In other more advanced plant hobbies, as with orchids, a complicated system of registering hybrids is usually set into place: all new crosses are given fancy names and registered with the society, and if a particular seedling merited distinction, a cultivar name would be given to that single plant.

This is so only halfway with carnivorous plants. When a cross is made, no matter how complicated, all the seedlings are still referred to

Sarracenia purpurea x flava

by its heritage, such as *S. (leucophylla x rubra) x (purpurea x flava)*. However, if a single seedling of this cross seems to merit distinction, then it can be given a fancy name and registered as a cultivar (cultivated variety) with the International Carnivorous Plant Society (ICPS).

If this sounds confusing, it is. Laws pertaining to the naming of artificially produced plants could fill a whole book, and here I can only present the most basic information. Eventually, as the hybridizing of *Sarracenia* becomes more and more complex, it will be impossible to call resulting plants by their ancestry, and growers will have to begin following laws similar to those followed by orchid growers. Thus complex crosses will be given fancy names for all resulting offspring, and fancy cultivar names given only to those rare, outstanding individuals that should be only reproduced vegetatively, to preserve their unique characteristics. Until the ICPS can take on the burdensome task of registering all crosses, and not just cultivars, the situation will likely remain controversial.

In the meantime, I would strongly suggest that anyone hybridizing the plants be careful to keep good labels and records of the crosses. Eventually pedigree will not be so important to the collector who simply admires a beautiful plant. But even if a plant is merely coded or numbered on its label, do keep file cards recording as much known data about the history of the plant as possible. For helpful tips on record keeping, see page 90.

Actual pollination techniques will be covered below under "Propagation." Here I will discuss what you can expect with the general results of hybridizing, as well as a few simple descriptions of some of the more popular representative crosses.

Remember that under the laws of genetics, 50 percent of the offspring will generally look intermediate between both parents, while the remaining plants will lean more toward one parent or the other. Variability is the rule, and extremes are certainly common, particularly when the ancestry of a plant is complex.

SIMPLE *SARRACENIA* HYBRIDS

Below are the Latin names of simple **Sarracenia** *hybrids found in the wild.*

S. x catesbaei	=	S. purpurea x flava
S. x moorei	=	S. flava x leucophylla
S. x popei	=	S. flava x rubra
S. x harperi	=	S. flava x minor
S. x mitchelliana	=	S. purpurea x leucophylla
S. x exornata	=	S. purpurea x alata
S. x chelsonii	=	S. purpurea x rubra
S. x swaniana	=	S. purpurea x minor
S. x courtii	=	S. purpurea x psittacina
S. x areolata	=	S. leucophylla x alata
S. x readii	=	S. leucophylla x rubra
S. x excellens	=	S. leucophylla x minor
S. x wrigleyana	=	S. leucophylla x psittacina
S. x ahlesii	=	S. alata x rubra
S. x rehderi	=	S. rubra x minor
S. x gilpini	=	S. rubra x psittacina
S. x formosa	=	S. minor x psittacina

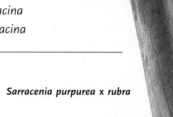

Sarracenia purpurea x rubra

RECORDKEEPING

Below are suggested codes for use with Sarracenia. *I have slightly amended Adrian Slack's codes from his book* Carnivorous Plants. *The general idea is to reduce the Latin name to one or two letters. Where subspecies, forms, and varieties are involved, an additional letter or two is added. Space will not allow me to list all of the varieties.*

p	=	purpurea
pp	=	purpurea ssp. purpurea
pv	=	purpurea ssp. venosa
pvb	=	purpurea ssp. venosa var. burkei
f	=	flava
fc	=	flava "Coppertop"
frt	=	flava "Red Tube" or "Burgundy"
ft	=	flava "Typical"
fv	=	flava "Veined"
r	=	rubra
ra	=	rubra ssp. alabamensis
rg	=	rubra ssp. gulfensis
rj	=	rubra ssp. jonesii
rr	=	rubra ssp. rubra
rw	=	rubra ssp. wherryi
a	=	alata
an	=	alata "Nigrapurpurea"
l	=	leucophylla "Typical"
lr	=	leucophylla "Red and White"
lg	=	leucophylla "Green and White"
o	=	oreophila
osm	=	oreophila "Sand Mountain"
m	=	minor
mg	=	minor "Okee Giant"
ps	=	psittacina
psg	=	psittacina "Giant"

THE SIMPLE HYBRIDS

Many of these can be found in the wild. All are greatly influenced by the subspecies, forms, or varieties of the parents. The following are plants with rather unique characteristics.

S. purpurea x flava

This is probably the most popular hybrid, although it is not a particularly good insect catcher, and the pitchers can topple if they collect rainwater. The plump pitchers curve upright, the undulating hood highly influenced by its *S. purpurea* parent. The flowers are usually pale red.

S. purpurea x leucophylla

Similar to the above, but much more colorful in the hood, which can be ruffled and mottled with pinks, whites, and reds, and highly veined. Red flowers.

S. purpurea x minor

An often reddish plant with low-growing curved pitchers that all face inward, and a monklike hood overhanging the mouth. The flowers are a dark orange red.

S. purpurea x psittacina

Strange, dark red, ground-hugging pitchers, with an unusual hood that curls inward on either side.

S. flava x leucophylla

Very handsome trumpets, mottled with extra color in the hood, and with orange flowers. Excellent pitchers throughout the season.

S. leucophylla x rubra

Clumps of narrow, colorful pitchers with ruffled lids, heavily influenced by the subspecies of *S. rubra* involved. Many red flowers.

S. leucophylla x minor

A very popular cross, with an undulating, overhanging lid, heavily dappled in reds and whites. Orange flowers.

Sarracenia x excellens, **the cross between** *S. minor x leucophylla*

S. leucophylla x psittacina

Extremely bizarre, the pitchers are curved with beaked heads. A poor insect catcher, but often very bright and colorful.

S. rubra x flava

These crosses usually produce handsome trumpets with rich red venation, and smallish, pale-red flowers.

Hybrids with **Sarracenia oreophila** are often extra vigorous and colorful. This is its cross with **S. purpurea** ssp. **venosa.**

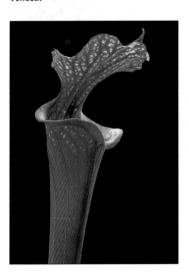

A burgundy form of **Sarracenia x moorei.**

Here are some general guidelines concerning the simple hybrids.

Most crosses between the upright trumpet species (S. flava, S. leucophylla, S. rubra, S. alata, and S. oreophila) produce attractive, tall, and colorful pitchers.

Hybrids with S. psittacina can be very weird and low-growing, and are often rather unattractive, as well as poor insect catchers.

The trumpet varieties crossed with S. minor inherit the overhanging hood of that species, and can be rather handsome. Light windows can also be inherited.

For color, nothing beats the influence of S. leucophylla.

S. oreophila crosses are almost always extra vigorous and beautiful.

Keep in mind the seasonality of the parents. S. flava, S. oreophila, and S. minor, for example, produce their best pitchers early in the year. S. leucophylla, S. rubra, and S. alata are often best in later summer. Crosses between these two groups result in strong pitchers throughout the season. S. purpurea and S. psittacina hold their leaves through winter in fairly good shape, and can influence offspring.

Pay close attention to the forms and varieties of the parents, which can add much beauty compared to the typical species. Among the most outstanding are plants such as S. oreophila "Sand Mountain", S. leucophylla "Red and White," S. purpurea "Red Form" and 'burkei', *S. minor* "Okee Giant," *S. alata* "Nigrapurpurea," and *S. flava* "Red Tube."

When a hybrid is labeled F-2, this means it resulted from a hybrid parent that was self-pollinated, and extremes in variability can be expected.

The more cold-hardy species can produce cold-hardy hybrids: *S. purpurea* ssp. *purpurea, S. rubra* ssp. *jonessi,* and *S. oreophila* pass on cold-tolerance to their offspring.

Although the rules have recently changed, the plant producing the seed is usually listed first in hybrid equations. New laws allow them to be alphabetized.

Complex crosses

You get to use your imagination here! I will only suggest that when labeling or recording your plants, try to use brackets and parenthesis, and use codes as the formula lengthens.

Here is an example of the progress of such hybridization.

First cross: *S. purpurea* x *flava*.

Second cross: *S. (purpurea* x *flava*) x *leucophylla*.

Third cross: S. [(p x f) x l] x *minor*.

If this last cross was the first of its kind, then it would be given a fancy name, such as S. x 'Godzilla'. If carnivorous plants were grown under a system similar to that of orchid growers, S. x 'Godzilla' would then be registered with the society, and anyone later duplicating the cross would have to call it by that registered name. My belief is that eventually the ICPS will organize such a system, and records will be important in order to trace and record the history of complex hybrids and how they should be named. This will be a daunting task, and I offer my best wishes to anyone willing to tackle it. A computer will certainly come in handy!

Sarracenia (purpurea x flava) x flava

Cultivars

This is a mildly easier topic to discuss, but it can still be confusing and many misconceptions can occur.

Cultivar means "cultivated variety."

A cultivar can be any outstanding plant species or hybrid that is so desirable it should be forever propagated only vegetatively—through division or tissue culture—to preserve its genetic makeup and guarantee it is an exact duplicate or clone of the originally selected plant. One cannot propagate cultivars from seed!

Sarracenia (leucophylla x minor) x (purpurea x rubra)

Cultivars can and should be registered with the ICPS, documenting the plant with a photo, description and history, if known. Cultivars are also legitimate if they are published in a book or catalog, and not ICPS.

Cultivars should be given a fancy name, but not in Latin. The name should be preceded by the letters cv. to identify it as a cultivar, or the name should be put into single quotes. On labels or tags it is wise to add the cv. to indicate that the plant is a registered cultivar. Common varietal or nicknames are best in double quotes, as in *S. flava* "Coppertop."

Cultivars among *Sarracenia* are rare but are beginning to gain in popularity. One problem has been the reliance on division to propagate the plants, which can take decades to produce sizable quantities, and thus the plants were often outrageously expensive. However, recent advances in tissue culture has made a once-bleak future look brighter, and I expect many famous and sought-after cultivars will, by the turn of this century, become very affordable and popular.

Some *Sarracenia* cultivars

S. x 'Willisii': Of very confused ancestry, this plant was produced by Vietch and Sons nursery in England in the nineteenth century. A beauty, it has curved, upright pitchers with

Sarracenia x 'Judith Hindle', before she turns plum red

a ruffled lid similar to a *S. purpurea* x *leucophylla* cross, but the pitchers are pink initially, turning a deep plum red.

The following seven clonal cultivars were produced by Adrian Slack. Mr. Slack owned Marston Exotics nursery in England before an unfortunate illness caused his early retirement.

Sarracenia x 'Daniel Rudd'
One of Slack's favorites. The bright red flowers can remain in petal for three weeks. The pitchers are coppery chestnut with darker veins. S. [(p x f) x l] x l.

Sarracenia x 'Evendine'
A clone of Slack's cross of *S. leucophylla* x (*flava* x *purpurea*). The pitchers at first are golden green and veined, later turning dark red.

Sarracenia x 'Judy'
Is *S. minor* x (x *excellens*), with a highly domed lid and many light windows.

Sarracenia x 'Lynda Butt'
Of unpublished ancestry. The pitchers are tall and narrow, with a ruffled lid and mottling around the mouth.

Sarracenia x 'Marston Mill'
Slender, olive-colored pitchers, widening to a highly decorative mouth and hood. Its parentage is S. [l x (p x f)] x f.

Sarracenia x *excellens* 'Lochness'
Another vigorous clone of this common hybrid.

Sarracenia x *moorei* 'Marston Clone'
A vigorous cultivar of the popular hybrid, with pale orange flowers.

Of my own cultivars chosen at California Carnivores, the following are noteworthy.

Sarracenia oreophila 'Don Schnell'
A beautiful clone of the 'Sand Mountain' form of the endangered species.

Sarracenia x 'Abandoned Hope'
This monstrous plant is a clone of a particularly vigorous *S. purpurea* ssp. *venosa* var. *burkei* x *flava*.

Sarracenia purpurea 'Red Ruffles.' See its description under the section on the Purple Pitcher plant.

Sarracenia x 'Judith Hindle'

One of the most beautiful cultivars yet produced, this plant was bred and grown by Alan Hindle, and chosen and named at California Carnivores. The compact pitchers have a wildly undulating hood, and start out green, dappled in whites and yellows. As they age, they transform to deep, dark red. Of the hundreds of CPs in my collection, this clone is probably the most popular. S. x 'Judith Hindle's' parents were two separate clones of S. (p x f) x l.

Sarracenia x 'Lamentations'

Of unknown origin, this hybrid has narrow, deeply maroon trumpets with upright, pointy lids.

Sarracenia (oreophila "sand mountain" x *flava*) x *leucophylla*.

Sarracenia x 'Extreme Unction'

Chosen from a cross of *S. m.* x [(*p* x *f*) x *f*], the plump pitchers are green, with a large domed lid netted scarlet, with cathedral-like windows along its back.

Larry Mellichamp of the University of North Carolina at Charlotte, with the assistance of Rob Gardner at UNC, Chapel Hill, have produced several distinctive clonal cultivars. Among them are:

Sarracenia x 'Dixie Lace'

Hardy to −6°F, if not colder, this complex cross has compact curved pitchers to ten inches, heavily veined in red on a pale yellow background, with a canopy hood.

Sarracenia x 'Jambalaya'

The pitchers are greenish with red veining, with flared, fan-like ruffled heads tinted red.

Sarracenia x 'Sultry Maid'

The narrow green pitchers are topped with a broad, flattened, wavy lid heavily mottled in green, white, and red.

Sarracenia x 'Sultry Maid'

CULTIVATION

(See Parts One and Two for further details)

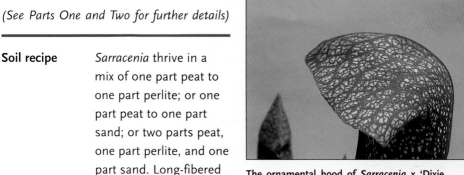

The ornamental hood of *Sarracenia* x 'Dixie Lace'

Soil recipe	*Sarracenia* thrive in a mix of one part peat to one part perlite; or one part peat to one part sand; or two parts peat, one part perlite, and one part sand. Long-fibered sphagnum is also excellent.
Containers	Plastic pots or glazed ceramics are best. They may be drained or undrained. Young plants do well in four-inch pots, mature plants in six- to eight-inch pots or larger.
Watering	Use the tray method for drained pots. Keep the soil permanently damp to very wet.
Climate	All, with one exception, are warm temperate, enjoying warm summers and chilly winters; tolerant of light frosts and brief freezes. *S. purpurea* ssp. *purpurea* require cold-temperate climates and can tolerate an extended deep freeze.
Light	Full to mostly sunny is best.
Dormancy	All require three to four months of winter dormancy, with reduced temperatures and photoperiod.

Outdoors	*Sarracenia* do well in temperate, warm-temperate, and Mediterranean-like climates. *S. purpurea* ssp. *purpurea* does best in temperate and cold-temperate climates. The southern species survive cold-temperate climates in bog gardens mulched in winter.
Bog gardens	*Sarracenia* are among the best for bog gardens. (See "Outdoors," above.) Mulch in colder zones.
Greenhouse	Excellent in cold houses, cool houses, and warm houses, and cold frames in warm-temperate climates. *S. purpurea* ssp. *purpurea* is best in cold houses.
Terrarium	Generally poor candidates due primarily to their size and dormancy requirements. However, good seasonal candidates are *S. purpurea*, *S. psittacina*, *S. rubra* and their hybrids, or young plants. Better under high-intensity lights. Dormancy must be respected.

Sarracenia flava

Windowsills	Good candidates for only the sunniest windows or solariums, but respect their winter dormancy. In order of best first: *S. purpurea* ssp. *venosa*, *S. psittacina*, *S. rubra*, *S. minor*, *S. flava*, *S. oreophila*, *S. alata*. The one requiring the most sun is *S. leucophylla*. All trumpet plants can be superb housefly catchers.
Feeding	Outdoors they are often gluttonous pigs, devouring ants, flies, wasps, beetles, and moths. Can usually be hand-fed crickets, sow bugs, or dried insects.

Fertilizers	Fertilizers for acid-loving plants are best applied foliarly.
Transplanting	Potted specimens should be divided and transplanted every three to five years, or when the growing points become crammed along the edge of the pot. This should only be done during dormancy.
Pests and diseases	Primary pests of American pitcher plants are aphids, scale, and mealybug. Orthene, Diazinon, and Malathion are the best controls. Seeds can be attacked by damp-off fungus. Treat with a fungicide.

PROPAGATION

Seed

Sarracenia flowers are not only among the most beautiful in nature, they are cleverly designed to enhance cross-pollination. Bees are their most common pollinator. Carrying pollen from a previous flower, the bees can only enter over the female stigmas between the petals, where the pollen is deposited. Once inside, they become dusted with fresh pollen. To exit, they push through the petals, thus avoiding the stigmas and self-pollination.

When the flowers open, they will remain in petal for seven to ten days on average. By lifting a petal, you will see the male anthers on the inside ceiling of the flower. The anthers, when ripe, will release their yellow, powdery pollen onto the floor of the upside-down umbrella style. To self-pollinate, collect this with a small brush, and deposit the pollen onto each of the female stigmas. You will see the stigmas, five of them, as tiny bumplike hooks on the inside tips of each point of the umbrella style. Deposit a dab of pollen onto each one.

The seed pod of *Sarracenia*

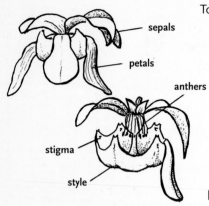

sepals

petals

anthers

stigma

style

The flower structure of *Sarracenia*

To cross-pollinate, carefully deposit the pollen onto the stigmas of another opened flower.

Be sure to label the flowers. It is best to repeat this procedure a few times for best seed set.

Pollen may be stored for several weeks, in the refrigerator, in packets of aluminum foil. It can be used on flowers that open later in the season.

When the petals drop off, the sepals and umbrella style remain, and gradually may lift upward, rather than remain nodding and upside down. The ovary, on the ceiling of the seed pod where the anthers were, will gradually swell over summer.

By autumn, the seed pod will turn brown and gradually crack open. The seed, up to several hundred, can be collected at this time. Each seed is brown to reddish tan, and about the size of a large pinhead. Separate the seed from the ovary, and store dry in a small paper envelope or an airtight plastic bag.

To germinate, the seed needs several weeks of chilly, damp stratification. It is usually best to sow the seed around February, onto its preferred soil mix or milled sphagnum. Do not bury the seed. Sow sparsely, and treat with a fungicide, as the seed is very susceptible to damp-off disease. Light frost is helpful during stratification.

After stratification, with warmer, partly sunny conditions, the seed will germinate. At the end of one growing season, the seedlings will have pitchers one to two inches tall. The plants will take, on average, about five years to reach maturity.

Division

Most mature *Sarracenia* readily produce offshoots and new growing points year after year. Some, such as *S. purpurea* and *S. psittacina,* are slow at this or never multiply, but others, such as *S. rubra,* may develop from one growing point to over fifty in a few short years. These clumps of plants can easily be divided.

This is best done during winter dormancy or
early spring as the plants come back into growth.
To divide a plant in summer or autumn will shock
it, and it may not recuperate until the following
year.

Remove the plant from its pot and wash away as
much soil as possible. You will be able to see clearly
the separate growing points from which the pitchers
emerge. The rhizome is often gnarled and branching,
the roots tough and wiry. By wiggling the growing
points you can usually make out where they join the
main rhizome. Snap these apart or cut them with a
knife. Be sure the separated growing point has a few
of its own roots.

If the divided plant had already begun growth,
you may want to soak the divisions in a vitamin B-1 solution such as Superthrive to overcome shock.

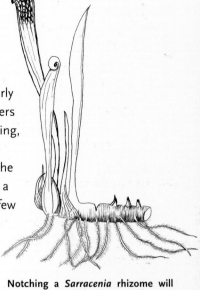

**Notching a *Sarracenia* rhizome will
usually encourage new growing points**

A healthy rhizome is white inside, similar to a potato.
Often, older parts of the rhizome are brown and
dead, and should be trimmed away.

Long, branching rhizomes with few growing points
may be cut further into pieces about two to three
inches long, even if no growing points appear on
that section. When potted up, these sections will
produce offshoots.

New growing points can be instigated in potted
Sarracenia when the rhizomes are long and old.
Clear away some soil along the top of the rhizome to expose it. With a sharp knife, cut into
the rhizome about halfway. Several cuts or
notches may be made. New growing shoots
will usually appear along these cuts. The following year the plant can then be divided.

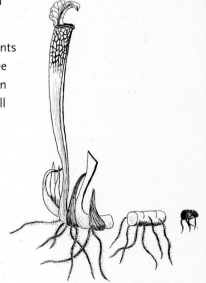

Division of a *Sarracenia* rhizome

When repotting divisions make sure the rhizome pieces are planted horizontally with the roots downward, the growing points at the soil surface. Cut off any emerging flowers from newly divided *Sarracenia,* as they will exhaust the plant.

Tissue culture

Sarracenia can be introduced in vitro through sterilized seed. Newly emerging flower buds and leaves can also be successful, but often with great difficulty. New methods are being developed to enhance this process, and are looking promising. This will greatly affect the propagation of cultivars, which have generally been in short supply.

— 3 —
THE COBRA PLANT
(DARLINGTONIA CALIFORNICA)

WITH THEIR BULBOUS GREEN HEADS, twisted red tongues, and long, tubular pitchers, the cobra plant is very suitably named.

The plant was discovered by botanist J. D. Brackenridge in 1841 just south of Mt. Shasta, California. On an expedition that was exploring the northwest, Brackenridge was reported to have just collected the plant when his group had an altercation with the region's Native Americans. Fleeing the area with his arms full of serpentine leaves, Brackenridge noticed a butterfly fluttering persistently after the bobbing heads, so attractive was the plant to its insect prey. John Torrey, who described it in 1853, named the plant after his friend Dr. William Darlington.

Cobra plants are native only to extreme Northern California and southern Oregon. They are primarily mountain plants, predominantly found in the Cascades, but populations exist down to sea level along the coast, often within sight of the Pacific. At the highest elevations, over eight thousand feet, the plants are covered with snow in the winter, while coastal stands of the plant may see frost only rarely. The climate could be considered Mediterranean-like to the extent that much of the precipitation falls in winter, while summers are mostly dry. Depending on the altitude, summer days may be hot inland or cool along the coast, but nights for native cobras in the summertime almost always are chilly.

Cobra plants may be found growing in sphagnum bogs in sunny patches of coastal forest, wet grassy meadows in the mountains, or on gravelly slopes of serpentine rock where water is constantly seeping. Typically, cobras colonize areas where springs are located and the water is usually cool and slowly moving. This is a key to understanding their cultivation.

Darlingtonia is very closely related to *Sarracenia*. There are striking similarities between it and *S. minor* and *S. psittacina*. Seedling plants are

The puffed hoods and red tongues of the aptly named cobra plant

tiny, with snakelike pitchers hugging the ground like little tubes with pointy tongues hanging from their ends. When two to three years of age, the pitcher leaves tend to become more characteristic of those of mature plants.

The leaves arise from the rhizome in tubular fashion, often with a gradual twist. The head of the leaf is a puffed hood of transparent windows. Under the hood is a circular opening, difficult to distinguish from almost any angle but below. It is from the front portion of the hole that the twisted, mustachioed "tongue" emerges, also known as the "fishtail appendage."

Most of its insect prey are lured to the plant by its colorful, nectar-baited tongue. Crawling insects also follow nectar trails that run up the pitcher's exterior. The nectar is the heaviest at the base of the tongue's attachment to the circular opening. At this point, insects may be lured to enter the hole by the brilliance of the sun shining through the hood's transparent light windows. To do so would be the prey's fatal mistake. For once inside the hood, escape is virtually impossible. An inner collar surrounding the entrance is similar to a lobster or minnow trap, making an exit almost impossible to find. Instead, the victim (most often a flying insect) is attracted to the windows in the hood, perceiving them (falsely) to be skylights offering escape.

The confused insect bounces around until it tumbles helplessly down the tube. It is not yet known if any drugs assist in the capture of prey. Regardless, hope for an escape is dismal, as the lower portion of the interior pitcher is lined with sharp, slippery, downward-pointing hairs.

Darlingtonia, unlike its cousins the *Sarracenia,* produces no enzymes to aid in the digestion of insects. But as insects become caught, water is secreted by the pitcher that drowns the victims. Bacteria and other microorganisms help break down the soft parts of the prey. This nutritional fluid is then reabsorbed by the plant.

That the plants do catch larger animals, such as the Pacific tree frog, is something I have witnessed among my greenhouse plants many times. It is possible that the frogs are tempted to enter the hood by the insects trapped there, but more likely these amphibians are simply seeking shelter.

Cobra plants often begin their growth for the season by developing flower buds at the growing point, even in winter. As the weather warms, the single nodding flower arises on a one- to three-foot-tall stem. The blooms hang upside down, in a similar fashion to *Sarracenia*. The sepals are long, pointed, and green; the petals are purplish red and are held together except toward their ends, where they allow for the entrance of pollinating insects.

Pitchers begin to grow in spring, developing in an upright, rosetted fashion with most of the leaves facing outward. The tallest pitchers are usually the first ones of the season and can be up to four feet tall in the wild, but usually half this in cultivation. Pitchers produced in summer are usually much shorter than the spring leaves. Grown from seed, maximum-sized leaves can take seven to ten years to develop. But the

plants are mature and can flower sooner than that.

This plant's most unusual trait is its ability to produce long stolons, or runners, underground. From the tips of the stolons, plants emerge that can reach maturity rather quickly. In the wild, cobras produce dense, impenetrable stands of these runners, sometimes at a great distance from the mother plant. At times these stands seem to run down a seeping slope like a river. In cultivation, these stolons may wrap around the interior of the pot several times before emerging as a baby plant.

Temperate plants, cobras are dormant in winter but can hold some leaves even under a blanket of snow.

The nodding flower of *Darlingtonia*

CULTIVATION *(See Parts I and II for further information)*

Cobra plants have a bad reputation for being difficult to grow. This is not far from the truth, but the difficulty can be overcome. You get a head start if you live in a climate with cool summer nights, if you can water your plants frequently, and if you can refrigerate the water (see "Watering," below).

Soil recipe	Use one part long-fibered sphagnum moss to one part perlite. Another good mix is two parts perlite, lava rock, and/or pumice to one part peat. The mix should be airy—the rock ingredients will help cool the roots.
Containers	Plastic pots can be used in a cool environment, but avoid dark colors such as black, which will warm considerably in the sunlight. For best results, use pale-colored, glazed ceramic or terra-cotta clay. Fibrous peat pots also work well.

	The roots can be kept cooler in larger pots, and even small plants will need room for stolon growth. Always use drained containers with holes; never grow cobras in small, undrained pots.
Watering	Use the tray method, but it is crucial that you continue to water the plant overhead. Always use cool water. People in hot climates should consider refrigerating their water. It often helps to flush the pot with chilly water when temperatures rise. Ice cubes of purified water on a very hot day, placed on the soil surface, can save a cobra's life.
Light	In the wild, cobra plants grow in full sun to partly shaded areas, with best coloration in the sun. In warmer climates, consider having the pots somewhat shaded, perhaps by other containers, if the plants are grown in sun.
Climate	A warm-temperate to temperate climate, preferably Mediterranean-like. Most *Darlingtonia* in cultivation originated from coastal Oregon, which is the milder portion of their range. Cool summer nights are preferred—you will have difficulty if your summer nights are very warm. Cobras are very tolerant of frosts.
Bog gardens	A superb bog candidate if conditions are similar to those under "Outdoors," below. May succeed in northerly latitudes such as the Great Lakes or New England if heavily protected in winter.
Greenhouses	Does well in cold houses, cool houses, and even warm houses, if night temperatures drop below sixty degrees in the summer. Succeeds in cold frames in warm-temperate to temperate and Mediterranean-like climates.
Terrariums	Impractical, but young plants may be worth a try in cool terrariums or under grow-lights in basements. Flush pots often with chilly water (see below).
Windowsills	Surprisingly good candidate for east-facing or sometimes sunless north windowsills. Flush pot often with cool or refrigerated water. Try ice cubes on hot days, or grow in an

	air-conditioned room. Cool nights are very helpful. Hot sun will warm pots to a dangerous level. Respect dormancy.
Outdoors	Generally succeeds well only in Mediterranean-like climates or high altitudes where summer nights are chilly. Excellent near the coast from Seattle to San Diego. Protect pots from hot sun. Water frequently; a turkey baster is helpful to recirculate water from the tray more easily. Drained pots submerged in the ground may also keep the roots cool.
Feeding	Sow bugs and crickets work well. Dried insects are easier, however.
Fertilizers	A light foliar feeding once or twice a month during the growing season works well. Use Miracid, Orchid 30-10-10, or epiphytic fertilizer.
Pests and diseases	Diseases are uncommon, but cobras can be attacked by scale, mealybug, and thrips. Aphids can attack newly emerging leaves, and caterpillars love new, soft pitchers before they harden off. Orthene, Diazinon, and Malathion control these pests.
	Deer have a peculiar fondness for the puffed heads of *Darlingtonia*. In their native habitat, cobras are sometimes called "deer licks" by the locals.

PROPAGATION

Division

You can divide large, mature clumps of *Darlingtonia* periodically. This is best done in winter when the plants are dormant. Be sure each growing point has its own root system. Pamper them with lots of overhead watering as the plants establish themselves.

Seed

Seed is a slow but possible way to produce cobras. Pollinate the flowers by hand to ensure good seed set. Separate the petals, and with a tiny paintbrush collect some pollen from the anthers, which you will find on the ceiling of the flower. Deposit this onto the star-shaped stigma, which lies at the bottom of the ovary. Seed is produced two to three months later, as the capsule becomes erect and brown, splitting open.

The small seeds are bristly, no doubt to encourage dispersal by animals. Store the seed dry in the refrigerator until the following winter. Sow them around February on long-fibered sphagnum. Then stratify the seed for a couple of months, keeping it damp and chilly. As spring approaches, the seed will begin to germinate. The plants will be slow growing. About three years later, the pitchers will be two to four inches long.

Stolon cuttings

This is by far the most reliable way to propagate cobras. Stolons can be removed from the mother plant in winter or early spring. The long runners should not be removed until a baby plant is visible at its end. You will notice small roots every few inches along the length of the runner. Cut the runners into sections, each containing a few roots. I like to lay these horizontally on a bed of sphagnum in a drained seed tray. Keep covered with a propagation dome, and water with cool water frequently. Soon pitchers will develop out of the stolon sections.

Tissue culture

Cobras can be propagated in vitro through seed.

— 4 —
THE SUN PITCHERS
(*Heliamphora*)

Heliamphora nutans

REMINISCENT OF DELICATELY sculpted vases, with tall stems of lovely, lilylike flowers, the sun pitchers of South America have a beautiful simplicity. Related to their cousins in the north, *Sarracenia* and *Darlingtonia,* these are the only pitcher plants of the southern continent, and their native habitat is as exotic and mysterious as the plants themselves.

When Sir Arthur Conan Doyle wrote his famous novel *The Lost World,* he chose as its location the remote and isolated tabletop mountains known as "tepuis." Doyle's prehistoric monsters had survived the millennia on these flat-topped mountains in the Guayana Highlands of Southern Venezuela, Guayana, and northern Brazil. The surrounding savannas are already four thousand feet above sea level, a cool tropical climate. The tepuis rise an additional two to four thousand feet above this—sheer cliffs and terraces that vanish into the clouds. Although no dinosaurs have yet been discovered, these islands in the sky have many strange species of life upon them, and among the most curious are the sun pitchers, *Heliamphora*.

The first species discovered was *H. nutans,* found by the German naturalist R. H. Schomburgk in 1839, upon Mt. Roriama. In 1840 the plant was named by G. Bentham, who chose the Greek words *helos* (marsh) and *amphora* (vessel or pitcher). But the similarity to *helios,* the sun, has given the genus its common name of sun pitcher. It wasn't until almost a century later that a second species was discovered, and in the 1950s and 1970s several more were found as explorations of the many tepuis became more frequent.

The tepui mountains of the Guayana Highlands sit in the cool clouds that arise from the humid, tropical

Heliamphora nutans

landscape below. These clouds condense as they rise, and the result is torrential and frequent rainfall, thunder, and lightning, with frequent high winds. The temperatures at the top can dip near the freezing mark but average in the fifties at night up into the seventies when the sun peeks through the clouds. The mountains are made of sandstone, and the rains collect in marshes and shallow pools along the surface, and end up cascading over the edges into often spectacular waterfalls. Angel Falls, for example, the tallest waterfall in the world, drops almost 3,500 feet from the top of Mt. Auyan-Tepui.

Vegetation is sparse on the mountain tops, and ideally suited for carnivores. Since the rains carry away the few minerals that exist, bladderworts and some sundews can often be found growing with the sun pitchers, as can the insect-eating bromeliad *Brocchinea reducta*. There is no real soil for plants to grow in on the tepuis, so these species are often growing in the decomposing debris of their own leaves, as well as the short clumping grasses and mosses that often accompany them. Two species, *H. heterodoxa* and *H. minor,* have migrated from the mountains to the warmer savannas below but grow in cool water marshes.

Of the several species, forms, and varieties known to exist, the basic structure is very similar. The pitcher leaves arise from a rhizome that is anchored by wiry roots. The pitchers themselves appear to be funnel- or bell-shaped structures that seem nothing more than rolled-up leaves joined by a seam at their front. Although lacking in the fancy ornaments of tongues, hoods and light windows like their North American cousins, the design of the sun pitchers is nonetheless a rather sophisticated trap.

Adapted to high winds, the pitchers are rather tough yet brittle. Scattered nectar glands appear externally, as a lure to insects. The most prominent structure is a smallish cap on the upper rear of the leaf, known as the nectar spoon. In strong light, these spoons are colorful and well developed, hanging over the wide, funnel-shaped mouth like a rudimentary hood. Although the nectar spoon does nothing to prevent the access of copious amounts of rainfall entering the leaf, it is so positioned as to protect the large glands found in the spoon, which secrete ample amounts of nectar.

Another curious yet invisible design is a rather narrow slit or pore found about midway along the front seam of the leaf. This allows excess rainwater to trickle free of the pitcher, keeping the water held in the leaf at a constant level.

The upper, interior walls of most *Heliamphora* pitchers are covered in fine, bristly, downward-pointing hairs, very similar to some species of *Sarracenia*. The mid part of the interior is completely lacking in hairs, the smooth walls offering difficult foothold for most insects. These hairs reappear near the bottom of the leaf, but are nearly always submerged in the pool of collected rainwater. Nectar glands also exist along the upper interior of the pitcher.

Adrian Slack commented that the small nectar spoon may be a well-adapted design to accommodate no more than one medium-sized insect, as he observed two houseflies jostling for a drink of nectar that almost cost the life of one fly. I have observed among my own *H. nutans* that immediately below the nectar spoon, where a falling insect may tumble, there is often a wet, dark splotch lacking in bristly hairs. I surmised this to be purposely slick, for an insect, falling from its perch at the spoon, would slip on this patch and immediately be dispatched into the pool of water below. There the insects drown.

There have been no drugs yet isolated from the nectar of sun pitchers, nor digestive enzymes. It is apparently bacteria that helps dissolve the prey that drown in the rainwater held by each leaf.

Curiously, the tepui mountains are not rich with insects for the plants to catch, and the plants may be competing for the few insects that are available with the many frogs also found on the mountains. Larger insects, like beetles, have often been seen entering and exiting the pitchers with minimal hassle. In fact, I've seen numerous photos of colorful, bug-eyed frogs sitting in the *Heliamphora* leaves, but not many photos of the leaves with insects within them. In my California nursery, I com-

Heliamphora nutans

monly find Pacific tree frogs nestled rather comfortably in the well of the leaves, staring in a trance at the nectar spoon above. The frogs often sit on the hairless splotch mentioned above. These frogs are never caught. However, it wouldn't surprise me if this turns out to be a further adaptation of the plant. The nectar spoon may allow the occasional frog to be literally spoon-fed insects—with a flick of its tongue, the frog can snatch a meal from the plant. However, the frog's presence may be a further example of "digestion by proxy," as sun pitchers may benefit from the excrement the frogs drop into the leaf. This symbiotic relationship would lessen frog and plant competition, while both would be rewarded.

The flowers of *Heliamphora* are showy and beautiful. Tall stems, often blood red in color, hold a row of large, bell-shaped flowers. The flowers have no petals, but have evolved tepals, which are midway between petals and sepals. The plants usually bloom in winter and spring, and the flowers open progressively along the stem. The anthers and stigmas mature at differing times, thus encouraging cross-pollination by bees. The tepals are usually snow white when they open, and gradually turn to pinks and greens over the many weeks that they remain on the stems.

THE SPECIES

The identification of species can be difficult for several reasons. Most are very similar to each other; their environment both in the wild and in cultivation can greatly affect the appearance of the leaves; they are very variable; and natural hybrids can also occur. True identification must rely on flower anatomy, which is beyond the scope of this work. Here I will review the general characteristics of the plants, some of which are still rare in cultivation.

Heliamphora nutans

This is probably the most common species grown. Native to Mt. Roraima and Mt. Duida, the pitchers are curvaceous and robust, averaging six to twelve inches in height. The nectar spoon is well developed, and the pitchers are dark green with a red border. Flower spikes are tall, reaching two feet in height. An easy and rewarding plant for the greenhouse and larger terrarium.

Heliamphora minor

An often diminutive species, the squat pitchers are usually two to six inches tall, but some forms can be twice as large. Usually pale green in color, tinted red in good light, the pitchers can form handsome, low-growing clusters. The nectar spoon is bright red and small. An excellent subject for the terrarium. Discovered in 1939 on Mt. Auyan-Tepui, colonies are also found in the surrounding warmer lowlands.

Heliamphora heterodoxa

Discovered in 1951 on Mt. Ptari-Tepui, this species also colonizes the lowland savannas. A handsome plant with a large, overhanging nectar spoon, the deep green pitchers can reach ten to twelve inches in height. Excellent in the terrarium. Most plants in cultivation originated from the warmer lowlands, but survive cooler conditions.

Heliamphora ionassi

Discovered on Mt. Ilu-Tepui in 1978, this beautiful species has only recently been introduced into cultivation. The pitchers flare widely at the mouth and can reach a height of eighteen inches. Their color is a pale yellow green, often suffused with red. The "Deep Red" form is burgundy along the exterior of the leaf, while the interior is a fuzzy, golden green.

Heliamphora tatei

Perhaps the most spectacular species, first described in 1931, there are now believed to be several varieties growing on Mt. Duida and a few other mountains. These plants are also new to cultivation. *H. tatei* var. *tatei* is the most unusual, for the large pitchers, over fifteen inches tall, grow from woody stems that can branch several feet. Variety *neblinae,* found on the mountain Cerro de la Neblina, was once thought to be a species. In general, the pitchers are tubular with highly developed nectar spoons. They are often lined with red venation, and in some, like var. *neblinae,* the pitchers can become beautifully crimson in strong light.

CULTIVATION *(See Parts One and Two for further details)*

Soil recipe	*Heliamphora* are very tolerant of a variety of wet, open, well-drained soils that are low in nutrients. An excellent mix is one part long-fibered sphagnum, one part perlite, and one part lava rock or pumice. Alternatively, the plants do well in two parts perlite to one part peat. Coarse New Zealand sphagnum also works well when it's not kept waterlogged.
Containers	Plastic, clay, or glazed ceramics that have drainage holes. Four-inch pots for young plants, six- to eight-inch pots for mature plants.
Watering	Use a shallow tray method with frequent overhead watering with cool, purified water. If watered daily, the pots need not sit in trays or saucers. Keep soil permanently wet.
Light	High light levels or partly sunny conditions are best for healthy, colorful plants. Avoid overheating pots.

Climate	Most are considered highland tropicals, and do best with night temperatures between 45 and 60 degrees; day temperatures between 60 and 80 degrees. Extremes tolerated are 35 to 90 degrees, but cooler day temperatures are preferred. High humidity is a requirement, as well as good air circulation. *H. heterodoxa* and *H. minor* from the lower intermediate zones do well with nights between 55 and 60 degrees and warm days, but appreciate cool overhead watering.
Outdoors	Very doubtful, unless you live in highland tropics. They might succeed on a cool, foggy, frost-free coastline like California, but would need protection from salty spray and hot, dry, offshore winds.
Bog gardens	Generally not suitable, for reasons cited under "Outdoors."
Greenhouses	Excellent for the cool house and warm house, near swamp coolers or under mist systems. Try not to exceed 85 degrees. A drop in night temperature is usually beneficial. The lowland varieties will also succeed in hothouses.
Terrariums	Excellent in cooler terrariums under grow-lights. If you live in a warm climate, terrariums in basements or air-conditioned rooms work well. Mist your plants often.
Windowsills	Very doubtful, due to the plants' high humidity requirements. Slightly possible if you live close to a cool beach, such as on the immediate Pacific Coast.
Feeding	Young plants will eat fruit flies and baby crickets; larger plants will enjoy sow or pill bugs, crickets, mealworms, and dried insects.
Fertilization	*Heliamphora* respond very well to foliar feeding. Try using Miracid, Orchid, or epiphytic fertilizers. Apply this once or twice monthly and the plants will grow fairly fast and flower regularly.
Transplanting	Easy, and best done in winter and spring. Soak in vitamin B-1 solution if bare-rooted.

Pests and diseases	Rarely attacked by scale. Fungus might be a problem in stagnant air and low-light levels. Slack mentions that copper-based fungicides are lethal.

PROPAGATION

Seed

Observation on the tepuis has indicated that it is bees that pollinate *Heliamphora* flowers, and that similarly to other species of plants, vibration is needed to release pollen.

The several flowers on a scape will open one at a time over the coarse of a few weeks. When a flower opens, the female stigma is receptive for a few days, but the male pollen is not mature until after the stigma looses its receptivity. Therefore, flowers must be cross-pollinated. When examining the flower of a sun pitcher plant, you will see a cluster of tubelike pollen sacs—the anthers. Rising from the center of this is a short, green stalk, the tip of which is the female stigma. The stigma turns brown when it is no longer receptive.

The tuning fork method works well to release pollen. Hold a piece of paper below the tepals and touch the pollen sacs with the vibrating fork. A small, dustlike amount of pollen will be deposited if the pollen is mature. Collect this with a small paintbrush and dab it to the green stigma of another, newly opened flower.

The flowers of *Heliamphora nutans*—a pleasure any time of the year.

Don Schnell has found that removing the pollen sacs and tearing them open will also release a small amount of pollen, without the use of a tuning fork. Using forceps, dab the whole sac gently to a fresh, receptive stigma. If pollination is successful, the ovary will swell, turn brown, and release its seed within two to four months.

The seed need no stratification and can be lightly scattered on milled sphagnum or their preferred soil mix. Keep humid and in bright light, and germination should occur in several weeks. A seedling will take several years to reach maturity.

Heliamphora may also be cross-pollinated among their species with ease, thus producing hybrids. Some hybrids already produced include *H. nutans* x *minor, H. heterodoxa* x *minor,* and *H. nutans* x *heterodoxa,* among others. These crosses have the combined characteristics of both parents.

Division

Sun pitchers have the pleasant habit of vigorously producing offshoots when grown well, thus producing handsome clumps over time. These can be easily divided when necessary.

I prefer to do this during winter and spring. Remove the plant from its pot and wash away the soil. You should be able to clearly distinguish the various growing points along the rhizome. Gently snap or cut these apart. Try to ensure each growing point has its own root system. Soak in a vitamin B-1 solution, such as Superthrive, and repot. Apply a light mist of fertilizer about two weeks later. Remove any flower stalks from a divided plant, because it will exhaust its recovery.

Tissue culture

Heliamphora have become much more common and affordable through the success of tissue culture. Plants may be introduced into flask through the use of sterilized seed.

— 5 —
THE SUNDEWS
(DROSERA)

"Evil little things they are, with their carnivorous habit. One wonders what crime the past lives of Drosera can have held, that now their race should be compelled to draw so ominous and unpleasant a [career] of murder and fraud. When will Sundews be free of the burden, through some self-sacrificing individual plant who shall starve to death rather than take life, and so redeem his race into happier paths of peace and virtue?"

—REGINALD FARRAR, *Alpine and Bog Plants*, 1908

IF AN INSECT EVER EVOLVED the brains to write a horror novel, the monster in that novel would probably be a sundew.

Sundews are innocent-looking and pretty, their delicate leaves sparkling with the promise of sweet nectar, but the foolish insect curious enough to give a sundew the slightest touch will suddenly find itself caught in a living nightmare. Doomed to a horrible death, the insect may struggle for a blessed few minutes or suffer for untold hours as it tries to break free of ensnaring, suffocating glue, grasping tentacles, and burning acids and enzymes; meanwhile, its precious bodily fluids are slowly sucked dry. Mother Nature hopefully had psychiatric care after she designed the sundews.

The *Drosera* are probably the most diverse genus of carnivorous

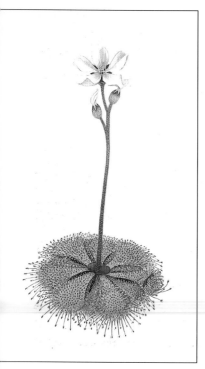

Drosera brevifolia

plants in the world. There are somewhere around 130 species found on almost every continent of earth. Sundews can be found in Canada, Alaska, and Siberia. They are denizens of bogs and swamps in much of Europe and North America. They lurk in tropical places such as Brazil and Queensland. And they haunt the southernmost regions of New Zealand and South America.

Sundews can be as tiny as a penny or as large as a small bush. Their tentacle-covered leaves come in a wide and imaginative variety of design: circular leaves, wedge-shaped leaves, leaves that are peltate or linear or as filiform as a thin blade of grass. Their leaves may be strapped-shaped, oval, or forked and branching like a dewy fern or lethal spiderweb.

Their adaptation to diverse climates is also rather inventive. While all sundews need wet, low-nutrient soils to grow, some have adapted to survive hot, dry summers and only grow during the cool winter rains. Others are found in bogs that are frozen much of the year. Still others grow in Mediterranean-like climates where temperatures may drop to near freezing at night and rise dramatically during the day.

A pleasant fact about sundews is that they often enjoy the same hunting grounds as many other carnivorous plants. Visit flytraps and American pitcher plants in North Carolina and you'll no doubt step on sundews in the process. Go to the tepui mountains in Venezuela to photograph the sun pitchers and *Brocchinea* and sundews will probably be in the picture. Sundews grow with *Cephalotus* in Australia, *Darlingtonia* in Oregon, and *Nepenthes* in Borneo. In fact, whenever you find wet, low-nutrient, acidic soils, chances are sundews will be there, the ubiquitous carnivorous plant.

Sundews caught the attention of European naturalists early on. Henry Lyte, an early British botanist, wrote of the peculiar nature of the plants in his "New Herbal" in 1578. Commenting (in Old English) on how the plants appeared to increase their dew the hotter the sun became, rather than the opposite, he mentions their Latin name to be *ros solis,* "which is to say in English, the Dewe of the Sonne, or Sonnedew." The word *Drosera* in Greek means "dewy."

In 1791, Charles Darwin's grandfather, Erasmus, thought the dew produced by the plants protected them from predators. That same year, William Bartram concluded insects were purposely caught, but for reasons he could not surmise. A German botanist, Dr. W. A. Roth, was the first to notice that the tentacles of sundews actually closed around prey.

But it wasn't until Charles Darwin himself took up the study of sundews that they were ultimately proven to be carnivorous. Darwin conducted

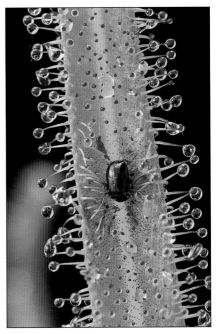

There's no escape for this beetle on a leaf of *Drosera regia.*

countless experiments on the plants for many years, and published the findings in his 1875 *Insectivorous Plants.* The bulk of the book was on his studies of the common round-leafed sundew, *Drosera rotundifolia.* At one point, Darwin wrote to his botanist friend, Asa Gray, that he cared more about sundews than the origin of all the species of life on earth. He also described them as being like animals in disguise. He found that the plants were more sensitive to taste and touch than any animal species he had studied.

Although the size and shape of *Drosera* leaves greatly vary, their insidious design and function are similar among all the species.

The leaves are generally flat, and their uppermost surface is covered with hundreds of stalked glands, or tentacles. The tentacles are hairlike filaments, at the end of which sits a small, usually reddish, gland. Most of these glands produce a tiny drop of dew, a clear, gluey mucilage that is extremely sticky and viscid. On some species of sundews, the glands on the outer edge of the leaf do not produce glue, and are instead called retentive glands, for reasons we shall see.

A small flying insect may catch sight of the glistening droplets and mistake them for a flower's sweet nectar. It alights upon the leaf and immediately panics. The "nectar" is glue, and the insect struggles to free itself. Instead, its legs and wings come into contact with more of the sticky drops, and the more it thrashes the further mired it becomes. It may lose a leg or a wing in the fight, or may pull partly free of one leaf of the sundew only to be caught by the tentacles of another.

Then a second lethal action comes into play. Within moments, some of the tentacles begin to move. If the insect struggles toward the edge of the leaf, the retentive glands along the edge begin to curl inwards, blocking the panicking insect's escape. If the insect happens to have been caught by some outermost glands, those tentacles quickly begin to move, carrying the victim toward the center of the leaf where dozens more glands await it.

Usually the prey of sundews suffocate when the breathing holes along their abdomens are covered in glue. But larger insects, such as crane flies, are sometimes caught by their long, thin legs, their bodies dangling help-lessly below the leaf. These victims usually die of exhaustion or starvation while the plant feeds on only the body parts it has caught.

Occasionally, larger insects escape—minus a few legs—only to die later. Sometimes they are finished

A crane fly realizes its mistake in landing on a staghorn sundew.

Tentacles have seized the crane fly's abdomen, and digestion begins.

off by spiders, who enjoy spinning webs around sundew plants. Spiders, too, are often caught, usually the consequence of their own greed, as they attempt to snatch a meal rightfully belonging to the sundew that trapped it.

Further movement in some *Drosera* species can be rather dramatic, although this movement typically enhances digestion rather than capture. Many sundews have the capacity to enfold their leaves around their prey. Varieties of sundews with thin, filiform leaves, or leaves that fork or branch, rarely have this ability, and rely strictly on the movement of tentacles for feeding. Others, with circular or strap-shaped leaves, may close around their meal like a clenched fist or jelly roll. Still others, like *Drosera regia,* may tie their leaves into knots around a larger meal.

The reason for this is apparently to get as many glands as possible into contact with their prey. For once an insect is caught, the highly developed glands begin to secrete a complex juice of enzymes and acids that rapidly cover the insect's body. This fluid, at times, can be rather copious and literally drip down the leaf. In a matter of hours or days, the digestive juices liquefy the softer parts of the insect. The glands then begin to reabsorb this nutritious, mineral-laden soup.

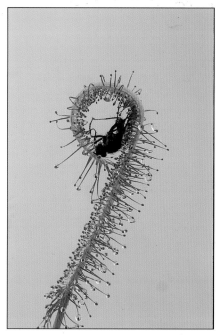

The movement of sundew tentacles and leaves is caused by a process similar to that of Venus flytraps, their relative. It is an amazing growth process. Cells along one side of a tentacle will grow and stretch, and the unequal length of the cells cause the tentacle to bend. Exactly how this occurs and how electrical signals notify nearby glands to start moving, even when an insect is some distance away, is still not clearly understood.

The speed at which sundews move is also variable, and differs depending upon factors such as tem-

The movement of cape sundews can be rather dramatic, as seen around this helpless fly.

perature, age of the leaf, species of plant, how much the insect struggles, and its nutrient worth. The tentacles won't react to a pine needle
falling upon them, but will slowly begin to move if they're repeatedly
teased with a toothpick. If you place a bit of cheese or chocolate upon
a leaf, initial movement may be slow but within a day or two the leaf
may be curled dramatically and literally drooling digestive juices. Typically, in about twenty minutes a number of tentacles may pin an insect
to the center of the leaf, while it may take twenty-four hours for a leaf
to completely curl around its prey.

Several sundews have retentive glands that move so rapidly the
results are startling. Species such as *Drosera pauciflora, D. burmanni,* and
D. scorpiodes can move 180 degrees within one minute, quickly secur-
ing an insect before it knows what has happened.

After digestion, the tentacles usually dry up and return to their normal upright position. The shriveled carcass falls from the leaf, is washed
off by rain, or simply remains as what should be a dire warning to
future prey. Dew drops reappear, and the leaf is ready for another meal.
Sometimes older leaves remain curled up even as the leaf turns brown
and dies. During their active growth cycle, most sundews continually
replace older leaves with new ones.

The flowers of sundews can be as varied as their leaves, and in some
cases are rather spectacular. Almost all *Drosera* flowers are five-petaled,
circular, and more or less flat-faced, with the female stigma surrounded
by male anthers. As a result, many self-pollinate and produce numerous seed. Others, however, never produce seed because they need cross-
pollination, and some varieties in cultivation are almost all of one
genetic clone. The predominant petal colors of sundews are whites and
pinks, but in some groups, such as pygmy and tuberous sundews, the
colors may range from orange to red to yellow to violet. Also, the inflo-
rescence of sundews is very variable, and while most produce tall flower
stalks with rows of blooms, others may be clustered or branching. Further, the size of the flowers can be rather dramatic, and in some unusual
species, the flowers may be as large or larger than the plant itself.

Due to the wide-ranging growth habits and habitats of sundews,
this chapter is arranged somewhat differently than the others. First, I
will discuss cultivation techniques in the most general of terms. I will
then review the grouping of plants by their characteristics and habitats, including descriptions of representative species and particulars

about their cultivation. This will be followed by information on their propagation.

CULTIVATION

(See Parts One and Two for further details)

Soil recipes	Almost all species thrive in a mixture of roughly half peat to half sand. Some will require a sandier mix than others. A few do best in long-fibered sphagnum.
Containers	Plastic containers with drainage holes are most suitable. Many species do well in undrained containers of plastic, glass, or glazed ceramic.
Watering	Most sundews thrive on the tray method, which keeps the soil permanently wet. A few prefer to be waterlogged. Winter-growing species require periods of complete summer dormancy, at which time the soil has to be dried out.
Light	Almost all sundews require sunny to partly sunny conditions. Very few prefer full shade.
Climate	As sundews grow worldwide, they come from varied climates: cold-temperate, temperate, warm-temperate, sub-tropical, tropical, and Mediterranean. Their preferred climates will be indicated under the species descriptions beginning on page 128.
Dormancy	Many sundews grow year round with no dormancy requirements. Others require cold winter dormancy or dry summer dormancy.

Drosera intermedia x brevifolia

Feeding	Sundews readily accept gnats, fruit flies, or small ants. Larger sundews will feed on houseflies, spiders, moths, etc. Strong insects such as crickets are generally unsuitable. Dried insects and pinhead-sized bits of hard-boiled egg, cheese, chocolate, and powdered milk are also accepted.
Fertilizers	Not necessary if the plants catch many insects, but most species benefit from monthly foliar-feeding with an acid or epiphytic fertilizer diluted to about a quarter of its normal strength. Never apply fertilizer to *Drosera schizandra*, *D. prolifera*, or *D. adelae*.
Greenhouses	Different greenhouse types will suit different types of sundews. Almost all thrive in warm houses and cool houses, where perhaps 80 percent of all *Drosera* species will be happy.
Terrariums / Grow-lights	Most sundews thrive in well-lighted tanks, but due to their preference for sun, they may need to be placed within inches of fluorescent bulbs. The closer to the lights, the more colorful and robust the plants will be.
Windowsills	Many sundews, such as cape sundews and rosetted sub-tropical species, thrive on sunny and humid windowsills. Your house's conditions will best determine suitable varieties. Surprisingly, even spectacular giants such as *Drosera regia* and *D. multifida* can be happy on windowsills if provided with cool, humid air and morning sunlight.
Outdoors	Sundews thrive outdoors in climates similar to their native habitats. The widest variety can be grown outdoors in warm-temperate, subtropical, and Mediterranean-like climates.
Bog gardens	Many sundews are ideal for bog gardens. Choose those suitable for your climate. Avoid most species requiring a dry summer dormancy.
Transplanting	Sundews can be happy in a container for many years. They are best transplanted when in a dormant state or in early seasonal growth.

Pests and diseases	Aphids are the primary pest. Wettable powder insecticides are safest. Flea collars in small enclosures work well. Some sundews can be attacked by fungus during winterlike conditions of low light and cool, dank temperatures. Apply fungicide. Never use soap-based insecticides on sundews.

CAPE SUNDEWS

From the cape of South Africa comes this marvelous sundew, a variable species that offers everything the plant lover could wish for. Cape sundews are large and handsome plants that are very easy to grow. They produce scores of showy flowers on tall stems and are so simple to propagate they often become a weed in collections. Their leaves move rather dramatically, and they are tolerant of a wide range of growing conditions. These are by far the most entertaining and popular of the *Drosera,* and a perfect beginner's plant.

Cape sundews grow best in a temperature range of forty to eighty degrees. They are very tolerant of extremes from freezing to a hundred degrees, but only for brief periods. The plants grow year round and have no dormancy requirements. If temperatures drop below freezing, the crowns will die away but the plants return from their roots and stems when conditions improve. Roots have been known to survive brief temperature drops to fifteen degrees.

Cape sundews will repeatedly send up tall flower stalks from spring through autumn. Each stalk can hold up to several dozen flowers, one bloom opening every day or so. The

Drosera capensis, a stem-forming variety

Cape Sundews (from left to right): *D. capensis* "Typical," "Alba," "Red" and "Narrow" form

flowers, up to three-quarters of an inch in diameter, usually self-pollinate and can produce copious quantities of seed that will readily germinate on any damp, peaty soil. The plants are also easy to reproduce via leaf and root cuttings. Continuous flowering can have an exhausting effect on the plants, resulting in smaller crowns by late summer, but the plants recuperate fully when blooming stops. For larger crowns, remove the scape as it develops; this will also prevent rampant seedling growth.

Cape sundews thrive in cold houses, cool houses, and warm houses; terrariums under grow-lights; sunny and humid windowsills; and outdoors as potted plants or in bog gardens in warm-temperate, subtropical, and Mediterranean-like climates.

Drosera capensis "Typical"

This variety is also known as "stem-forming" and "wide-leafed". The plant gradually forms scrambling stems several inches long with a cluster of leaves at the apex. The green leaves are strapped-shaped at the end of wide, lengthy petioles, and are covered with bright red tentacles. Individual leaves are three to six inches long or larger, resulting in crowns that can reach over a foot across.

This form can be pruned back by cutting off the crown of leaves in late winter or spring. Shoots will develop from the remaining stem, eventually producing large, multiheaded, bushy plants.

The flower of *Drosera capensis*

The flowers are bright pink on stalks one to two feet tall, and produce enormous quantities of seed.

Drosera capensis "Narrow"

Similar to the above in almost all respects, except that tall stems are rarely produced, resulting in neater, more compact plants. The leaves and petioles are rather narrow, about a quarter inch in diameter.

Drosera capensis "Alba"

This very pretty form is similar to the narrow-leafed variety, except that the flowers are white and the tentacles transparent with pale pink glands, giving the plants a ghostly appearance. Stems may gradually form over time.

Drosera capensis "Red"

This stunning variety is entirely reddish maroon in color, with deep pink flowers. In all other respects, it is similar to the narrow-leafed form. This variety requires lots of sun or very high light levels to maintain its rich coloration, which may fade in winter or when the plants are grown too far from grow-lights.

ROSETTED SUBTROPICAL SUNDEWS

Many sundews from various parts of the world fall into this category, which for the sake of convenience I will call "subtropical," although they can also be found in warm-temperate, Mediterranean-like, and tropical climates.

The basic form of most of these *Drosera* are low-growing plants with leaves that fan out into a rosette-like pattern. They typically have leaves that are pressed flat to the ground, although some may hold their foliage in a more upright fashion, or even form a short stem, with old, dead leaves forming a skirt around their base. Usually these rosetted species average one to three inches in diameter, although a few may be smaller or larger.

Rosetted subtropical sundews are all pretty plants, while a few are spectacular.

The Alice Sundew, *Drosera aliciae*

They are usually as easy to grow as cape sundews, and many will also spread like weeds from ample seed production. A few are short-lived perennials, meaning that older rosettes die off after a couple of years and the plant reproduces by seed. Almost all can easily be propagated by leaf cuttings. Some have thick roots also useful for propagation.

With a very few exceptions, this class of *Drosera* grows throughout the year without any dormancy requirements. While most grow in frost-free climates, many are tolerant of brief freezes into the twenties. The rosettes will die during these light frosts, but usually new plants come up from the thick, protected roots. For best results, grow them in frost-free environments.

Rosetted sundews produce flower stalks throughout much of the warmer months of the year. The stalks may be a few inches tall, but in some plants may rise to one or two feet, quite tall for such small plants. In some, a scape of flowers open, one at a time, over several weeks. Typically, these flowers are small, barely a quarter inch across, but in some can be quite showy and large. A few exceptional species have very large blooms almost as big as the plant itself. While many self-pollinate and produce seed, others never do and must be propagated from leaves or roots. Invariably, the flowers of rosetted subtropicals are colored pinks or whites.

As a group, these sundews perform extremely well in cool and warm greenhouses. Many are exceptional plants for a humid and sunny windowsill. They are also great for the terrarium under grow-lights, but for best results should be no more than several inches from fluorescent bulbs. They are great outdoor plants if you live in an almost frost-free climate.

Some of these species look so similar to each other that even long-time growers have difficulty telling them apart. Also, new varieties are still being found in countries such as South Africa, and these plants may be circulated under nicknames for many years. For many growers, pedigree is not quite as important as simply having a handsome rosetted sundew to look at!

Drosera aliciae

Possibly the most popular rosetted species, the Alice sundew comes from the Cape Province of South Africa. The handsome rosettes are up to three inches across, producing a mound of pale green, wedge-shaped leaves with crimson tentacles. The leaves curl dramatically around larger prey. The substantial flowers are deep pink, around a half inch in diameter, and on stalks over a foot high. This species often produces offshoots from its roots, eventually producing attractive clumps of plants. It also returns well from light frosts. Easily propagated from abundant seed, or leaf and root cuttings.

One of the most popular rosetted sundews, *Drosera aliciae*

Drosera spatulata

This widespread and variable species is found from southern Japan to Australia and New Zealand. Many forms are grown, which are usually known by their location. The rosettes are flat, with spoon- to wedge-shaped leaves typically one to two inches across. In good light the entire plant can be flushed red. The small flowers are pink or white, and usually self-seed. The "Kansai" form from Japan is most popular, with spoon-shaped leaves and pink flowers. "Kanto," also from Japan, is very attractive with narrow, wedge-shaped leaves. "Hong Kong" forms have rosettes about one inch across, with pink or white blooms. The form from the eastern coast of Australia is virtually indistinguishable from "Kansai," but may have either white or deep pink flowers. New Zealand forms also have small rosettes with leaves that are almost circular.

D. spatulata "Kansai"

Drosera capillaris

The pink sundew is very common in the southeastern United States from Virginia to Florida to Texas. Forms are also known from Central and South America. The rosettes are usually one to two inches across with almost circular to sometimes spoon-shaped leaves, often reddish in color. Flowers are usually pink. An "alba" form is all green with white flowers. This species usually performs as an annual or short-lived perennial, returning from seed after hard frosts. It is very commonly seen growing with other carnivores in the southeast, such as *Sarracenia, Dionaea,* and *Pinguicula.*

Drosera brevifolia

Uncommon in collections, this tiny sundew has a range similar to *Drosera capillaris*. It looks like a miniature *Drosera spatulata* "Kanto," with bright red, wedge-shaped leaves. The whole plant is barely one-half inch across, and very pretty in dense colonies. Short lived, the plants often die away in winter, returning from seed.

A story I've enjoyed is how this diminutive sundew has sometimes been found growing in the damp cracks of sidewalks in Houston, Texas during the wetter parts of the year!

Drosera slackii

This magnificent *Drosera* was discovered in the early 1980s in the coastal mountains of the cape of South Africa and named for Adrian Slack,

who introduced it to cultivation. The beautiful rosettes can be large, from two to four inches across, and can form a short stem draped in dead leaves. Deep crimson in color, the leaf blades are almost circular with broad petioles, and they move dramatically over prey. The flowers are more than one inch in diameter, a deep pinkish violet, but rarely produce seed. However, it is easily propagated from roots and leaves, and is slowly clump forming. Although they will grow in peat, I find it is easier to establish the plants in long-fibered sphagnum. They can do very well on windowsills.

One of the finest of recent discoveries, *Drosera slackii*. Discovered by Frank Woodvine, it was named by Martin Cheek after Adrian Slack, who introduced it into cultivation.

Drosera cuneifolia

Another handsome South African sundew that, with its wide petioles, reminds me of *Drosera slackii*. But the leaf blade is even wider and with rounded corners. The leaves are bright green with pink tentacles.

Drosera dielsiana

A small sundew from South Africa, this plant was named after Diels, who wrote the first monograph on sundews early in the twentieth century. The roundish leaf blades have a fairly wide petiole, and the flowers are pink.

Drosera montana

The "Mountain Sundew" comes from South America. For many years, plants were grown under this name that actually appear to be a form of *Drosera spatulata*. *Drosera montana* is variable but usually has wedge-shaped, reddish leaves with blunt ends.

Drosera hamiltonii

This peculiar sundew grows with *Cephalotus* in southwestern Australia. The flat rosettes have pale, olive brown leaves that are shaped like rounded paddles and sparsely covered in red tentacles. Although it flowers infrequently, the blooms are purplish and over one and a half inches across, almost as large as the rosette itself. The flowers put on quite a show, but do not seed; the plant propagates from its roots and leaves.

Drosera collinsiae

A very pretty sundew, this South African species has upright, spoon-shaped leaves on long, thin petioles. The leaves are bright green with red tentacles. This species has a brief winter dormancy and the pink flowers usually self-seed.

Drosera burmanni

This curious species is a tropical annual that grows in northern Australia and Southeast Asia. It lives only for a few months during the warm rainy season, seeds prolifically, then dies off when the soil dries out, returning from seed when the rains return. In cultivation, it is easy to grow during any stretch of warm weather. The plants are about one inch across, with deeply dished, wedge-shaped leaves, usually green or pinkish, and small white flowers. After flowering, the plant dies, so be sure to collect the tiny seed. The seed will also tolerate a light frost. Most amazing are the long retentive glands, which can close around prey in less than one minute.

Drosera villosa

This South American species is variable, but typically has attractive rosettes two to five inches across with arching, strapped-shaped,

Drosera hamiltonii

Rosetted Sundews (clockwise from top corner): *Drosera venusta, D. hamiltonii, D. capillaris* "Alba," *D. spatulata* "Kansai," *D. cuneifolia, D. intermedia* x *brevifolia, D. spatulata* "Kanto," *D. intermedia* "Cuba." *D. aliciae* in the center.

hairy leaves, often reddish in color. I have never been able to maintain this plant through winters in my greenhouse, and suspect it may do better in more tropical conditions.

Drosera intermedia x brevifolia

Hybrids are rare among sundews, but a colony of this plant was discovered in the 1980s in North Carolina. A very attractive plant, the leaves are golden bronze and shaped like elongated spoons. It does not go dormant, as does its parent, *Drosera intermedia*. Propagate by leaf cuttings.

Drosera x henryana

A hybrid between *Drosera capensis* and *D. aliciae,* this good-looking plant has upright, strapped-shaped leaves. However, I have never been able to maintain them for more than a year, which is puzzling since the parents are both easy.

Drosera roraimae

From Venezuela, this species is often found growing with *Heliamphora* and *Brocchinea*. A reddish sundew with spoon-shaped leaves, it is notable for its tall stems, usually cloaked with dead leaves.

Drosera glabripes

From South Africa, this sundew can form long, scrambling stems, with the rosette of green, spoon-shaped leaves at the apex. The rosette averages three inches across. I have found it difficult to maintain long-term.

Drosera venusta

A robust South African species with rosettes two to four inches across, this recent discovery is reminiscent of *Drosera aliciae.* The long, oval-shaped leaves are semierect and golden green in color, which sets off the bright red tentacles rather well. The flowers are pink on tall wiry stems.

A flower stalk emerges from *Drosera venusta*

TEMPERATE SUNDEWS

Sundews that grow in climates that experience various amounts of cold weather in winter survive frost and snow by dying down to buds called hibernacula (from the word "hibernate"). Some of these species have wide natural ranges and their length of dormancy and cold tolerance is based on where the plant or seed originated. You should therefore pay attention to location data, if available, when considering which forms of these species you wish to grow.

For example, one species, *Drosera intermedia,* is actually pan-climatic, growing from Canada south all the way into South America. Plants originating from Wisconsin are cold-temperate, may experience a dormancy lasting six or seven months, and can survive temperatures well below zero degrees. Representatives of *D. intermedia* from Louisiana would be considered warm-temperate, being dormant perhaps three to four months and surviving only light frost and brief freezes. *D. intermedia* from Cuba are tropical, having no dormancy and an inability to withstand freezing temperatures.

Most of these species are easy to grow if you allow them the dormancy they require. If you live in a warmer climate, you can always remove the hibernaculum once the plant dies down, and refrigerate it over winter in an air-tight plastic bag with a few strands of damp sphagnum moss. When dormant, these plants usually lose their roots as well as leaves, and this is the best time to transplant them. They are easy to propagate from leaf cuttings and seed. Most do best outdoors, or in cold and cool greenhouses.

Drosera rotundifolia

This is the plant made famous by Charles Darwin's tireless and hideous experiments upon it. The round-leafed sundew is a common inhabitant of almost every sphagnum bog found in the northern latitudes. Its range is from Alaska through much of North America as well as

Europe and Asia. The rosettes average three inches in diameter, with dished oval leaves at the end of long, thin petioles. The flowers are white. Specimens from Northern California, Oregon, and the New Jersey pine barrens can have rosettes up to five inches across with dime-sized leaves. In cultivation, the species grows best in long-fibered sphagnum.

Drosera anglica

The "English Sundew" grows in bog habitats in Japan, North America, (including Alaska), and Europe. Similar to *Drosera rotundifolia* and often growing side by side with it, *D. anglica* has long, paddle-shaped leaves held more upright. An unusual colony is found in Hawaii on the island of Kauai. These plants are tropical, smaller in stature, and do not go dormant, making them ideal for terrariums.

Left to right: Drosera anglica, D. rotundifolia, and D. linearis, which was once called D. longifolia

Strangely enough, evidence suggests *Drosera anglica* is a fertile hybrid between *Drosera rotundifolia* and *Drosera linearis* (below). The mystery is why *Drosera anglica* is so widespread while *Drosera linearis* is presently restricted in its range.

Drosera x obovata

The natural hybrid between *Drosera rotundifolia* and *D. anglica* can be rather robust and handsome, looking intermediary between the two. Sterile, it must be propagated by leaf cuttings.

Drosera intermedia

The temperate forms of this beautiful sundew are found in Europe, eastern Canada, and the United States. The tropical forms that do not go dormant occur from central Florida south into the West Indies and South America. The temperate forms of this species most often grow semiaquatically around lakes in pure peat covered in a few inches of water. The plants will form stems several inches high with small, spoon-shaped leaves on narrow petioles with white flowers. The whole plant is often a lovely maroon color. Tropical forms, such as those from Cuba, have smaller compact rosettes perfect for the terrarium. Very large forms are often found in New Jersey, the Carolinas, and the Gulf states. I like to grow these in undrained bowls of waterlogged peat moss. Propagate from seed or leaf cuttings.

Drosera x beleziana

The natural hybrid between *Drosera rotundifolia* and *D. intermedia* is another vigorous plant with large, upright, spoon-shaped leaves. Sterile, it must be propagated by leaf cuttings.

Drosera linearis

This strange sundew grows primarily in alkaline marl bogs around the Great Lakes area, often with *Sarracenia purpurea*. It has three- to four-inch linear leaves on long, upright petioles, and white flowers. Difficult to grow without a sustained, frozen winter, I have had limited success using a medium of one part sand to one part vermiculite, refrigerating the plants for a full six or seven months dormancy. Folks in cold winter climates would probably find it easier to grow outdoors. The plants reportedly can adjust to acidic peat soils.

Drosera filiformis

This very unusual and pretty sundew from North America is also controversial, for there is confusion about

Drosera x beleziana

its status in taxonomy. Is it one species with two forms, or two species, or two subspecies? Here I will follow the latter interpretation.

Thread-leafed sundews make nice additions to bog gardens, and the larger forms look beautiful in hanging pots in a greenhouse. Their dormant buds are large, blackish, and hairy. They can be propagated by seed or leaf cuttings, with the exception of the cultivar 'California Sunset', noted below. They also gradually form large clumps that can be divided.

Drosera filiformis ssp. filiformis

This is found in scattered locations from New England to North Carolina, with one peculiar colony, sometimes called "Florida giant", in northern Florida. In its typical habitat, such as the New Jersey pine barrens where it is most common, the plants have long, thin, threadlike leaves from six to ten inches tall, covered in red tentacles. The flowers are pink and almost one inch across. The "Florida giant" form has leaves twice as tall. Very recently a colony in Florida was discovered with solid maroon leaves.

Drosera filiformis ssp. tracyi

This plant is found along the Gulf states, and is very similar to the above except the tentacles are green and the leaves reach twenty inches in length. A large, showy, warm-temperate sundew.

Drosera filiformis ssp. filiformis "Florida giant"

Drosera filiformis x 'California Sunset'

This is a beautiful hybrid between the two subspecies produced by Joe Mazrimas and published in 1981. Vigorous and clump forming, it resembles both ssp. *tracyi* with reddish glands and ssp. *filiformis* "Florida giant." Since *Drosera* x 'California Sunset' is a cultivar, it should only be reproduced through leaf cuttings and the seed should be destroyed.

Drosera x hybrida

This rare sundew is a hybrid between *Drosera intermedia* and *Drosera filiformis* ssp. *filiformis*. Found occasionally in the New Jersey pine barrens, it is sterile and can be reproduced through leaf cuttings. Clump forming, it produces narrow, tapered thin leaves a few inches long on short, upright petioles. It needs a few months of fairly cold winter weather, or the dormant buds may rot.

Drosera arcturi

This rare cold-temperate species grows in alpine regions of New Zealand and Australia, where its mountain habitat is often snow covered in winter. The plants prefer sphagnum moss, and

The flower of *Drosera filiformis* x 'California Sunset'.

they die down to their roots rather than form hibernacula. The peculiar, strapped-shaped leaves are three to four inches long and an odd purplish brown color. My own attempt with this plant failed, as my winters are too warm to sustain its dormancy.

THE FORK-LEAFED SUNDEWS

This group of sundews is restricted to the east coast of Australia, with one species found also in New Zealand. Usually referred to as varieties of one species, *Drosera binata,* their taxonomy is still doubtful. Current research will hopefully clarify the matter, and thus the names of some forms may change. Most of the names have been used for convenience, and have no legitimate value.

Forked sundews are all magnificent and showy species. They grow from tropical to warm-temperate climates, in wet swamps and on dripping cliffs that may experience frost in winter.

The plants have thick black roots, from which long petioles arise. The leaves themselves branch into two or many points, depending on the species. Often, the branching, tentacle-covered leaves resemble large, ferny spider webs. The flowers also are large, usually white but sometimes pink, in clusters on tall stems. As they rarely produce seed in cultivation (they need to be crossed with other clones and most plants in cultivation originated from single individuals), growers usually remove them due to their exhausting effect on the plant.

Forked sundews have been popular plants since Victorian times.

The larger forms look best in large, hanging pots that are watered daily, or in pots that sit in hanging bowls of water. They also do well on the tray system, but the drooping leaves of most forms will have their beauty masked. Forked sundews succeed quite well planted in undrained containers too, such as oversized brandy snifters or tall flower vases, which give ample room for their leaves to hang luxuriously.

In suitable climates, they are unbeatable for the bog garden, but avoid windy areas. They make attractive flycatchers for very sunny porches and patios. Most are too large for the average terrarium, but can succeed if dormancy is respected and the light levels are high enough. Sometimes they do well on windowsills—but only with several hours of sun and in humid conditions. In cool and warm greenhouses, they are unsurpassed.

These *Drosera* do equally well in peat and sand mixes or long-fibered sphagnum. They are easy to propagate from root and leaf cuttings. Young plants, and the first leaves of the season on older ones, usually fork once, such as *Drosera binata,* but will rapidly attain their full form in time.

Drosera binata

Considered by many to be the ancestor of all forked sundews, this species is actually uncommon in its native Australian swamps. It is also found in New Zealand. More upright and compact than its sisters, *Drosera binata* has leaves up to a foot tall that fork once. Often called "T-form," the leaves are actually Y-shaped, and are green with intensely red tentacles or entirely red. The plant spreads into massive clumps. Dormant in winter, it is tolerant of brief freezes to fifteen degrees, but if the roots freeze completely, you may loose the plant. The flowers are white.

Drosera dichotoma "Giant"

A personal favorite of mine, this is one of the most massive of *Drosera.* The leaves are olive to bronzy yellow, with nearly transparent tentacles and pink glands. The wiry petioles can be a foot in length, and the leaves branch from four to

Drosera binata in an undrained, glazed ceramic pot

twelve points, sometimes two feet in diameter. (Visitors to my nursery have involuntarily screamed when they've accidentally backed into my four-foot-diameter specimens!) A superb flycatcher, this species has a brief winter dormancy and is as cold-tolerant as *Drosera binata*. Outdoors in full sun, the leaves are colorful, smaller, and held erect. The flowers are white and best removed. The larger the pot, the more massive the plants become.

Drosera dichotoma "Giant"

Drosera dichotoma "T-form"

A smaller, handsome version of the above, the leaves on this form fork only once.

Drosera dichotoma "Small Red Form"

This plant has yet to be truly identified, but is more similar to the *multifida* varieties below than to *dichotoma*. It is a low-growing species, with fine, branching leaves up to a foot across, deep red in color. A striking difference in this forked sundew is that mature plants set seed after flowering, and then go dormant in late summer, while the viable seed sprout everywhere and can spread like a weedy cape sundew. The mother plants return the following year.

Drosera multifida

More tropical in nature, this large sundew can survive light frost but is best kept warmer, as it will not go dormant. The large, olive-colored, drooping leaves branch a dozen or more times and have crimson tentacles. A pink-flowered variety has a brief dormancy.

The flowers of *Drosera multifida*.

Drosera multifida "Extrema"

Perhaps the most beautiful of the forked Drosera, this form was found on Stradbroke Island off southern Queensland, where it may now be extinct due to mining activity. A lovely plant with pendulous leaves over a foot long, they branch enormously, forming globose webs with forty to seventy points! In strong light the whole plant is a rich maroon color. The white flowers are best removed. Keep over forty degrees to avoid dormancy. The plants will return from brief, hard freezes.

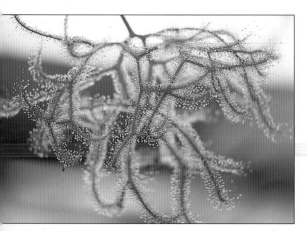

A branching leaf of *Drosera multifida* "Extrema" acts like a spider web to catch its prey.

Drosera x 'Marston Dragon'

Adrian Slack created this attractive, large hybrid between *Drosera dichotoma* "Giant" and *Drosera multifida* "Extrema". The leaves are unusual in that the forked tendrils are hooked, reminding Slack of the taloned feet of a Chinese dragon. The leaves are dark green with red tentacles, and fork to eight or so points. No dormancy required.

SOME TROPICAL SUNDEWS

Sundews from truly tropical places are not as common as one might think, in spite of their exotic appearance. I have already discussed some of these in the previous sections. Many forms of *Drosera spatulata* come from tropical climates, as do *Drosera burmanni, D. villosa, D. anglica* "Hawaii", *D. multifida* "Extrema", and forms of *Drosera intermedia*. But even some of these sundews are also tolerant of occasional chilly temperatures or even frost, and *Drosera burmanni,* an annual, can be grown as a summer plant in temperate climates.

Here I will discuss *Drosera* that are best grown warmer year round. Some of these, too, may tolerate chillier temperatures, and as growers experiment with them we may learn more of their tolerance extremes. But suffice it to say, the following sundews generally do best when temperatures remain above fifty to sixty degrees, as in a terrarium under grow-lights or in warm and hot greenhouses.

Three Sisters from Queensland

I call these "the three sisters" because not only are they related, but they also grow in similar conditions: humid, shaded, tropical rain forest with little temperature extremes. All come from Queensland, Australia, usually along the damp, mossy edges of slow-moving streams. Although rare in nature, they are very popular in cultivation, not only for their unusual appearance but because they are ideal for the potted terrarium under grow-lights. They despise strong, direct sunlight. They prefer being grown in long-fibered sphagnum. They are easy to propagate from leaf and root cuttings, rarely producing seed. They are happiest with high humidity and a temperature range of fifty-five to eighty degrees. These three sundews also do well on sunless, north-facing windows if placed under a bell jar or in a small tank. Warning: Fertilizer will fry the leaves of these plants and must never be applied.

Three sisters from Queensland. *Clockwise from upper left: Drosera schizandra, D. prolifera,* and *D. adelae*

Drosera schizandra

Commonly called the notched sundew, this odd plant produces a flat rosette of leaves that are broad and nearly oval. But as it grows older the leaves may elongate and develop a notch at the end, achieving a heart-shaped form. The tentacles are sparse and weak, catching mostly gnat-sized insects. The beautiful and delicate rosettes are typically four to six inches in diameter. The plants commonly form clumps that develop from their roots. A short scape produces unusual, small, red-petaled flowers.

Drosera prolifera

The "hen and chicks" sundew has oval to kidney-shaped leaves up to three-quarters of an inch across, held semierect on long, thin petioles. Most peculiar are the flower stalks, which run along the ground carrying a few

The flowers of *Drosera adelae* are like miniature red stars.

small red flowers, ending in a small baby plant if the tip touches the ground. Over time, with frequent flowering, many new plants take root around the "mother," and sometimes the flowers produce seed. The dime-sized leaves will fold around prey like a sandwich.

Drosera adelae

The lanced-leafed sundew is the errant sister, for she can take somewhat brighter light, less humidity, and cooler temperatures. A lovely sundew for the terrarium, she can also occasionally thrive on bright, humid windowsills (for example, a bright bathroom). The leaves are arching, long and pointed. In lower light, the plants are green and can reach a foot across. Brighter conditions will develop stiffer, shorter, bronzy leaves. The stunning flowers look like bright red stars, and many dozens can appear on stalks a few inches tall. *Drosera adelae* is a spreader: older plants may die away and be replaced by many offspring that come up from the roots. A curious fact is that originally only plants with dull, yellow white flowers were known. After the introduction of the red-flowered form (which some believed was a new species because the flower structure also seemed different), the pale-flowered form seemed to disappear, or turn red. On several occasions I have been given fresh material of the older variety, but these in time also turn red!

THE WOOLLY SUNDEWS

An exciting development in the past two decades has been the discovery of many new sundews in the remote, vast areas of northern Australia. For a long time one species, *Drosera petiolaris,* the woolly sundew, was the only type formally described. But now, thanks to the enthusiastic work of people like Allen Lowrie and Katsuhiko Kondo, a whole group of related *Drosera* known as the petiolaris complex is beginning to enter cultivation.

Many of these plants are still mysterious and rare, and are only now beginning to be identified and named. Some of them currently are known by location names only, but this is rapidly changing as the plants are formally described. Cultivation techniques are also being explored.

Many of these sundews are notable for their unusual petioles, and leaf blades densely packed with long, fine tentacles.

Northern Australia has a warm, tropical climate marked by six months of rain and six months of drought. These sundews grow in sandy areas that are wet to waterlogged during the rainy season. When the soils dry out during the annual drought, most of these plants die down to their thick, often hairy, bulblike stems for several months of dormancy. However, in cultivation the plants remain in growth if they are kept wet.

To grow these types, I recommend a soil recipe of two parts sand to one part peat. Peat pellets also work well. Use the tray system in brightly lit terrariums or sunny greenhouses. Temperatures are best between sixty and ninety degrees. Propagation is by leaf cuttings, division, and sometimes seed. They can be grown outdoors in warm climates.

All of the following sundews are beautiful and unique, and vigorous hybrids are common. Here are some of the more popular forms.

Drosera petiolaris

The original species, this plant was discovered by J. Banks in Queensland during Cook's voyage around 1770. Fond of waterlogged conditions, the rosettes are a few inches across with many erect leaves that have long, narrow petioles and small, spade-shaped traps with very long retentive glands. The flowers are dark pink.

Drosera dilatato-petiolaris

Although recognized by L. Diels in 1906, Kondo formally described this species in the 1980s. Common in damp areas around Darwin (on the coast of Northern Territory), this clump-producing species has medium-broad green petioles and

Drosera petiolaris x dilatato petiolaris

Drosera falconeri **growing in peat pellets**

small, circular red traps, most of which lie flat along the ground. Clumps can be over a foot across. The flowers are white.

Drosera falconeri

Discovered around 1980, this desirable species has short, broad petioles with immense, oblong traps over an inch wide. The leaves are pressed flat to the ground and the whole plant is a deep maroon color. It is now known to be common in the coastal areas of the Northern Territory.

Drosera lanata

A pretty species with clusters of low-growing leaves that have long, thin petioles and small, circular leaf-blades. The leaves and center of the rosette are covered with dense, silvery, woolly hairs.

Drosera ordensis

This stunning sundew was discovered by Allen Lowrie and was called *petiolaris* 'Kununurra'. The rosettes are three to six inches in diameter and can form clumps over a foot across. The leaves are erect with long, wide petioles so densely covered in silvery hairs that they appear white. The small, circular traps are golden green. Large flowers can be pink or white.

Drosera paradoxa

This unusual form is very similar in appearance to *Drosera petiolaris* except the leaves are hairy, like those of *Drosera lanata*. In the sun the plants grow in pincushion-like rosettes on the ground. When shaded by bushes, they can grow to a foot tall, leaning among other plants.

Two other tropical species from northern Australia deserve mention. Both behave as annuals, renewing themselves from seed during the wet season, but may grow longer when kept wet. Follow the cultivation techniques for the woolly sundews, above.

Drosera indica

This species is also found in other tropical countries such as Africa and India. The plants look surprisingly like *Byblis liniflora* and are often mistaken for them. *Drosera indica* produce a scrambling stem several inches in length. Long, linear leaves covered with tentacles radiate out from this stem in all directions. The flowers can be white, pink, or even orange. A pretty and delicate species for the hothouse or terrarium.

Drosera banksii

This curious-looking, small species appears similar to the climbing tuberous *Drosera* discussed earlier. However, these plants produce no drought-resisting tubers and instead die away during the dry season. The plants are erect and a few inches tall. They produce a few cup-shaped, peltate leaves on thin petioles. Propagate from seed.

THE PYGMY SUNDEWS

Pygmy sundews, almost all of which originate in southwestern Western Australia, are a fascinating and complex group of plants. Most of these plants are true miniatures, rarely larger than a penny, although a few can be somewhat larger in size. All are beautiful, diminutive jewels, best seen in colonies with the aid of magnifying glasses. There are probably around forty or so species, including a few hybrids.

The climate of Western Australia is considered warm-temperate to subtropical and Mediterranean-like. This means the summers are very hot and very dry. Winters are cool, with night temperatures in the thirties and forties and day temperatures between fifty and sixty-five degrees. Most of the rain falls during the winter months, and it is then that the flora of the region does its most vigorous growing. This is also true of the carnivores from this region of the world. As the hot days of summer approach, most of the plant life goes dormant while desertlike conditions prevail. The soil is predominantly sand.

Pygmy sundews are typically small rosetted plants rarely over an inch in diameter. The leaves radiate outward on short petioles with small, tentacle-covered traps that are circular to spoon-shaped. The tentacles can be very long around the edge of the leaf, and move quickly when small prey are trapped. The center of the plants usually have a

Now you know why they're called pygmy sundews. This one is *Drosera nitidula x pulchella*.

147

cone-shaped structure of shiny, dense hairs called stipules. In summer, when pygmies are dormant, the plants fold up to these heat-reflecting tufts of hair.

A most curious fact of pygmy sundews is their ability to produce gemmae, or brood bodies, an asexual method of reproduction. Each gemma is pinhead sized or smaller, and may be similar in shape to the scales of a fish or small beads.

Clusters of gemmae arise out of the stipules, forming crowns of these brood bodies in the center of the plant. This occurs in autumn as the days get cooler and shorter and the winter rains begin. Each gemma is held by a tensely coiled hair, and when struck by a rain-

In autumn, gemmae arise from pygmies like a crown.

drop, the gemmae explode outward—sometimes shooting many feet from the mother plant! Each gemma quickly takes root and rapidly grows into a new plant, genetically identical to its parent. The production of gemmae makes pygmy sundews easy plants to propagate.

The flowers of the pygmies are also interesting. While some flowers are small, many are large, showy, and in a wide range of colors. Some flowers are larger than the plants themselves. However, in cultivation they rarely produce seed so most growers rely on the dependable production of gemma for propagation. To the delight of growers, many of the flowers are also highly fragrant, a pleasant bonus for such tiny plants.

The typical life cycle for pygmies in the wild is as follows. After their summer dormancy, as the rains begin in autumn, a few leaves are produced, followed by gemmae. By early winter the gemmae is scattered and the plants grow vigorously in their wet, sandy soil. Winter and spring are their most active growing season. By late spring the plants flower and are cross-pollinated by insects. By early summer, seed is set, the soil dries out, and the plants go dormant. Seed germinates the following wet season. In some low-lying areas, pygmies may be flooded and killed in springtime after heavy rains. But a few plants always survive on higher ground, and the following winter they rapidly replenish their colonies through massive gemmae production, only to be killed off again the following spring.

Most pygmy sundews are easy to grow in cultivation. Fortunately, when kept wet year round, most species don't require a dry summer dormancy. Therefore they can be enjoyed year round and more or less grown like typical subtropical rosetted sundews.

Pygmy *Drosera* grow well in a half-sand to half-peat mixture. Even better is a mix of two parts sand to one part peat. Grow them on the tray system unless I indicate otherwise below. A sunny position is required. All thrive in cool and warm greenhouses. They also do well in terrariums grown close to the lights, but shorten the photoperiod in autumn for gemmae production. They are superb outdoors in pots and bog gardens in warm-temperate, subtropical, and Mediterranean-like climates, and will spread in bogs to form glittering, beautiful colonies. They are generally tolerant of brief, light frosts into the mid twenties but perform even better in frost-free climates. On windowsills they require very sunny conditions.

Although pygmy *Drosera* primarily catch small, gnat-sized insects, very large prey such as crane flies, moths, and houseflies are also caught. Sometimes, dense colonies of the plants act in a group effort to overpower prey. Struggling insects leave behind legs and wings in their attempt to escape the long and rapidly moving tentacles. The individual plants feast on whatever insect parts they can grab.

The following are some of the most popular varieties.

Drosera callistos

A handsome pygmy up to one inch in diameter with elliptic leaf blades and large, shiny, orange flowers. If this species goes dormant in hot summers, keep the soil just barely damp.

Drosera closterostigma

Bright red rosettes up to two-thirds of an inch in diameter. The large flowers are white with red centers.

Drosera dichrosepala

This species has half-inch rosettes of spoon-shaped leaves clustered atop a slow-growing stem. The white flowers are sweetly perfumed. Keep them almost dry if they go dormant.

Drosera eneabba

Bright red rosettes up to one inch, with pretty pinkish white flowers with scalloped edges.

Drosera ericksonae

Named after Rica Erickson, whose beautifully illustrated *Plants of Prey* was a popular book on Australian CPs. Large, golden rosettes over one inch across, with circular pink flowers that occasionally produce seed.

Drosera leucoblasta

Small reddish rosettes of circular leaves less than one inch in diameter. Bright orange flowers are as large as the plant. This species may go dormant in summer.

Drosera mannii

A beautiful, vigorous pygmy with broad petioles and elliptic red traps. The large flowers are a pearly pink or white.

Drosera occidentalis ssp. occidentalis

One of the tiniest, and a favorite of mine (under a powerful magnifier!). Minute, fine, sparse leaves deep red in color, with pink flowers.

Drosera paleacea ssp. paleacea

Rosettes a half inch across with many small, white, perfumed flowers.

Drosera pulchella

Robust rosettes up to over one inch in diameter, with flowers ranging from white to pink to orange. The broad petioles and reddish orange, circular leaves are very attractive.

Drosera pygmaea

The only pygmy found outside Western Australia, this tiny species is also found in southeastern Australia, Tasmania, and New Zealand. Fascinating for its small, bright red to green rosettes, and minute, four-petaled white flowers.

Drosera rechingeri

This species has stunning white flowers with yellow borders.

Drosera scorpiodes

This is a "giant" pygmy, exceptional for its large rosettes that measure almost two inches across, and its tall, rootlike stems. The dished, lancelet leaves have exceptionally long tentacles. I grow two forms. The larger form, with white flowers, grows rapidly but is short lived, dying away af-

Pygmy Sundews

The flowers of *Drosera manni*.

The tiny rosettes of *Drosera occidentalis* ssp. *occidentalis* are barely a quarter of an inch across.

Drosera pulchella

A giant among pygmies—*Drosera scorpiodes*

ter two to three seasons. By contrast, my plants from the smaller form with dark pink flowers have grown for over seven years, and have stems several inches tall.

Although probably extinct in the wild, *Drosera nitidula x occidentalis* is one of the most popular in cultivation.

The pearly pink flowers of *Drosera nitidula x pulchella* appear for months at a time.

The following two pygmies are probably the most popular in cultivation. Both are vigorous hybrids.

Drosera nitidula x occidentalis

Bright reddish rosettes up to a half inch in diameter. The flowers are white with bright red stigmas. Now believed to be extinct in the wild due to habitat destruction, this may be the most widespread pygmy in cultivation.

Drosera nitidula x pulchella

My favorite of all the pygmies. The deeply colored rosettes are very robust, up to one inch across, and similar to its parent, *Drosera pulchella*. It grows as easily as any cape sundew, and the lovely flowers are a showy, pearly pink.

THE TUBEROUS SUNDEWS

Western Australia is home to another large group of sundews that share the same wet winter–dry summer habitat as the pygmies. These are the tuberous *Drosera*. Instead of dying down to protective cones of stipule hairs to survive the dry heat of summer, these plants have adapted to a dormancy underground, where they hibernate as small tubers.

The tuberous *Drosera* are about as strange and as beautiful as sundews get. The fifty or more species come in a wide range of growth habits: Erect sundews have self-supporting stems with small, tentacle-covered leaves scattered along their length, sometimes reminiscent of little trees. Climbing sundews grasp and loop over bushes and other plants as though they were vines. Fan-leafed sundews can be so elaborate in their design they can appear like several different sundew species all glued together. Tuberous sundews can also be rosetted, often covering the sandy soils with dense mats of carnivorous leaves, a lethal landing platform from which few insects can escape.

The tubers of these plants may be pea- to walnut-sized. They can extend underground at a depth of a few inches to a couple of feet. The tubers can be brightly colored in oranges and reds. They are often covered with insulating papery sheaths, each layer marking a year's growth. It is in the tuber that the plant stores its energy reserves.

On the top of the tuber is a small "eye," not unlike that of a potato's. As autumn approaches, a vertical stolon grows from this eye to the soil surface, even when the soil is still dry. Usually along this stolon are the plant's roots. Sometimes the root mass is so thick it forms a "chimney" through which the tuber grows and recedes each season. Energy from the tuber gives the plant its resources to develop above ground during the cool, wet winter. For five or six months the tuberous sundews catch insects and flower and do all the things happy carnivorous plants do. Then summer approaches, and the days get longer, hotter, and drier. The plants turn brown and die back, and all the minerals and energy of the plant return down the withering stolen into the old tuber. Usually the tubers get larger each year. Often the plants produce more food than one tuber can store. In this case, new stolons develop horizontally from the mother tuber, and new tubers are grown. Some species don't return to their old tuber but create a new one each season adjacent to the dried shell of the older.

Tuberous sundews are still uncommon plants in cultivation, but they are growing in popularity as more plants are propagated and

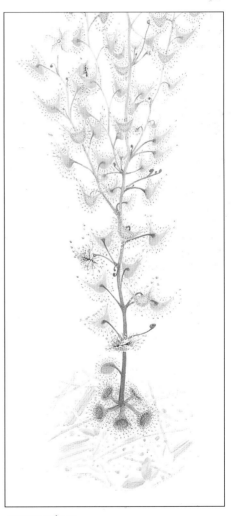

Drosera peltata

as growers become less intimidated by their unfair reputation of being difficult. I have found this group to be challenging but fairly easy to grow. The most problematic obstacle is obtaining plant material. Currently, most plants in cultivation are grown from seed or tubers imported from Australia. Propagation can be difficult because most of the species don't produce seed in cultivation and are difficult to grow from leaf cuttings. Production of additional tubers is a common but slow affair.

If you obtain a potted, established tuberous sundew, consider yourself lucky. If you receive tubers imported from Australia and you live in the northern hemisphere, remember that the seasons are reversed so most likely you will receive your dormant plants during Australia's summer (December to March), which is the northern hemisphere's winter growing season for these plants. Therefore, due to the plant's biological clock, the tuber begins to grow as summer starts. This first crucial year of seasonal adaptation is the most challenging aspect of establishing the plants.

Drosera peltata with prey. The tentacles pull the victim into the cup-shaped leaves.

When you receive your tubers, store them in airtight plastic bags with a few strands of barely damp sphagnum moss and keep them at room temperature in a dark place such as a drawer. Check them weekly until you notice the stolon's growth beginning from the eye of the tuber.

Pot them using five- to eight-inch drained, plastic containers in a mix of pre-wetted two parts sand to one part peat. With your finger, make a hole in the center of the soil about two to four inches deep. (Some large tubers may need bigger pots and deeper holes.) Using forceps, lower the tuber into the hole so the eye is facing upwards. (Remember, the eye is where the stolon is emerging.) Then fill the hole with pure sand, but don't pack it tightly. Set the pot on the tray system, maintaining the water level around one inch.

Within a few weeks, the plant should emerge and develop quickly into its full size. Most tuberous *Drosera* do not continually grow new leaves all season long. The plants produce all their leaf growth rapidly and retain those leaves for the duration of the season.

The objective is to sustain the plant during a shortened summer growing season. Keep the plants as cool as possible, for example, near swamp coolers in the greenhouse or in a cool terrarium under grow-lights. Usually, during this first season of adjustment they grow for around three months, from around April or June until July or August. Feed the plants insects during this time. When the plants turn brown and die back, remove the pot from the water tray. Set the pot in a shady place in moderate temperatures—for example, under a greenhouse bench. The soil must now dry out completely.

Usually the plants remain dormant through autumn and return to growth in wintertime. Do not set the pot back in the water tray until you see the stolon emerge from the soil. Sprinkle water overhead so the soil returns to a wet condition. Allow the plants to grow normally until another cycle of dormancy sets in.

When adjusted to the northern hemisphere, tuberous sundews begin to grow (usually) between October and December. They go dormant between April and June. The plants enjoy sunny conditions in cool and warm greenhouses during the winter months, in temperatures best kept on the cool side: forty to fifty degrees at minimum, sixty to seventy-five degrees maximum. I imagine they would thrive in the cooler, potted terrarium on a winter photoperiod (but I have not yet tried this). Remove the pots during summer dormancy and dry them out. Tuberous sundews make nice winter replacement plants if you remove dormant temperate species from your tank, such as Venus fly-traps or winter-dormant sundews.

Some growers prefer to remove the dormant tubers from their pots every summer, storing them dry in airtight plastic bags. I prefer to leave them potted, but I transplant them every three years or so. This is usually necessary to separate additional tubers that have been produced.

You might be able to grow tuberous *Drosera* as outdoor potted plants if you live in a frost-free Mediterranean-like or subtropical climate such as the immediate California coast or central Florida. Protect the plants if temperatures drop below freezing. Never leave pots of dried, dormant plants in direct sunlight, as the heat will desiccate the tuber. Cool, sunny, humid, south-facing windowsills may also be a place to try these plants in winter.

The flowers of tuberous sundews are usually very pretty, often large, and very sweetly fragrant. Some species flower early in their growth cycle, while others late—just prior to dormancy.

ERECT TUBEROUS SUNDEWS

These sundews produce stems that are usually self-supporting, but may occasionally lean on other plants. The leaf traps are often small, barely a quarter of an inch across, yet are often strong enough to catch a house-fly of equal size.

Drosera peltata

This is one of the easiest to grow and most popular of the tuberous sundews, and the only species found outside Western Australia, growing also on the east coast of that country, New Zealand, India, and much of Southeast Asia. The two outstanding attributes of this plant are that it

Drosera peltata

often produces seed in cultivation, and the tubers usually survive damp to wet conditions during dormancy. The typical forms of *Drosera peltata* usually produce a basal rosette of nearly oval leaves early in the season, not unlike a normal rosetted sundew. Then the climbing stem emerges, carrying several shield-shaped, peltate leaves along its length. The stems average six to ten inches tall. At the top of this stem, the plants have a few small pink or white flowers. Often the stem continues to grow after blooming. I prefer to briefly dry out the pots during dormancy, but have also grown them in bog gardens in my greenhouse. *Drosera auriculata,* an almost identical plant, is now considered a subspecies. In Australia, *Drosera* peltata often comes up in winter-wet lawns around homes in the suburbs, often succumbing to the lawn mower!

Drosera gigantea

This is the king of tuberous sundews, and one of the largest of all *Drosera*. Fortunately it is also simple to grow, and is my favorite in this group. It also survives damp dormant conditions. The red tubers can approach 1 $^1/_2$ inches across, and larger plants are best grown in five-gallon pots. This incredible sundew grows in the form of a small tree, with lateral branches from the stem holding many small, shieldlike leaves. The clustered white flowers come early and the foliage is golden green to bronze. Mature plants are nearly three feet in height.

Drosera andersoniana

A small, lovely species that forms a basal rosette similar to that of *Drosera peltata*. The stem reaches up to ten inches tall, with circular, peltate leaves. The whole plant can achieve a rich red color in good light, with white to pinkish flowers topping the stem.

Drosera gigantea, an easy tuberous sundew that grows like a small tree. This specimen is nearly three feet tall.

Drosera huegelli

A charming plant usually under a foot tall with a few cupshaped leaves hanging bell-like on the upper half of the stem. The flowers are large and white.

Drosera marchantii

There are two subspecies of this plant, one with pink flowers (ssp. *marchantii*), another with white (ssp. *prophylla*). The stems are rather stiff with circular, peltate leaves.

Drosera menziesii ssp. *menziesii*

A handsome plant with an undulating stem, circular leaves and pink flowers. This often reddish variety can approach a foot in height.

Drosera microphylla

A typical erect sundew with circular, peltate leaves, but the startling flowers have large golden sepals and red petals.

CLIMBING TUBEROUS DROSERA

These plants scramble over surrounding vegetation with wiry, flexible stems sometimes many feet in length. Some of their tiny leaves cement themselves to other plants with their tentacles, and these leaves usually have longer petioles than the others.

Drosera macrantha

Another of my favorites, this species is easy to grow. Its seed germinates easily, although cultivated plants have yet to produce seed on their own. Ultimately reaching four or five feet in length, the small leaves are cup-shaped and the one-inch flowers are white or pink. Seedlings remain in a small rosette the first year of growth, forming short stems by the second year. One specimen of mine has remained in the same gallon-sized pot for over seven years, and puts on quite a show each winter and spring.

Drosera macrantha ssp. macrantha can scramble and climb for many feet. Some of its leaves have cemented themselves to the branch for support.

Drosera modesta

This greenish climber, almost three feet tall, has shield-shaped leaves with extra long tentacles and white flowers.

Drosera subhirtella

Rather fine, reddish plants with circular peltate leaves and lovely yellow flowers. The ssp. *subhirtella* reaches fifteen inches in length, while the ssp. *moorei* remains under ten inches.

FAN-LEAFED TUBEROUS DROSERA

These are some of the most highly developed *Drosera* in the world, and some are quite robust and unusual.

Most produce basal rosettes of rather flat oval to elliptic leaves, from which one to several stems grow, often with whorls of folded, fan-shaped leaves along its length.

Drosera stolonifera

There are several sub-species of this plant, all of which are magnificent and easy to grow. *D. stolonifera* ssp. *stolonifera* is my favorite,

Drosera stolonifera **ssp.** *stolonifera*

a thick-stemmed, robust species with whorls of reinform leaves that are somewhat cupped or folded. Several stems may appear, each around six inches long, with leaves in several groups of three to five scattered along the stem's length. The large flowers are white. *D. stolonifera* ssp. *compacta* is rather smaller, deep red, with compact stems and nearly funnel-shaped leaves. *Drosera stolonifera* ssp. *humilis* is a delicate, reddish plant whose stems are semierect, the small leaves on thin petioles. *Drosera stolonifera* ssp. *prostrata* has interesting stems that trail along the ground, and whorls of nearly oval leaves. Another handsome variety is ssp. *rupicola,* with coarse stems and large leaves that fold over prey like a sandwich.

Drosera ramellosa

This small golden green plant is like a miniature version of *Drosera stolonifera* ssp. *stolonifera*. From a leafy rosette arise two four-inch stems of folded, fan-shaped leaves.

Drosera platypoda

A fan-leafed species I have longed to grow but have never tried, the plants are erect, up to eight inches tall, and

Drosera ramellosa

golden green in color with red folded leaves held close to the stem. The flowers are white.

ROSETTED TUBEROUS SUNDEWS

Like many of their cousins around the world, many tuberous sundews grow as rosettes of flat leaves pressed to the ground. The differences are that the leaves of rosetted tuberous *Drosera* are all produced early in the season and they are often large and nearly circular, often with short petioles.

The leaves of rosetted tuberous sundews are incapable of movement. Fragrant flowers usually appear after the leaves are formed. As a rule, the blossoms are white, and may appear clustered or as multiple single blooms.

Drosera macrophylla, a rosetted tuberous sundew

Drosera macrophylla

An easy and handsome plant for cultivation, the large leaves are teardrop-shaped and the rosettes are four to six inches across. Multiple, sweetly perfumed flowers appear before the rosette is fully developed.

Drosera rosulata

Neat rosettes of obovate leaves around two inches across make this an attractive sundew, particularly when the single, short-stemmed flowers are open in the rosette's center. The leaves have a pronounced, depressed, reddish midrib.

Drosera tubaestylus

This species is also easy to cultivate. The rosettes are barely one and a half inches across, and the teardrop-shaped leaves are bronzy red in color. Inter-

Drosera rosulata

estingly, this plant sometimes sends out stolons from the center of the leaves toward the end of its growing season. These stolons anchor into the ground around the mother plant prior to dormancy, where they produce tubers that develop into new plants the following season.

Drosera zonaria

An interesting and beautiful sundew with small rosettes of twenty to thirty closely held leaves arranged like overlapping shingles. The margins of the leaves are usually reddish. The plants commonly form underground stolons and develop into compact colonies.

Drosera orbiculata

A strange tuberous species, the leaves are almost circular at the end of long red petioles. Each rosette is about two inches across with four to six leaves. This species was discovered in 1980.

Drosera lowriei

Another new species named after Allen Lowrie, who has done so much to widen our understanding of Australian CPs. Similar in leaf arrangement to *Drosera zonaria,* the leaves are reddish and spoon shaped, and are reduced in size toward the center of the rosette.

Drosera bulbosa

There are two subspecies of this pretty sundew. *D. bulbosa* ssp. *bulbosa* looks rather similar to *Drosera rosulata* but with raised midribs on golden leaves. *D. bulbosa* ssp. *major* reaches five inches across and has uncommon variants with pink flowers and maroon-tinted leaves.

Drosera erythrorhiza

There are several subspecies of this plant, all producing five to twelve oval to obovate leaves. Some of them are: *D. erythrorhiza* ssp. *erythrorhiza,* with two-inch rosettes of broadly oval leaves that often form dense colonies from underground stolons. *D. erythrorhiza* ssp. *magna* has large rosettes up to five inches across, with wide oval leaves that turn reddish with age. It rarely produces dense colonies. *D. erythrorhiza* ssp. *squamosa* is the most beautiful and rare. The two-inch rosettes have leaves with a distinctive red band along their margins.

Drosera whittakeri

This popular tuberous sundew grows not in Western Australia but further east in Victoria and South Australia. It is odd because it not only grows in woodland forest habitats but has a summer dormancy even though the soil remains damp. The two-inch rosettes have oval leaves on wide petioles, with large, fragrant white flowers. Grow as other tuberous *Drosera,* but keep soil slightly damp during its dormancy.

SOUTH AFRICAN WINTER-GROWING SUNDEWS

Although most South African sundews grow year round in permanently wet areas, some of the most unusual species from this Mediterranean-like climate go dormant when soils dry out, usually from midsummer to midautumn. This dormancy period is rather similar to the tuberous Australian species I have just reviewed; however, instead of tubers, these plants die down to thick, wiry roots from which they return the following season. Further, the rest period is usually somewhat shorter than that of the tuberous varieties, averaging around three months. All are easy to grow. I use a soil medium of half sand to half peat, and otherwise grow them similarly to their tuberous cousins. However, when the plants die back I prefer to dry out the pots for about two months, then I keep the soil barely damp until new growth appears. I then return the pots to the water tray.

Drosera cistiflora

This variable species is particularly unusual and famous for its enormous flowers. When growth begins, the plant forms a two- to three-inch rosette of narrow, tapered leaves pressed flat on the soil surface. After a

couple of months, a stem eight to twelve inches tall is formed, with narrow, tapered, strap-shaped leaves along its length. When the plants are several years old, they may flower. The single, sensational blooms are large, cup-shaped, and two to three inches across, in colors ranging from purple to rose to white to deep red. My plants have never produced seed, and in my experience the plants die after flowering. However, *Drosera cistiflora* is easily propagated using the early rosetted leaves as cuttings.

Drosera cistiflora has the largest flowers in the genus.

Drosera pauciflora

This is another impressive species closely related to *Drosera cistiflora*. It produces large, pale green rosettes of broad, wedge-shaped leaves up to four inches across. The translucent tentacles are among the fastest moving in the genus. Sometimes the rosettes creep along the ground on wiry stems, but they never climb. The very rarely produced flowers are equally impressive as those of *Drosera cistiflora*. I have grown this plant for a dozen years, and just once (the first season I grew them!) I was treated to a mass flowering that lasted many months. It was a sight I will never forget, but strangely the plants have never repeated this perfor-

Drosera pauciflora

mance. The flower colors are as variable as *Drosera cistiflora*, but my plants did not die off as with that species.

Drosera trinervia

A small species with flat rosettes of narrow, wedge-shaped leaves. The small flowers are white.

Drosera hilaris

I have never grown this species, but I have seen impressive-looking photos of it. It looks similar to a robust *Drosera capensis* but has long, oval, undulating leaves.

THE KING SUNDEW

Drosera regia, the king sundew, is in a class of its own. In nature this impressive plant is very rare—only a few colonies in South Africa are known. It is believed by some to have distant relations to the Venus flytrap.

The plant is large, with stiff, sword-shaped leaves that arch outward in a rosette pattern. The leaves can approach two feet in length, and the plants gradually form stems and can develop offshoots from their thick roots. On younger plants the leaves are capable of moving dramatically, twisting in knots around large prey. On older plants only the tapered ends of the leaves move. The tentacles are substantial and produce thick globules of mucilage that can overcome even large and powerful insects. The flowers are deep pink, one and a half inches across, and held in a cluster on a stalk as long as the leaves. They can

The king sundew, *Drosera regia*

have an exhausting effect on the plant so I usually remove them.

Drosera regia enjoys a rather open soil, so grow it in large pots of one half long-fibered sphagnum to one half perlite. Peat can be substituted for the sphagnum. It grows best in cool, frost free climates, or in cool and warm greenhouses. Terrariums need to be large to accommodate it. I have seen surprisingly beautiful specimens on cool, sunny windowsills near the coast in California, where they appear to have a voracious appetite for houseflies.

In winter *Drosera regia* greatly reduces the size of its leaves, and occasionally crowns die back, but the plant returns from its thick roots. Leave large plants undisturbed for several years, and grow them permanently on the tray system. Leaf cuttings fail on this species, but it takes well from root cuttings. Rather than disturb the whole plant, which can set it back, I prefer to cut roots from the base of a potted specimen and gently pull these from the soil. Plants have also been propagated in tissue culture.

PROPAGATING SUNDEWS

Propagating Drosera can be achieved through various methods—most of which are easy and fun while others can be rather challenging.

Seed

With those species that readily produce seed, this method is a rather simple affair. Some, such as cape sundews, will self-seed in such quantities that the plants can become troublesome weeds. Others may need a little coaxing. Many sundew flowers self-pollinate upon closing, but with those from which you want good seed-set, it is wise to tease the flowers with a toothpick while they are open. The seed pods mature in several weeks.

I prefer to separate the seed from their pods and store them in small, airtight plastic bags (jewelers have supplies of these) or paper envelopes. Seeds lose their viability at room temperature, so refrigerate them.

Sowing times are simple. Almost all sundew seed is best sown in late winter or early spring. The exceptions are tuberous and other winter-growing species, which should be sown in early autumn.

Most species germinate best with a period of stratification. This means that after sowing, the seed should experience several weeks of damp and chilly conditions. Light frost is often beneficial, even for the winter-growing varieties. However, after germination protect the seedlings from frost. If damp-off occurs, use a fungicide.

Drosera adelae

Sow the seed sparsely on the medium the plants prefer. Do not cover the seed with soil. High humidity is beneficial for germination, so use covered seed trays or airtight plastic bags placed over pots. (Various take-out plastic food containers work well for this.) The medium need not be deep for germination; one to two inches is adequate.

After stratification, place the containers in bright conditions, or place them close to grow-lights. Avoid hot sun or the containers may overheat. The seed will usually germinate in four to eight weeks. Remove the covers at this time. When the plants are of manageable size, they may be pricked out using forceps and planted in their permanent pots. Try not to break the small roots.

Leaf cuttings

This is a fascinating way to reproduce sundews, and larger plants can be grown more quickly. This method works for nearly all species. *Drosera regia* and *D. burmanni* are two exceptions, and many tuberous *Drosera* produce too few leaves to be used for cuttings and have such short growing seasons they can run into problems.

Leaf cuttings work best when taken early in the growing season. Snip off the leaves at their petioles. With the woolly sundews, I've had better success plucking the petiole from the plant with its base intact.

Lay the leaves flat, tentacle-side up, on a peat and sand mix, long-fibered sphagnum, or milled sphagnum. Using pinches of the soil, secure the leaves at their ends but do not cover the tentacles to any great extent. Long leaves, such as those of *Drosera filiformis* or the forked sundews, can be cut into segments about two inches long.

Keep the cuttings in covered containers to ensure high humidity. Place in very bright light, but not direct sun, or place them under grow-lights. After several weeks tiny plantlets will appear, usually from the tentacles. Check the cuttings frequently and resecure them if movement causes the backs of the leaves to lose contact with the medium.

One method I have used to enhance leaf cuttings is to dip them in a solution of Superthrive (one drop per cup of water) before laying them out.

Also, many leaves will bud when floated in small covered cups or petri dishes filled with pure distilled water. Change the water weekly or if algae appears.

Drosera binata

Root cuttings

This method is also easy and can result in mature plants within one season. It works best with sundews that have long and thick roots, such as the cape sundews, most rosetted subtropicals, forked sundews, and *Drosera regia*. Root cuttings work best when taken early in the growing season or at the tail end of dormancy, if the plants have one.

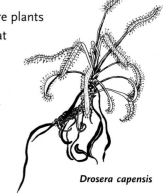

Drosera capensis

Remove the plant from its soil and cut off healthy roots. These roots are generally black with whitish tips. The mother plant can be repotted. Cut the roots into pieces around two inches long. Using covered containers similar to those for leaf cuttings, lay these root pieces horizontally on medium about two inches deep. Cover the roots with no more than a half inch of the medium. Keep the containers covered and in very bright light. After several weeks the plantlets should appear. When a few leaves come up, remove the covers and place the plants in sunnier locations. They can usually be potted up within a few months of sprouting.

Gemmae

The most reliable way to propagate the pygmy *Drosera* is by the brood bodies they produce in autumn. The only tricky thing is removing the gemmae. If the pygmies are in pots, remove the pots from the water tray and allow them to drain for several hours. Then hold the pots upside down over a sheet of plastic or paper. Using a toothpick, tease the crowns of gemmae in the center of each plant. Mature gemmae will pop and shoot off onto the sheet. Collect them with a slightly moistened fingertip. By gently rubbing your finger and thumb together, the gemmae can be sowed like seed onto soil where you will permanently grow the plants. They will reach maturity by springtime.

In situations where the growing containers cannot be overturned, such as bog gardens, most gemmae can be removed gently with a moistened fingertip or small wet paintbrush.

Drosera burmanni

Since pygmies will grow wherever the gemmae are placed, you can be clever in growing them. One lady I know, using a large garden bowl, tediously placed individual gemma with forceps in precise positions. Months later the scores of small dime-sized rosettes spelled out the word "sundews" rather neatly!

Tissue culture

Most sundews are easy to start in vitro by the use of sterilized seed.

— 6 —

THE WEST AUSTRALIAN PITCHER PLANT

(CEPHALOTUS FOLLICULARIS)

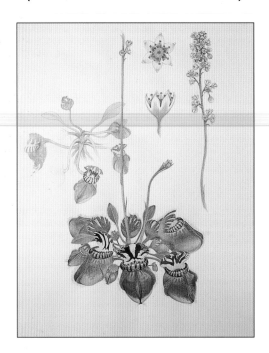

ONE OF THE MOST DESIRED carnivorous plants in cultivation, *Cephalotus* is a curious pitcher plant of compact growth with bristly, colorful traps that are seemingly yawning for a bite to eat.

The first published account of this pitcher plant was in 1806 by the naturalist La Billardière, who had accompanied the French explorer d'Entrecasteau on an expedition to southern Australia some years before. A monotypic genus, the Latin name refers to both the structure of the flower as well as the leaf.

The plants grow naturally in a narrow coastal strip around Esperence Bay in extreme southwestern Australia, a range barely 250 miles long. A Mediterranean-like climate of warm, dry summers and cool, wet winters belie the fact that the plants grow in permanently damp areas on the edges of swamps. The summers are cool, being near the coast, and light frost is occasional in the winter. The plants often grow in clusters under the partial shade of sedge grass in wet, open areas. Sometimes colonies grow only a few feet from saltwater beaches, clinging to mossy banks where fresh water trickles. It is often found accompanied by *Drosera hamiltonii*. The soils are peaty sand.

Seedlings grow slowly into low-growing plants that spread through creeping, branching, underground rhizomes. *Cephalotus* is peculiar in that it produces two main forms of leaves. As the days grow longer in spring, several noncarnivorous leaves emerge from each growing point, probably to aid in photosynthesis. These are pointed, oval leaves on short petioles, a rich, shiny green in color. As summer arrives, the pitchers develop, starting as fuzzy knobs at the ends of elongating petioles that slowly inflate and open as a pitcher trap. Occasional third and even fourth kinds of leaves may form, perhaps representing primitive leaves. Some may appear as hollow cups with forked edges, or similar to the foliage leaf but with unusual projectiles emerging from them. Only the pitchers catch insects.

The plants slow or stop their growth in winter but are evergreen perennials—older leaves and pitchers dying off as new ones form the

The thimble-sized pitchers yawn patiently for food.

following year. Flowers usually occur in summer. The stalks are surprisingly long for such a small plant and may be two feet or more in length, semierect, or leaning along the ground. Clusters of the small flowers appear scattered along the upper part. They lack petals, are of a pale green in color, and are less than a quarter inch across.

The pitchers, though small, are elaborately designed. In the typical form of the plant, the traps are one- to one-and-a-half inches in height. A much-sought-after larger form exists, called 'Giant', with pitchers two to three inches in size.

Reminiscent of an Indian moccasin standing on its toe, the pitchers all face outward in a rosette pattern. Hairy bristles are on the lid and along three rows of ribs on the pitcher's front. These are no doubt "guide hairs" that lead an insect toward the open mouth. Nectar glands lure the prey—usually small ants—toward a ridge of sharp, incurved teeth. At the base of these teeth the nectar is the heaviest, and insects will often lean over the slippery teeth to get a better taste.

The rain-protecting lid hangs over the mouth of the pitcher much like a canopy. Transparent light windows on this lid are similar to those found on *Darlingtonia* and some *Sarracenia* pitcher plants. But here these window panes are not meant to deceive a way of escape. Instead, they allow light to enter the pitcher cavity. The light shines on the otherwise murky pool of digestive juices that lie at the bottom of the leaf, making the depths of the trap more inviting to insects.

Unique among pitcher plants, *Cephalotus* has a bright white collar that overhangs the well of juices. This collar is slippery and is also baited with nectar. Insects hanging on the downward curving teeth may attempt to taste the nectar on this waxy, almost funnel-shaped collar. The prey slips and tumbles into the digestive fluids below.

Even if a frantic insect manages to scale the walls of this watery pit, it cannot bypass the overhanging collar and escape. Soon the insect drowns, and is slowly dissolved in a bath of acids and enzymes.

In the sun, Australian pitcher plants can develop a beautiful coloration of reds and purples. Shaded, the pitchers may grow larger but remain greenish in color. Although the lids don't close to capture prey, in drying conditions of low humidity they may slowly fold downward, covering the mouth, perhaps to discourage the evaporation of its digestive juices.

CULTIVATION *(See Parts I and II for further information)*

Soil recipe	West Australian pitcher plants do best in a mix of one part peat to two parts sand and/or perlite.
Containers	Plastic containers are best, but they also do well in terra-cotta or glazed clay. Always use drained containers; shallow undrained containers will rot their roots.
Watering	Use the tray method. *Cephalotus* dislikes long periods of being waterlogged, so it is best to allow the water in the tray to evaporate before adding more.
Light	From full sun to part shade. The more sun, the more color in the pitchers.
Climate	*Cephalotus* does best with moderately warm summers and cool to chilly winters. The plants may die in long periods of very hot weather, and they enjoy cool summer nights. They are tolerant of brief, light frost down to twenty-two degrees, but may be killed in lower temperatures.
Greenhouses	Thrives in cool and warm greenhouses.
Windowsill	Does well in partly sunny windows of fairly high humidity. Mist often.
Outdoors	A fine potted specimen for partly sunny decks, patios, and porches in Mediterranean-like and warm-temperate climates. Appreciates cool nights in the summertime.
Bog gardens	Does well in deeper bogs that are not waterlogged continuously.
Terrariums/ Grow-lights	Excellent as a potted specimen year round in the unheated greenhouse-style terrarium. Colorful and vigorous under grow-lights.
Feeding	Small sow or pill bugs, tiny ants, or dried insects work well. Wingless fruit flies or baby crickets can also be fed to your plant.

Fertilizers	Occasional misting of foliage can be beneficial. Use Miracid, Orchid, or Epiphytic fertilizer.
Pests and diseases	Aphids are rare on *Cephalotus* due to the bristly nature of developing pitchers and tough foliage leaves. The primary pest is scale. Use Orthene, Diazinon, or Malathion for control. Fungi attack is a sign of low light and stagnant, overly humid air. Use a fungicide to control.

PROPAGATION

Although the West Australian pitcher plant is fairly easy to propagate through various methods, it is slow-growing plant and is still rather scarce and much sought after by hobbyists. Plants offered for sale by nurseries—when you can find them—are often on the young side and may take a couple of years or more to reach maturity.

Seed

The tiny flowers open on the tall stalk a few at a time. For best seed set, it is wise to use a small paintbrush and tease each flower on a daily basis, transferring pollen from one to another. In several weeks most pods will produce a few hairy, brown fruits—a few seed in each one.

The viability of the seed is not long, so if you refrigerate them, do so for no more than two to four months, or sow immediately. Sow on their recommended soil, or on milled sphagnum. It is best to stratify the seed, keeping them damp and chilly, for two to three months. With increased light and warmer temperatures, the seed will start germinating after several weeks. Some seeds may take a few months to germinate. Slow growing, the rosettes will increase by about one inch a year.

Leaf cuttings

This is a faster way to grow larger plants more quickly than seed. Remove leaves or pitchers from the rhizome by gently tugging them by the petiole, trying to get as much of the whitish leaf base as possible. Lay these right-side up on a damp mix of one part peat to one part sand, or use milled or long-fibered sphagnum. Place pinches of medium lightly over the broken base of the petioles to keep the cutting in place. Cover with clear plastic or use a propagating tray. Keep bright, and maintain cool to moderate temperatures. Plantlets will appear usually at the cut end of the petiole in several weeks. After a few months, when a small root system has formed, plants can be transferred to small pots. A mature plant can be attained this way in about two to three years.

Root cuttings

Mature plants can be produced this way somewhat faster than by leaf cuttings. Remove a large plant from its medium in late winter. Rinse off all soil. The thick rhizome and its wiry roots may be used for cuttings (as well as the leaves), or you may simply trim some of these away, leaving much of the mother plant intact, and later repotted. Cut the rhizome and roots into pieces one to two inches long. Lay these on the soils recommended for leaf cuttings, but cover them with about a half inch of the medium. Keep bright, damp, and covered with clear plastic. Shoots will appear in several weeks. After a few months, separate and pot them.

Division

Use the same method as under "root cuttings" when your plants have produced several crowns. While dividing these growing points, you may take some leaf and root cuttings as well. Keep bright and humid as the divisions recuperate.

Tissue culture

Cephalotus can be propagated in vitro primarily through sterilized seed. Removal from flask and introduction into soil can be difficult, and plantlets should have well-developed roots for best success. Plants from tissue culture can be slow to attain a large size.

— 7 —
THE DEWY PINE
(DROSOPHYLLUM LUSITANICUM)

A prize-winning dewy pine grown by Geoff Wong.

THE ALLURING AROMA OF HONEY exuded by the dewy pine is the insidious trick used by this plant to catch flying insects, suffocate them, and eat them.

A most unusual plant, *Drosophyllum lusitanicum* was known by locals as a "flycatcher" for centuries, before studies by Charles Darwin and, later, Dr. A. Quintanilha proved the plant to be carnivorous. Even more surprising, recent DNA studies suggest that this plant (the only species in its genus) may share distant ancestors with *Nepenthes,* the tropical pitcher plants of Asia. Closer relatives are the sundews and Venus flytraps.

What is most striking about the dewy pine is that it is an exception within the carnivorous plant world. Far from being a denizen of a swamp, the dewy pine is native only to limited areas of Portugal, Spain, and Morocco, where it grows on dry, alkaline coastal hills. The soil is usually sandy gravel caught between boulders and chunky rock, where the most runoff from rain flows. Inhabiters of a Mediterranean climate, dewy pines get most of their rain in winter. The dry summers are cooler along the coast, due to persistent fogs. The summer fog seems to be vital to the plant—it appears to absorb fog through its leaves as the moisture condenses.

Dewy pines produce several bright yellow spring flowers that scatter their seed in summer on dry soil. When winter rains arrive, the soaked seeds begin to germinate. The seedlings grow quickly, sending their roots deeply into the gravelly soil. It is believed that the plant produces a chemical to inhibit the growth of other dewy pines from growing within several feet of itself—a strategy due no doubt to water conservation.

Dewy pines produce a cluster of narrow, linear leaves around eight to ten inches in length. Their upright nature resembles a tuft of pine needles, hence their common name. As these leaves die, they produce a skirted thatch around the slowly scrambling, woody stem. Often the plants produce offshoots from their stems, resulting in a branching, semiprostrate plant that looks like a small, scrubby bush.

The long, thin leaves are highly developed. A shallow fold, or furrow, runs along the length of the leaf on its upper side. The undersurface of the leaf is lined with several rows of stalked glands that are tinted red.

A drop of mucilage, or glue, is secreted by each gland. This glittering drop not only magnifies the red color of the gland but produces a heavy aroma of bee honey, making the whole plant smell rather sickly sweet. Since the leaves are held more or less upright, this sparkling reddishness combined with its promising scent invites insects to alight upon its leaves for a taste of nectar.

The unfortunate insect immediately finds itself mired in an oily fluid. Unlike the sticky glue of sundews, this mucilage readily pulls off from the glands, adhering to the struggling insect. Larger, stronger prey such as flies frantically move up or down the leaf, trying to free themselves. As they do, they pull drop after drop of the viscid fluid from the glands. Soon they are overwhelmed, the breathing holes along the sides of their bodies smothered in the clinging liquid. The insect soon suffocates. Tiny prey like gnats are usually overwhelmed in a single drop.

Next, sessile glands along the narrow leaf surface secrete digestive juices under the dead body of the prey. Strong enzymes dissolve the soft parts of the insect. This fluid trickles down the leaf, where it is reabsorbed like a soup of nutrients for the plant.

The dewy pine is a perennial plant that can live for many years if properly grown. It is still fairly rare in cultivation, mostly due to the trickiness of seed germination, which is the only way the plant can be propagated currently.

CULTIVATION *(See Parts I and II for further information)*

Soil recipe	Use a mix of equal parts perlite, sand, and vermiculite. If you have some, a fourth part of pumice or lava rock is a good additive to this mix.
Containers	Dewy pines can be grown in large plastic pots, but I prefer terra-cotta clay pots about ten to twelve inches in diameter.
Watering	Dewy pines require a drier soil than most carnivorous plants and should never be kept on the tray system with the pot immersed in water. Always allow good drainage. In greenhouses and other controlled environments, water the plants about once or twice a week most of the year. I like to keep the medium dampish for several days at a time during the winter months. In summer, occasional misting of the leaves is beneficial but not necessary. It is crucial that after spring flowering the soil is kept on the dry side for a few months.
Light	*Drosophyllum* does best in full sun most of the day.
Climate	Dewy pines grow naturally in a Mediterranean-like climate that is warm-temperate. The warm, dry summers have cool foggy nights; the winters are chilly and wetter. The plants can survive brief heat waves of 100 degrees, as well as

short freezes down to twenty degrees or sometimes even colder. There is no dormancy.

Greenhouses	An excellent candidate for the cold house, cool house, and warm house.
Outdoors	If you live in a Mediterranean-like climate such as California, western Australia, or South Africa, this is a wonderful potted plant for your deck or patio. Prolonged wet soils in winter are not harmful. You can also grow the plant outdoors in other temperate areas in a sunny place protected from too much summer rain, such as a covered porch. Cool nights in summer are appreciated.
Terrariums/ Grow-lights	Difficult but possible in only the largest of tanks or under Halide lights as a potted plant.
Windowsill	Quite possible, but only on the sunniest windowsill or solarium.
Bog gardens	Impossible, but should do well in Mediterranean-like coastal climates as a potted plant submerged in the ground in a drained container. The plants might be able to be naturalized in gravelly soils in places such as coastal California or western Australia. In these Mediterranean-like climates, one might dig a hole and fill it with soil (see soil recipe, above) and try a dewy pine in the drier parts of a garden.
Feeding	Dewy pines will catch an abundance of flies, moths, gnats, and mosquitoes when grown outdoors. Dried insects applied to the leaves will make your dewy pine drool in appreciation.
Fertilizers	Not necessary if the plants catch plenty of insects. A foliar feeding of heavily diluted epiphytic or orchid fertilizer can be beneficial, but do not apply this more than once every month or two.
Pests and diseases	I have never experienced pests on my *Drosophyllum*, but should any occur I would try Diazinon or Orthene as a

method of control, or I would place a flea collar very close to the problem. Diseases are mostly fungus or stem rot, which may affect plants that are kept too wet or are in a humid, low-light, stagnant-air environment.

PROPAGATION

The most frustrating problem with *Drosophyllum* is getting the germinated seedling plants to survive the first few crucial months of their lives. A second disappointment is that currently the only successful way to propagate the plants is by seed. Leaf-cuttings, root-cuttings, and division all fail. Tissue-cultured plants from seed may be a possibility.

Dewy pines usually flower in spring or early summer, but in cultivation can bloom sometimes as late as early autumn. The handsome, bright yellow flowers are about one inch in diameter, and will self-pollinate upon closing. But for heavier seed set, tease the flowers with a toothpick or brush when they open (which is only briefly). Several flowers will open over the course of a few days.

A few weeks later the seed pod cracks open, revealing a number of large, coarse, black seed. The pod itself is an unusual cone-shaped structure, opaque tan in color.

I prefer to store the seed dry in the refrigerator until autumn. Scarification of the seed is helpful, so I usually rub the seed firmly between sandpaper until the hard surface is lightly scraped. Next I soak the seed in water for a few days.

Sow the seed, without burying it, in a small tray of shallow vermiculite. Keep it damp to wet, and seed should start germinating within days to weeks.

Check daily, and immediately upon germination (within a few days) gently remove the sprouting seed and lay it upon the surface of the soil in its permanent pot. Keep the soil damp for a few weeks as the seedling establishes itself. Then begin to allow the soil to dry out between waterings. The plants will grow rapidly; keep them in a sunny location. I find that even container plants inhibit the growth of plants nearby, so I usually keep the pots several feet away from each other.

The plants will be of flowering size in one to two years. Although some people trim the dead skirt of leaves, I find it rather attractive and leave it on. Never attempt to transplant your dewy pine; root disturbance often leads to its death.

— 8 —
THE RAINBOW PLANTS
(*Byblis*)

Byblis liniflora

IN MYTHOLOGY, Byblis was the granddaughter of Apollo, who fell in love with her twin brother. When he rejected and fled from her, Byblis wept bitter tears and turned into a fountain.

Glittering and often delicate, *Byblis,* the rainbow plants, can sometimes appear as frosted sprays of water, and in sunlight can sparkle with multicolored hues. Their shining leaves and pretty flowers mask their deadly nature, as they catch and kill countless tiny insects who make the fatal mistake of alighting upon them.

180

For over a century only two species were known (from Australia and New Guinea), but recent discoveries by Allen Lowrie may add several species, subspecies, or forms to the genus. James Drummond, the famous Australian botanist, discovered *Byblis gigantea* in the nineteenth century. In 1905, a woman named A. Nikon Bruce fed plants of *Byblis liniflora* tiny bits of hard-boiled egg, and when the egg dissolved in a few days concluded that the plants were carnivorous.

Because of their flower structure and glands, rainbow plants were at first assumed to be related to butterworts and bladderworts of the family Lentibulariaceae, but finally were given their own family, *Byblidaceae*. Recent DNA research by Steve Williams has shown that their closest relatives are indeed the butterworts, found far from the Australian continent.

The two primary species and their newly discovered forms all have similar structure and trapping mechanisms. The plants have narrow stems that sometimes branch and trail along the ground or lean and climb nearby grasses or other plants. The leaves are fine and linear, radiating in all directions from the stem. The whole plant is covered with two types of glands. The first are stalked, hairlike glands, which are capped with a clear, sticky glue. Small insects like gnats and mosquitoes become trapped in the glue and struggle to escape. Eventually these insects die from exhaustion or are suffocated.

It is then that the second glands come into action. These sessile glands lie flat along the leaves, and they secret the digestive juices that dissolve the soft parts of the prey.

Strangely enough, no enzymes or bacteria have been found yet in these juices, but some scientists theorize that fungi may play a role in digestion. Furthermore, *Byblis* plays host to assassin bugs, similar to *Roridula,* and the plants may benefit from the bugs' secretion in the same way. Further study is needed to discover the details of the carnivorous nature of *Byblis*.

BYBLIS GIGANTEA

This species grows in the coastal regions of southwestern Australia: from about 50 miles south of Perth to an area nearly 400 miles north of Perth. The climate is Mediterranean-like, with cool, wet winters and hot, dry summers.

Byblis gigantea

The plants are perennial and the seedlings grow rapidly, sending roots deep into the sandy soil. The seeds usually germinate when the rains of late autumn begin, but they need a quick-moving brush-fire in summer to chemically condition them to germinate. In the wild, seed may lay on the ground for several years before a fire moves through. But during the rainy season subsequent to a fire, hundreds of seeds will sprout. The seedlings can grow so fast they can be flowering by the following spring, just before the onset of the hot, dry summer.

The giant rainbow is really no larger than a small bush. Stems grow from a woody base one or two feet tall. The linear leaves average about ten inches long. The handsome flowers are more or less flat faced, deep pink to violet blue in color, about one inch across, and on stalks that look similar to the leaves. To release their pollen, the vibration of insect wings is usually required, the pollen spraying on the insect in a little cloud. The insect then deposits the pollen onto the next flower.

Byblis gigantea usually grows on the sandy edges of wet winter swamps. When summer arrives and the soil dries out, the stems of the plant die down to the woody base, and the plant remains dormant until the rains return the following autumn. *Byblis gigantea* grows year round, however, in cultivation and in some areas where the soil is always damp.

There are a few forms of this species. The typical one has fairly short stems with leaves clustered at the growing point. The more recently described "Enneabba" and "Cataby" forms have taller stems with leaves more sparsely arranged along them.

BYBLIS LINIFLORA

The little rainbow plant is an often beautiful species, and in its typical form grows as a tropical annual.

It is found in northern Australia, from Western Australia through the Northern Territory and into the Cape York Peninsula in Queensland. The species is also found in southern New Guinea. The climate is tropical and warm all year, but is marked by a monsoonal wet summer with a drier winter.

Plants of *Byblis liniflora* typically grow in sandy areas bordering summer wet streams and water holes. The small, poppylike seeds germinate rapidly with the warm rains, and the plants grow very fast, flowering sometimes within weeks of germination.

The plants are small, delicate, and scrambling, their stems approaching twelve inches in length and sometimes longer. The leaves are threadlike and a few inches long. The whole plant is densely covered in sticky hairs, and in sunlight can put on a rather spectacular show, glittering like frosted miniature Christmas trees.

The flowers are profusely produced during the life span of the plant, many small, quarter-inch blooms hovering amid the leaves. They are the exact color of amethyst, and will open in sunlight over several days. They self-pollinate themselves before withering.

A few forms have been discovered that may turn

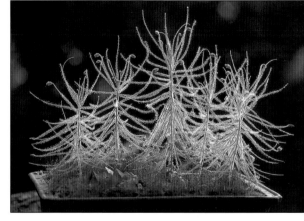

Byblis liniflora at sunrise

out to be entirely new species. From the Darwin area (in the extreme north of the Northern Territory) are maroon plants called "Darwin Red." Another has been named ssp. filifolia. More are likely to be identified.

CULTIVATION *(See Parts One and Two for further details)*

Both species are easy to grow, but **B. gigantea** *is definitely the more difficult to get started, as the seed needs to be treated before germination.*

Soil recipe	Both species do well in a mix of two parts sand to one part peat. You can also add an additional part of perlite, lava rock, or pumice.
Containers	Plastic works well, but if you use fire to germinate seed of *B. gigantea,* use clay or glazed ceramic. Use four- to six-inch pots for *B. liniflora* (the plants can live longer in deeper pots); six- to ten-inch pots for *B. gigantea.*
Watering	Use the tray method, but allow the water to evaporate before replenishing. Keep the soil just damp and not permanently waterlogged.
Light	Full to partly sunny for both species.
Climate	*B. liniflora* does best in tropical climates, but its annual nature allows you to grow it during any span of several months of warm weather. *B. gigantea* does best in Mediterranean-like climates that are almost frost free, with cool summer nights, but may succeed in subtropical climates. Dry summer dormancy is not necessary in cultivation.
Outdoors	*B. gigantea* does well in almost frost-free Mediterranean-like climates. *B. liniflora* will usually grow well with several months of warm weather, or in tropical areas.
Bog gardens	Excellent in bog gardens. Best in higher areas of the bog. Pay attention to climate requirements of the species (see above).
Greenhouses	*B. gigantea* thrives in cool and warm greenhouses. *B. liniflora* does best in warm houses, hot houses, and stove houses, but can be grown from late spring until autumn in other houses, too.

Terrarium/ Grow-lights	Excellent for *B. liniflora*. *B. gigantea* is too large for most tanks, but worth a try in larger terrariums or under high-intensity lights.
Windowsill	Both are surprisingly good for sunny windows.
Feeding	Small insects such as gnats and fruit flies.
Fertilizer	A light monthly misting with an orchid or epiphytic fertilizer helps.
Transplanting	Any root disturbance can shock and kill *B. liniflora*. *B. gigantea* can be successfully transplanted when necessary. Soak the rootstock in a vitamin B-1 solution to overcome shock.
Pests and diseases	On very rare occasions, mealybug or aphids may attack *B. gigantea*. Damp-off fungus can be a hassle with seedlings; treat with a fungicide. Snails and slugs like baby plants.

PROPAGATION

B. liniflora is simple to propagate by seed. Although the flowers will usually self-pollinate, I like to tease them with a toothpick to ensure good seed set. A few weeks later, the brown pods will split, revealing up to two dozen seed. Store these dry in the refrigerator and sow in spring. Or, after a rest period of a few weeks, the seed will germinate in any warm, bright environment, such as under grow-lights. Simply scatter the poppylike seed on the surface of their preferred soil mix, and keep it warm and damp. Typically, *B. liniflora* will die off in the winter months, but in terrariums and sometimes windowsills they can live two years or longer. The form

The flower of Byblis gigantea

"Darwin Red" apparently needs fire or smoke treatment, as with *B. gigantea* (see below).

The flowers of *B. gigantea* can be tricky to pollinate. I have found the tuning fork method to be the best. Touch the vibrating fork into the center of the flower while holding a sheet of paper under the petals. If the pollen is ripe, it will spray a cloud of pollen grains onto the paper. Collect this with a small paintbrush. The pollen must be dabbed onto the stigmas of a separate flower, as self-pollination seems to fail. Seed will be produced in several weeks.

It is believed that the chemicals released by smoke is what triggers seed germination in *B. gigantea*—not the heat of fire. There are several methods used to achieve this in cultivation.

Lightly press the seed onto the damp soil surface in a clay or ceramic pot. Place a small loose pile of dried grass, hay, or paper towels over the soil. Light with a match and gently blow on the fire to ensure a good, smoky blaze. When the fire burns out, allow to cool and gently blow off excess ash. Lightly sprinkle with water. Germination should follow in a few weeks.

Alternatively, sow the seed as above and place a burning cigarette on the soil. Cover the pot with a clear plastic bag and allow the smoke to become dense. The cigarette will usually extinguish itself before too long. Leave the bag on the pot until the smoke eventually clears.

Although I have not yet tried it myself, liquid smoke, available at grocery stores and used to flavor meats, might also work with *B. gigantea*. I would suggest soaking the seed in this product, or try placing a few drops of the liquid onto your sowed seed.

Smoke discs have recently been developed to enhance seed germination of certain plants. These paper discs are soaked in water along with the seed. One source for this product is the National Botanical Institute, Private Bag X7, Claremont, 7735, South Africa. Inquire about their *Kirstenbosch Instant Smoke Plus Seed Primer*.

Finally, gibberellic acid can be used to germinate *B. gigantea* seed. It is available through companies specializing in science and biological supplies. Gibberellic acid is a powder you dissolve in water at a ratio of about 1 part acid to 1000 parts water. I find that about an eighth-inch of the acid on the end of a toothpick dissolved into about one cup of water works well. Soak the seed for twenty-four hours in this solution before sowing.

Division and root-cuttings

Larger plants of *B. gigantea* can be divided. Remove the plant from its pot and rinse away most of the soil. The woody rhizome will usually have multiple growing points. Cut these apart with a sharp knife, trying to assure that each piece has a few roots attached. Soak in a vitamin B-1 solution, then repot the divisions.

Root cuttings can also work. Cut the oldest, thickest roots into pieces about two inches long. Lay these on their preferred soil mix, and lightly cover with pinches of soil. Keep damp and humid, as in a propagating case, in bright light. Plantlets usually appear in several weeks.

— 9 —
THE BUTTERWORTS
(PINGUICULA)

Pinguicula vulgaris

> *"Well, it's a cross between a butterwort
> and a Venus fly trap."*

—SEYMORE KRELBORN TO MR. MUSHNICK,
when asked where his person-eating plant, Audrey Junior,
came from. *Little Shop of Horrors* (1960)

A CUSTOMER VISITING MY NURSERY once described the butterworts as "the Shirley Temples of the carnivorous plant world." I must disagree. Butterworts are Patty McCormicks (the sweet, pretty child who played Rhoda Penmark in *The Bad Seed,* a devilish girl who enjoyed pushing little old ladies down stairs). The fact that Seymore Krelborn, in the original production of *Little Shop of Horrors,* admits that one of the parents of Audrey Junior was indeed a butterwort, boggles my mind. I can only imagine Charles Griffith, the screenwriter, perusing his encyclopedia under "carnivorous plants" and suddenly exclaiming, "Butter-wort! Now that sounds pretty disgusting!" And thus history in sci-fi horticulture was made.

As for real history, butterworts were brought to the attention of Charles Darwin in the early 1870s. A gentleman named Mr. Marshall mentioned to the carnivorous-plant-obsessed Mr. Darwin that he noticed many small and struggling insects upon the leaves of butterworts growing in England. Darwin investigated, and sure enough discovered another genus of insect-eating plants.

S. Jost Caspar, in the mid 1960s, wrote a large monograph on butterworts that accumulated all the information on the genus known up to that time. A botanist in East Germany, Herr Caspar was amazed to find out that some of the plants had achieved windowsill popularity in the outside world when the Berlin wall fell in the late 1980s. More recently, much information has been gathered by the studies of Dr. Donald Schnell on the U.S. species, and particularly by Juerg Steiger in Switzerland. The most exciting development in the 1990s has been the establishment of the International Pinguicula Study Group, based in England, to promote the popularity of pings (as they are affectionately referred to) in cultivation.

Pinguicula, in Latin, means "little greasy one." While butterwort is their common name, more recently some growers have begun to call them "pings." There are around seventy species known, many of them rather recent discoveries. Pings grow throughout much of the Northern Hemisphere, from the Arctic Circle down through Siberia, Europe, and North America. They reach their climax in Mexico, where the most spectacular forms exist. A few more species exist down through South America.

Butterworts are typically small, herbaceous plants a few inches in diameter. Like many other CPs, they grow in a rosette fashion. The leaves of almost all species are flat, with slightly upturned margins. The leaves arise out of the center of the plant, and as they mature they press themselves rather firmly upon the ground, although in a few species the leaves may be held semierect or arching. The leaf shape of butterworts may be narrow and tapered to a point, or be rather oblong to nearly oval. Only a few unusual forms have leaves nearly filiform, and in some species the upturned margins may be lacking or even curved downwards. The color of the leaves is almost invariably pale to green, but some sun-growing pings may have leaves that turn bronzy or reddish. The roots are usually few and short.

As their Latin and common names suggest, the leaves of butterworts have a distinctly buttery or greasy feel to them. At a glance, the leaves appear perfectly innocent. But examined closely with a magnifying lens, one can see that the surface of the leaves is covered with thousands of minute, nearly transparent glandular hairs that rise a tiny fraction of an inch above the surface. The glands at the top of the hairs produce a small drop of sticky glue. A second gland also litters the leaf surface. These are flat, sessile glands, and in the right angle of light, when viewed under a lens, they appear as shallow depressions, like small, dished craters. These sessile glands are dry—until prey is caught.

Butterworts sometimes have a slight, musty, almost fungoid or earthy aroma that may or may not attract prey. The stalked glands can catch sunlight, and thus the leaf surface can glitter or shine, sometimes producing a shimmering rainbow effect that may also be a lure for prey.

Their victims are generally very small insects such as gnats, springtails, and fruit flies. Rarely can pings catch anything approaching the size of a housefly, although sometimes this does occur. The strongest prey I have ever witnessed caught by a butterwort, to my amazement, was a newly hatched praying mantis.

When an insect alights upon a butterwort leaf, it immediately realizes its mistake: it is mired in the glue of the stalked glands. As it struggles to break free, it pulls more and more drops of glue from the glands until it is overwhelmed and hopelessly stuck.

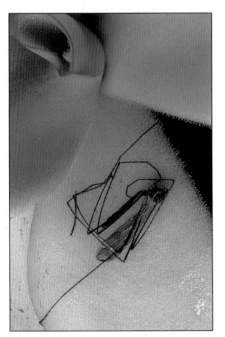

Butterworts only rarely catch prey as large as this unfortunate cranefly.

The strength of this glue is powerful—the panicky insects often leave behind twitching legs in their attempt to escape. Minute insects like springtails can be overcome by one or two stalked glands.

It is then that the sessile glands come into play. Almost immediately after the insect is caught, these glands begin to secrete a liquid of acids and enzymes. Soon the dying or dead insect is wetted down by this secretion and digestion begins. The soft parts of the prey dissolve, and the victim is reduced to a pulpy mass, sometimes in a matter of hours. The secretion of digestive fluids can be so copious it can sometimes be seen trickling down the leaf. The sessile glands soon reabsorb this fluid, now rich in nutrients.

That butterworts produce a strong bactericide was noticed quickly by Darwin. Parts of dead insects and bits of meat he fed to his pings that were not wetted by the digestive juices were soon attacked by fungus. The digested food was bacteria-free.

In fact, this antibacterial property has long been known by northern Europeans. For generations, butterwort leaves were applied to the sores of cattle to promote healing. The leaves were also used to produce a unique curdling effect in goat's milk to produce a ropy, yogurtlike cheese.

Some species of pings also have the power of movement. This is most often seen in species from temperate climates, and is almost entirely lacking in tropical forms. Over a period of a day or so, after the capture of substantially sized prey, the margins of the leaf, already upturned, may curve inward or over their precious food. This has nothing to do with capture but is believed to be helpful in preventing the digestive fluids from drooling off the leaf. Another possible explanation is that it helps prevent the victims from being washed away by the rain. Many butterworts can even "dish" their leaves under prey, giving their juices a convenient place to pool.

Three forms of *Pinguicula moranensis*

The most wonderful thing about *Pinguicula* in cultivation is their flowers. Most of the species in this genus have flowers that are pretty, but the flowers of the tropical forms are extraordinary; they can rival orchids or African violets in their beauty and brilliant color. Many put on quite a beautiful show in the springtime, and some may be in bloom so often and for so long, they can provide many months of pleasure.

The flowers of butterworts may be funnel-shaped, cupped, or flat-faced, with long or short spurs. The petals appear as two lips: the upper lip divides into two lobes while the lower lip divides into three. In the throat of butterwort flowers are many hairs, often called beards, which in some species may be rather pronounced. During their flowering season, pings usually send up a succession of individual blooms on single stalks.

Since pings grow on nearly half of our planet, their climates obviously differ greatly. In the north, their habitats are often frozen or frosty in winter, and they can sometimes be found accompanied by sundews and pitcher plants. But in the more tropical countries of Mexico and the Caribbean, butterworts have adapted to survive long periods of drought. Some, found growing in alkaline dry areas of Mexico, are even companions of cacti and other succulents. There are also species that grow epiphytically on trees (as do the tillandsia air plants), and a species has been found growing in mossy patches near glaciers in the Arctic.

For convenience's sake, this chapter will be divided into three sections that are based on the pings' habitats. Specifics on their cultivation and propagation can be found on pages 213–218.

TEMPERATE PINGS

Butterworts from temperate climates survive long, cold winters by dying down to small, cone-shaped hibernacula. These "resting buds" of tightly held leaf scales often lose their roots in winter and are easily moved about by water at this time, which aids in their distribution. The hibernacula also produce, around their bases, gemmae, or brood bodies, which look like miniature resting buds. Scattered about, they grow into new plants and are very helpful in propagation.

Temperate butterworts come into growth in spring, producing flat, often starfishlike rosettes of narrow, tapered leaves with strongly upturned margins. Spring is also their flowering time, and several blooms arise singly on stalks a few inches tall. The flowers are typically cone-shaped with long, funnel-like spurs. The petals are usually short, and most often colored purple, violet, or white, with hairy beards at the entrances of their throats.

Temperate pings can be found in boggy moors of acidic, peaty soils in North America and Europe, but most often they grow on wet, dripping, gravelly cliffs and grottos, often amid mosses and ferns. In areas such as the Great Lakes region, they can be found in flat, damp, rocky soils at the water's edge, sometimes accompanied by *Sarracenia purpurea* ssp. *purpurea* and *Drosera rotundifolia*. Often, the soils that temperate pings grow in are more neutral to alkaline than acid. The habitats in which they grow are usually sunny, but the butterworts are often partly shaded by grasses, ferns, and other low-growing vegetation. The water trickling through their gravelly soils is usually cool groundwater.

The dormant winter bud of *Pinguicula longifolia* with gemmae around its base

Pinguicula vulgaris

This is the species Charles Darwin studied, and it is very widespread, growing in North America, Europe, and northern Asia. It likes rocky areas, and is often found around waterfalls and lake margins, growing in both acid and alkaline soils. The rosettes are up to four or five inches across, of greenish yellow leaves that appear narrow due to their strongly incurved margins. The flowers are about

Pinguicula vulgaris in Ontario, Canada.

Temperate Pings

Pinguicula macroceras ssp. *nortensis*

Pinguicula grandiflora is an easy temperate species with lovely spring flowers.

The flowers of *Pinguicula longifolia* ssp. *caussensis*

one inch long, violet with a white throat. There are a few geographical forms from Europe. *P. vulgaris* f. *bicolor* has petals that are white and purple; *P. vulgaris* f. albida has white petals; *P. vulgaris* f. *alpicola* has flowers that are twice the size of the typical species.

Pinguicula macroceras

This species was once considered a variant of the above, but is now considered a separate species. It grows in western North America, Japan, and Russia. The flowers are more opened than those of *P. vulgaris,* and the lower lobes are longer. *P. macroceras* ssp. *nortensis* is found in northwestern California and southwestern Oregon. Its flower has an elongated lower-center lobe, and plants growing in full sun in serpentine gravel, often with Darlingtonia, can have leaves a rich chocolaty red coloration.

Pinguicula grandiflora

This is a lovely species when in flower, and much easier to grow than the above two species. Native to Europe, it is found in hilly, mountainous regions in Ireland, France, Switzerland, and Spain. The foliage is rather similar to that of P. vulgaris, but can be larger. The beautiful flowers are up to one and a half inches long, with broad lobes of rich violet and deep purple veins. *P. grandiflora* f. *pallida* has pale bluish petals with a purple-ringed white throat. *P. grandiflora* ssp. *rosea* has pale rosy colored flowers.

Pinguicula longifolia

A favorite of mine, this is another easy temperate species that does not require the frigid winters of *P. vulgaris*. It grows in the Pyrenees of southern France and northern Spain. The foliage is similar to the *P. grandiflora* and *vulgaris*. The flowers of *P. longifolia* ssp. *longifolia* have long spurs, with pale violet petals, white throat, and hairy lower lobes. *P. longifolia* ssp. *caussensis* has very pale flowers and a broad lower-center lobe, while *P. longifolia* ssp. *reichenbachiana* has small flowers with a prominent, hairy, white throat.

There are many other temperate butterworts that require rather similar cultivation techniques. Some of these are:

Pinguicula corsica

I enjoyed growing this Mediterranean island species for several years, and found it similar to *P. grandiflora* and *P. longifolia*. The flowers have rounded lobes of very pale violet with darker veins.

Pinguicula alpina

A small plant barely two inches across, this species is common in the mountains of Europe but can be found in lower elevations in Scandinavia and Scotland. The leaves are short and triangular, and the handsome flowers are white with bright yellow throats. When dormant, this species does not loose its roots—so transplant it with care.

Pinguicula ramosa

From the mountains of northern Japan, this rare species has small, spatulate-shaped leaves. Most unusual are the white flowers, which can appear in twos and threes on a stalk. Almost extinct, this plant has appeared on a Japanese postage stamp. Only two colonies remain.

Pinguicula villosa

This tiny species grows in the Arctic regions of Asia, northern Europe, and North America. I have never known anyone who has grown it, but success might be had by keeping the plants for nine months or so in your freezer (unnecessary, of course, if you live someplace like northern Alaska!). These tiny plants are under one inch in diameter and grow only a few reddish leaves in their short season. The minute flowers are white to pale purple, with yellow dots on the lower lobes.

Pinguicula vallisneriifolia

I have not had the pleasure of growing this unusual species from southern Spain. The summer leaves are very narrow and almost eight inches in length. The flowers are pale bluish purple and the lobes are rather rounded. This species usually grows on shady wet cliffs and has a rather spidery appearance. Very peculiar are the stolons it grows that produce new plants.

WARM-TEMPERATE PINGS

There are a number of butterworts that do not form winter resting buds because their climates are less severe. I will refer to these as warm temperate even though some grow in temperate or subtropical conditions. Most of these species prefer permanently wet, acidic soils, and can take various degrees of light frosts. Hard freezes can kill them, but even when this occurs in the wild, plants survive from seed. Many are short-lived perennials, dying off after a couple of years, and at least one is an annual. Like most other butterworts, they usually grow in sunny locations lightly shaded by surrounding vegetation.

The largest group of warm-temperate butterworts grow in the southeastern coastal plain of the United States, and most share their habitats with *Sarracenia, Drosera, Dionaea,* and *Utricularia.* This unfortunately does not mean they are as easy to grow as their companions. These species usually grow best in outdoor bog gardens in suitable climates, or in cool and warm greenhouses. It is a good idea to keep up propagation of these plants if you wish to keep them in your collection, since most are short lived. Most of these have pretty flowers that can be self-pollinated for seed.

The leaf rosette of **Pinguicula caerulea**

Pinguicula caerulea

The violet butterwort is found from the coastal plain of North Carolina south into southern Georgia and most of the Florida peninsula. It forms a handsome rosette of pale green leaves up to four inches across. The leaves are oval with strongly incurved margins, making them appear narrow and pointed. The one-inch-long, funnel-shaped flowers are usually violet with many purplish veins and a yellow, protruding beard. Some variants are pure purple. The lobes are deeply incised, giving the appearance of many petals. This species is probably the easiest to grow of the warm-temperate pings, and can survive for many years. It is excellent for a bog garden.

Pinguicula lutea

This species looks identical to the above, except that the flowers are a bright sulfur yellow. Its range is also similar, except it extends along the Gulf Coast almost to New Orleans. I have found it difficult to maintain long-term in cultivation. Usually the plants flower for many months while the plants wither away.

Pinguicula primuliflora

This is a popular species in cultivation, and in nature is found in coastal areas of the Florida panhandle west into Louisiana. The leaf rosettes are similar to the above, but appear narrower. The plants are often found in mostly shaded areas of very wet peat and sphagnum, often along the edges of streams and ponds. While the plants are short-lived and prone to rot, they spread by producing plantlets at the tips of their leaves, which is helpful for propagation. Keep them shaded from hot sun. The beautiful flowers have incised petals that are pinkish violet with white centers and a yellow beard.

Pinguicula primuliflora cultivated in live sphagnum moss

Pinguicula planifolia

This large species is unique. Its six-inch-wide rosettes of pointed, lanced-shaped leaves turn a purplish red color in sunny locations. Like *P. primuliflora*,

Warm-Temperate Pings

The flower of *Pinguicula lutea*

The flower of *Pinguicula primuliflora*

The flower of *Pinguicula caerulea*, more purple than veined.

Pinguicula planifolia

it enjoys wet, peaty soils, and is sometimes flooded by shallow water. The flowers are attractive, pale violet, and seem many petaled due to the deeply incised petals with a protruding yellow beard. Unfortunately it is difficult to maintain long-term, although it fairs best in sunny, wet bog gardens. Occasionally it produces leaf buds late in the season. It is found in the western Florida panhandle to Louisiana.

Pinguicula pumila

A diminutive butterwort rarely approaching three-quarters-of-an-inch across, this tiny ping grows in the coastal plain from the Carolinas, south through the Florida peninsula, and west into Texas. It is a pretty miniature that is fairly easy to grow, and often self-seeds. The tiny flowers can be purple, yellow, or pink. I grow a pretty blue form from Georgia.

Pinguicula ionantha

I have never grown this endangered species from the central Florida panhandle. The rosettes approach six inches across, the margins of the leaf barely rolled along the sometimes kinked margins. It is fond of very wet areas. The petals are usually white, nearly oval, and indented at their ends. A prominent yellow beard protrudes from the throat.

In other parts of the world are a few butterworts that also maintain their leaves year round.

Pinguicula lusitanica

A personal favorite of mine, this is another tiny species that often behaves like an annual but produces abundant seed and is very easy to grow. Its habitat is wet, peaty areas along coastal Europe—from England to Spain to northwestern Africa. The rosettes are usually around an inch across, although they are sometimes larger. The elliptical leaves are deeply rolled, translucent, often pinkish and veined in red. Hairs along the center of the leaf force insects (often springtails and gnats) to be trapped along the glandular margins. The small, funnel-shaped flowers are pale pink. *P. lusitanica*

The shadows of insect prey are visible through the leaf margins of *Pinguicula lusitanica*

grows well in cool and warm greenhouses, terrariums, windowsills, and in bog gardens. Since it grows fast from seed, it succeeds as a summer annual outdoors in cold-temperate climates, but you should collect seed to sow the following year.

Pinguicula hirtiflora

I have not had the pleasure of growing this species from the Mediterranean, notably south Italy. The foliage is rather similar to that of *P. vulgaris,* but the stunning flowers are large and purplish, turning white in the center, with a bright orange throat. Pollinate them for seed production.

Pinguicula crystallina

My one attempt to grow this species from Cyprus failed. Similar to *P. hirtiflora,* the flowers are rose to pale blue, with leaf rosettes up to two inches.

Pinguicula antarctica

This species is the most southern-growing ping, coming from coastal, marshy areas at the southern tip of South America. The cool, wet climate where this species is found was once described to me as Seattle-like. The oval leaves are oblong and pointed, in rosettes rarely approaching two inches across, with small lavender flowers. I grew this rare species successfully for a couple of years in my cool house, but I neglected to pollinate the flowers for seed and ultimately lost it.

The following butterworts are still rare in cultivation, and I have not had the opportunity to try them, but suspect they would be successful in the cool or warm house. All are from South America.

Pinguicula elongata

An intriguing species from the highlands of Columbia and Venezuela, this plant undergoes a dry season when it forms a noncarnivorous, short-leafed, succulent rosette. During the wet months it produces long, narrow leaves a quarter inch wide and around six inches long. The flowers are violet with purple veins. I suspect it would do well grown similarly to the tropical pings I will discuss below.

Pinguicula calyptrata

Native to the northern Andes, this species has oblong leaves in two-inch rosettes with small lavender flowers.

Pinguicula involuta

From the southern Andes, this species grows in chilly, wet climates, with small rosettes two inches across and flowers that range in color from white to violet.

Pinguicula chilensis

Similar to the above, this is also an Andean species found in Chile and Argentina. The small leaves are oval, and the flowers are blue or white with blue veins.

Tropical Pings

Butterworts reach their height of diversity and beauty in Central America and the Caribbean. While thirty years ago the number of *Pinguicula* species in the world was estimated to be around thirty or forty, that number has doubled over the last few decades as intrepid botanists and collectors scoured the hills and canyons of Mexico, searching for these plants in the most unlikely of places—and finding them. While the companions of carnivores in other parts of the world are commonly plants such as sphagnum mosses, cranberries, and bog orchids, it is not unusual to find butterworts in Mexico growing with agave, succulents, and tillandsia. Instead of searching out wet, peaty soils to find butterworts, collectors look for dry cliffs of gypsum or moss-covered tree trunks. If you happen to be in Cuba or Haiti searching for pings, you might have better luck looking up instead of down.

P. moranensis

The incredible adaptability of *Pinguicula* in this region of the world is further shown by the fact that most species in the tropics are part-time carnivores. Mexico and the Caribbean are not equatorial places, but lie on the edge of the subtropical zone. While warm most of the year, the winters can be very dry, and the summers wet. What's a carnivore to do, with no water to help make all those glues and digestive juices? Turn into a tuber underground, like a winter-growing sundew? Tropical butterworts have a different strategy. When the rain stops falling, most turn into succulents. They give up their large, sticky summer leaves, quit the wholesale massacre of gnats and small flies, and instead transform into drought-tolerant rosettes of harmless, dry leaves, inconspicuous and plain. Well, not quite, for it is during this otherwise boring succulent stage that most tropical pings do penance by sending up their colorful, glorious flowers. In this way, they are truly redeemed.

Mexico, where more butterworts grow than any other place in the world, is a diverse country. States like Oaxaca in the south are warmer and wetter than Tamaulipas in the northeast, where the Gulf coast of Mexico meets Texas. While the warm-temperate *P. pumila* is found in the wetlands of eastern Texas, traveling south along the Gulf coast the genus does not reappear until about 100 miles south of the Texas-Mexico border. More rain falls in Mexico's coastal areas, while the interior mountains are not only drier, but cooler. Mexican butterworts can be found at high elevations where the dry winter nights can be surprisingly chilly, while the summers are warm and wet.

Another curious fact is that not all of these tropical butterworts are closely related to each other, as one might suppose. Mexican species such as *P. esseriana* and *P. ehlersiae* are more closely akin to north-latitude species such as *P. grandiflora* and *P. villosa* than they are to famous Mexican varieties like the *P. moranensis* complex. Botanists group *Pinguicula* species by the similarity of their flower structure, but this can be rather controversial. To further compound the problem, many butterworts that were described and named in the 1800s are now either lost in cultivation, grouped with other species, or have yet to be rediscovered in the wild. Some species, such as *P. moranensis,* have many different forms found in countless canyons and valleys that may or may not be species in themselves. The taxonomist's headache turns into the horticulturist's nightmare, as species' names change or are eliminated. Also, travelers to Mexico often return with seed or plants (not realizing this is against Mexican law) and introduce them into cultivation, while data on the plants is virtually nonexistent. As an example, over the years I have been given so many plants described as *"P. moranensis,"* some with dubious site identification numbers (Site one #2, Site two, #4) that I simply code them with a letter in hopes that someone will eventually tell me what it is I am growing! My first *"P. moranensis"* I lettered 'A', and at last count I was on letter 'O'. That's fifteen plants that may or may not be *P. moranensis.*

This confusion is slowly resolving itself with the growing interest in tropical butterworts. A few varieties are appearing in the general nursery trade as companions to Venus flytraps and purple pitcher plants (often with cultivation instructions certain to guarantee the death of the poor plant). Also, societies such as the International Pinguicula Study Group, based in England, are working toward the goal envisioned by some CP growers, such as Adrian Slack, who dreamed that one day these beautiful plants may achieve a status similar to that enjoyed by *Saintpaulia,* the African violet.

In the following pages I will avoid the nitty-gritty, technical floral descriptions of most of these plants, and try to keep it simple, so as not to lose the beginner. Tropical pings are a fun and easy group of plants to grow.

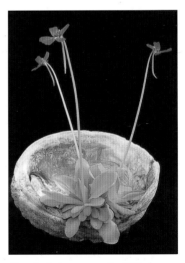

Pinguicula moranensis

Pinguicula moranensis

This is the most popular species to grow, in all of its forms and varieties. They make excellent windowsill, terrarium, and greenhouse plants, and can be in flower for many months of the year. The many different forms vary in leaf shape and size, but typically have carnivorous summer rosettes up to four to eight inches in diameter, the leaves oval to oblong, from pale green to suffused in red. The leaf margins are slightly incurved. In winter and early spring, the rosettes transform into succulents from one to three inches across. These noncarnivorous leaves are spoon- to wedge-shaped, tough and thick, and may number from a few to many dozens. *P. moranensis* are usually in flower twice a year. The flowers are usually pink, but there is also a white flowered form called "Alba". Many blooms, some lasting several

Pinguicula moranensis "G" in an abalone shell. Three seasons of leaves are visible: newly emerging summer leaves, winter succulent leaves, and a few old summer leaves from the previous year.

The flower of *Pinguicula moranensis* "G"

weeks each, appear from the small succulent rosette almost continuously during winter and spring. When the summer leaves appear, the plants usually stop flowering for a couple of months. By late summer, they experience a second flowering period. The summer leaves persist through autumn, but by early winter they die away and return to their succulent growth.

Of the many varieties I grow, I have never been able to make a positive match with similar forms grown in other countries. Of my own letter-coded plants, here are some of the best:

"A" produces the largest summer rosettes, sometimes measuring over eight inches across, with leaves heavily mottled in red. The flowers are enormous—over two inches in length—pink in color, with much white streaking toward the throat. The winter growth is a compact rosette of short, thick leaves. This variety occasionally clumps.

"D" is a handsome variety, with large, pale green, oval summer leaves and a tight winter rosette of thick, succulent leaves. It never clumps. The large flowers are pale pinkish lavender, the lobes almost rectangular.

"G" is the most popular form I grow, and can be in flower almost continuously, except during the transition times between summer and winter rosettes. The summer leaves are green and oval, and the winter rosette is short lived, with a few spoon-shaped leaves one to two inches in length. This form regularly clumps. The beautiful

The flowering winter rosette of *Pinguicula moranensis* "A" growing on lava rock.

flowers are deep pink with some white toward the throat. This variety is somewhat tolerant of wetter winters, and rarely succumbs to rot.

Many forms of *P. moranensis* come from Oaxaca, and are named after their location of discovery (or sometimes site numbers). A beautiful form called 'Site one # 2' has summer rosettes up to four inches across, with densely compacted winter rosettes of numerous narrow and curved leaves. The striking flowers are narrow lobed and deeply purple pink, with a white "tongue" at the base of the middle lower petal. The two outer lower petals have a curious twist. A form called 'Mitla' has extremely narrow purplish lobes, described by Adrian Slack as spidery. 'Huahuapan' has lilac-colored narrow petals with darker streaks. 'Vera Cruz' has flowers a deep rose color. In 'Site two #6', the smallish flowers are pink and rounded, the lower petals indented with white streaking toward their base.

Pinguicula agnata

There are several forms of this species in cultivation, and some are so different in appearance they may warrant separate classification. None form true winter succulents, although their leaves may get smaller in size. In all *P. agnata* forms, the leaves are thick and fleshy and lack upturned margins. The true *P. agnata* from the Mexican state of Hidalgo has green, almost strapped-shaped leaves that gradually press to the ground. The small flowers are pretty, with oblong petals purplish-blue, and white at their bases, with a wide green throat and short spurs. A variety known as 'Pale Flowered' form has petals almost pure white, with only the slightest hint of purple around the yellowish throat. I grow a few other forms that have rounded, teardrop-shaped leaves that are often reddish in summer sun. In these, the flowers are almost round-petaled, flat-faced, and tinted purplish, with bright greenish yellow throats. One form has flowers that are occasionally scented like violets. It was introduced into cultivation by Leo Song of Cal State University and the folks who discovered it in the wild (owners of a now defunct nursery). The 1987 discovery by Alfred Lau, called *P.* 'Ayautla', is a magnificent plant no doubt related to the *P. agnata* complex. It was recently named *Pinguicula gigantea*. The rosettes are very large, with arching, buttery yellow leaves that are sticky on both their upper and lower surfaces—the only such butterwort yet known. The handsome flowers are tinted violet with a striking purplish edging. The plants were found in Oaxaca, growing on sheer rock cliffs in hot tropical sun, accompanied by tillandsias.

Pinguicula potosiensis

This plant has pale green summer leaves three or four inches long and slightly pointed. The winter rosettes are densely compacted, with many dozens short, narrow, succulent leaves. The medium-sized flowers are pur-

Tropical Pings

CLOCKWISE FROM ABOVE LEFT:
The flower of the true form of *Pinguicula agnata*. A beautiful but dubious form of *Pinguicula agnata*. Rosettes of *Pinguicula agnata* pale flower form. *Pinguicula gigantea*, the only butterwort yet known to be sticky on both sides of the leaves.

ple, with slightly rounded lobes. This plant has been distributed as *P. moranensis* 'B'.

Pinguicula esseriana

This is a popular miniature Mexican ping of recent discovery. It is from Tamaulipas, and is surprisingly tolerant of frost. The one-inch rosettes are compact, with numerous short, thick, spatulate leaves with sharply upturned margins at their apex. In winter the leaves are similar, but lose their margins and stickiness, being rather like the succulent leaves of a jade plant. The pretty, short-petaled flowers are lilac-pink and rather cupped-shaped, with long, downward-pointing spurs.

The flower of **Pinguicula potosiensis**

Pinguicula esseriana

Pinguicula ehlersiae

The rosettes of this species from San Luis Potosi are larger than the above and copper colored in strong light. The rather different flowers are flat-faced, with rounded petals a lovely mauve.

Pinguicula reticulata

This recent discovery, also from San Luis Potosi, is now famous among collectors for its beautiful flowers. They are cone-shaped with short spurs, the nearly rounded petals white with many violet veins, and have a hairy yellow throat. The leaves are rounded with rather long petioles, and there is little difference between summer and winter growth.

Pinguicula laueana

Mr. Alfred Lau and his wife run a boys home on charitable donations in Vera Cruz, Mexico. He is well known for his many discoveries of Mexican flora, and among the finest was his discovery in 1978 of this species, which entered cultivation in the early 1990s. From the Mixe Highlands of Oaxaca, *P. laueana* has summer rosettes of oval reddish leaves. In winter the succulent growth is reduced to flat rosettes of smallish, overlapping

The brilliant flower of **Pinguicula laueana**, the only reddish bloom yet known among butterworts.

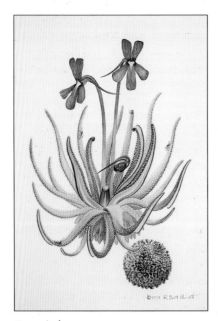

P. gypsicola

leaves. But its glory are its flowers, rather *P. moranensis*-shaped but of a stunning, rich, orange-red, the only red-flowered butterwort yet known.

Pinguicula gypsicola

This strange Mexican ping is rather difficult to maintain in long-term cultivation. It grows on gypsum cliffs that remain bone-dry most of the year, at which time it stays in a succulent growth of many dozens of tiny, densely compacted leaves nearly flat on the ground. But its brief summer foliage is most unusual. The carnivorous leaves are long and narrowly lance-shaped, around three inches long by a tenth of an inch wide. The flowers are rather similar to those of *P. moranensis,* with narrow, dark pink petals. This species must be kept dry during its succulent growth.

Pinguicula heterophylla

The summer leaves of this species are rather similar to those of *P. gypsicola:* thin, spidery, and arching. It is very odd in its having a long dormancy underground as an almost onionlike "bulb." It must be kept bone-dry during this rest period.

Pinguicula macrophylla

I've had better luck with this species, which also disappears to an underground, bulblike dormant bud for much of the year. The summer leaves, at the end of rather lengthy petioles, are large and oval. The summer flowers are deep purple with rounded lobes.

Pinguicula rotundiflora

Closely related to *P. reticulata,* this species was described in 1985. The summer leaves are rounded at the ends of long petioles, with upturned margins. The tiny winter leaves are also spoon-shaped, but densely clustered. The flowers are cone-shaped, with pale violet, rounded petals and a darker throat.

Pinguicula colimensis

This butterwort is rare in cultivation. Many plants grown under this name are actually forms of *P. moranensis.* The true species grows on gypsum cliffs near Colima in Mexico. In winter the plant goes dormant underground as a small green "bulb" wrapped in dead leaves. The summer leaves are pale green, papery thin, and lack upturned margins. The flowers are large and beautiful, with wide, overlapping, dark-pink petals, giving the flower a full, circular appearance. The long spur is thin and curved downward.

Pinguicula heterophylla

Pinguicula hemiepiphytica

From Oaxaca and described in 1991, this species has long been grown as a type of *P. moranensis.* It usually grows in moss upon cliffs or tree trunks. The flowers are similar to those of a typical *P. moranensis,* but with more oval pink petals and a thicker spur. The oval summer leaves are pale green to copper. The distinctive winter rosette is a dense mound of pointed, spatulate-shaped, small leaves, often tinted bronze.

Pinguicula acuminata

This strange Mexican species has spoon-shaped leaves similar to those of *P. macrophylla,* and also disappears to an underground "bud" during winter. However, they are not related, and this species sends up winter flowers directly from underground. The stalks can be red, the rounded petals pure white, gradually turning pale lilac as they age.

There are a few tropical species that keep carnivorous leaves year round, growing in permanently damp conditions.

Pinguicula lilacina

A widespread Mexican species, the oblong leaves have downturned margins. The pretty flowers are large and lilac colored, with a darker throat. A yellow beard hints at its relationship to butterworts from the southeastern United States.

Pinguicula zecheri

This handsome species has arching, elliptical leaves. The frequent flowers are beautifully deep purple with a veiny white throat. Also from Mexico.

Pinguicula filifolia

This is an unusual tropical species from western Cuba, primarily on the Isle of Pines. My one attempt to grow it failed when winter arrived, probably due to cold temperatures. It grows in sand at the edge of fresh-water lagoons, often accompanied by silver saw palmetto, a swamp-loving palm. *P. filifolia,* as its name suggests, has narrow, threadlike leaves. Several color forms of the flowers exist: white, blue, purple, and lilac.

Pinguicula albida

This Cuban species is related to *P. filifolia* and *P. agnata,* and maintains rosettes of oval green leaves year round. The white petals are beautifully contrasted against the orange, starlike throat.

Pinguicula jackii

Another Cuban species, with four-inch rosettes of oval leaves; the flowers are blue.

Pinguicula lignicola

This is an odd and rare species, also from western Cuba. A true epiphyte, it grows in trees and bushes attached to branches and twigs. The tiny rosettes of narrow leaves are barely one inch across. The large flowers are beautiful and white with orange centers, similar to *P. albida.* I have not yet grown this, but imagine it would be easy if grown as tillandsia air plants are grown—on bark or branches, with frequent misting and overhead watering in a hothouse.

Pinguicula cladophila

This epiphytic species is similar to *P. lignicola,* but the rosettes can reach two and a half inches. It grows in mossy forest in Haiti.

BUTTERWORT HYBRIDS

While a few temperate butterworts occasionally produce natural hybrids, none are known among warm-temperate and Mexican species. Among the latter this may be due to the isolation of most species amid Mexico's many mountains and canyons. Ironically, however, many Mexican species readily hybridize artificially in cultivation, and often produce beautiful plants with increasingly showy flowers. The future of *Pinguicula* in horticulture, aside from further new introductions from the field, may lie in the production of ornamental hybrids, a development that has already created promising hints of what is to come. When one realizes the beauty and diversity of African violet (*Saintpaulia*) hybrids, all resulting from two species with blue and purple flowers, ping possibilities are mind numbing.

Pinguicula moranensis x ehlersiae

This beautiful cross results in plants having diamond-shaped summer leaves that turn coppery in the sun. It clumps prolifically, producing mounds of plants over time. The flowers have rounded, oblong petals of a rich bluish pink. Two cultivars have been named: *P.* x 'Sethos' has a starry white throat; *P.* x 'Weser' has darker veins and a white streak at the base of the lower central lobe. In winter the leaves get smaller.

Pinguicula agnata x gypsicola

Leo Song of California State University in Fullerton first crossed these plants. The tissue-cultured clone is frequently sold in the mass-market. The beautiful summer rosettes have arching, strapped-shaped leaves that turn reddish in good light. The winter rosettes have many small blunt leaves, and during this time the plant must be kept rather dry or it is prone to rot. The pretty flowers are pale purple and funnel shaped, with light veining.

Pinguicula x 'Gina'

Produced by Miloslav Studnicka of the Czech Republic, this lovely clone is the result of crossing *P. agnata* x *zecheri*. The agnata-like leaves have upturned margins. The flowers have pale violet, oval petals with dark purple margins, and a deep purple mouth with yellow throat.

Pinguicula moranensis x gypsicola

Several variable clones of this cross have been named, and all must be kept winter-dry. *P.* x 'George Sargent' has lilac flowers, undulating strap-shaped leaves, and large winter rosettes of many small leaves. *P.* x 'Hameln', x 'Mitla', and x 'Mola' have wider summer leaves.

Pinguicula agnata x (moranensis x ehlersiae)

I grow a couple of attractive clones of this cross, produced by Leo Song. The leaves are short and rather oval, with full-petalled, pinkish blue flowers with darker veins.

Butterwort Hybrids

LEFT: *Pinguicula moranensis* x *ehlersiae,* a vigorous and clump-forming hybrid. RIGHT: A clump of *Pinguicula agnata* x *gypsicola,* the sticky glands clearly visable on its leaves. This hybrid needs a dry winter to succeed. This photo shows the early summer leaves which lengthen considerably later in the season.

LEFT: *Pinguicula* x *mola.* RIGHT: *Pinguicula* x 'John Rizzi'.

Pinguicula rotundiflora x *esseriana*

This cross produces nice, compact miniatures with small, pinkish blue flowers, intermediate between the parents. The winter rosettes are small clusters of tiny, succulent leaves.

Pinguicula x 'John Rizzi'

In my California greenhouse in the summer, hummingbirds frequently make a beeline for our flowering Mexican butterworts, probably because the birds are familiar with pings from their winter sojourn south of the border. This sometimes results in seed which I usually destroy, not knowing their pedigree. Once, however, I grew some plants from seed collected from a *P. moranensis* variety dubiously marked 'Superba'. Some of the resulting plants I sold before maturity, nicknamed "hummingbird mix." Our friend, the namesake of this cultivar, grew one of these plants to flowering size. Its exceptionally large, full blooms of deep pink petals warranted its preservation. The oval summer leaves are undulating and virtually marginless.

CULTIVATION *(See Parts One and Two for further information)*

Soil recipes	Temperate species: Use a mix of two parts peat, one part sand, and one part perlite. Warm-temperate varieties do well in a soil of one part peat to one part sand. Mexican and tropical species enjoy a more open mix of equal parts sand, perlite, vermiculite, and peat. Some growers add dolomite or gypsum to this, although I have not found it necessary. But when it's handy, I add an additional part of lava rock or pumice.
Containers	Plastic or glazed ceramics with drainage holes suit most varieties. Warm-temperate species can also do well in undrained containers, but you should let the water level fluctuate without drying out the soil. Mexican species do best in well-drained containers, but I have also grown them in shallow, undrained ceramics with very careful watering. I also enjoy growing Mexican pings in abalone shells (they enjoy the calcium) and chunks of lava rock that have large nooks and crannies. I use the recommended soil for these, but I top-dress the medium with a few strands of long-fibered sphagnum to keep it intact. Large-leafed varieties look best in wide, shallow containers.
Watering	All temperate and warm-temperate species should be grown permanently wet on the tray system, with frequent overhead watering. Use chilly water for your temperate

pings. The Mexican varieties can be kept on the tray system with overhead watering while they have carnivorous foliage in summer and autumn. When the rosettes change to their small succulents in winter, keep the soil on the dry side, dampening them only slightly and occasionally. You can usually tell how dry a species enjoys its winter by the size of its succulent leaves. The tighter, smaller leafed rosettes such as *P. gypsicola* or the bulblike *P. heterophylla* and *P. macrophylla* require bone-dry conditions. Species with larger winter leaves, like a few of the *P. moranensis* varieties or *P. agnata,* enjoy winter soils just slightly damp. Cuban species should be kept wet year-round, with only slight winter drying.

Light	Most *Pinguicula* enjoy partly sunny locations or very bright light. Don't roast temperate pings in summer.
Dormancy	Temperate butterworts require chilly to frosty winters while they hibernate as dormant buds. Warm-temperate species usually survive light winter frost but are best protected from severe cold, and usually slow or stop growth in winter (but maintain their foliage). Mexican species that turn into succulents in winter are not truly dormant, but those that form "bulbs" are.
Climate	As the name classifications suggest, temperate, warm-temperate, and tropical butterworts can be grown outdoors in their appropriate climates. As a rule, the Mexican varieties withstand cooler, drier winters than equatorial climates, and can survive winter-night lows in the forties. The only Mexican butterwort I accidentally exposed to freezing temperatures was *P. esseriana,* which was unharmed after a dry freeze of several nights in the low twenties.
Feeding	Butterworts feed on small insects such as gnats and tiny springtails. You may feed your plants wingless fruit flies or small ants, or occasionally apply bits of dried insects to their leaves.

Fertilizers	Temperate and warm-temperate butterworts can occasionally be foliar-fed a very diluted acidic fertilizer. The Mexican species greatly benefit from foliar feeding once or twice monthly during their carnivorous growth, using an epiphytic or orchid fertilizer diluted to about a quarter of its normal strength. Warning: Fertilizer applied to the flowers of Mexican species will mar them with unsightly white spots, so apply it only to the leaves.
Greenhouses	Temperate species generally do best in cold houses, or they can be placed under benches during winter in cool houses and warm houses. Warm-temperate species enjoy cool-house and warm-house conditions. Mexican species can survive cool houses, but thrive best in warm-house or hothouse conditions. Some Mexican species may grow in stovehouse facilities, but none are truly equatorial.
Windowsill	Temperate species are totally unsuitable as houseplants, but some warm-temperate butterworts such as *P. lusitanica* make good candidates, occasionally, on windowsills. Many of the Mexican butterworts make ideal plants for partly sunny windows, and are charming for their pleasant winter and summer flowers. Those that excel are *P. moranensis, P. agnata, P. esseriana,* and *P. ehlersiae,* plus the vigorous hybrids and cultivars.
Terrariums / Grow-lights	Forget temperate varieties here. Some warm temperates do nicely, such as *P. lusitanica, P. caerulea,* and *P. primuliflora,* but do best with cooler winters. Most of the Mexican species thrive under grow-

The leaf rosette of an unidentified form of *Pinguicula moranensis*

lights, in a tank or not, at room temperature. Use the pot-and-saucer method to allow for drier winter conditions.

Outdoors	See the Climate section, above. Mexican pings can be grown outdoors or on porches during the warmer months of the year, moving to windowsills for winter. The largest butterworts I ever grew were dinner-plate-sized *P. moranensis,* grown under the dappled sun of redwood trees during the summer in coastal Northern California. In places like southern Florida, Mexican pings would thrive outdoors year-round.
Bog gardens	Temperate and warm-temperate pings make interesting species for the outdoor bog garden in appropriate climates. They do best when lightly shaded by *Sarracenia* or ornamental bog grasses.
Transplanting	Butterworts are not as fragile as they look, but shouldn't have root disturbance during active growth. Transplant and divide gemmae of temperate species in late winter, or just as the new leaves appear in spring. Warm-temperate species and Caribbean varieties, likewise, are best disturbed at this time. Mexican species can be transplanted and divided during the end of their succulent growth. Sometimes these plants lift themselves out of the soil with their ground-hugging summer leaves, surviving for months as their leaves protect their exposed, short roots. When this occurs, you should break away the down-curved, older leaves and reinsert the roots in soil. Most potted butterworts should have their soil changed every two to three years. A quick soak in Superthrive during transplanting will encourage new roots.
Pests and diseases	These are few. Slugs and snails can attack pings, but they usually move on after a bite or two. Rarely do aphids attack the undersides of newly emerging leaves; if they do, use Orthene or Diazanon. Flea collars in close proximity to the plants also control insect problems. In Europe, mites can attack Mexican pings, causing pale, deformed new leaves. Dicofol is an effective cure. Fungus can attack

pings that are grown in dark, stuffy, overly humid terrariums and greenhouses, usually in winter. Apply Captan or similar fungicide, but, even better, change their environment.

PROPAGATING PINGS

Propagating butterworts is a fairly easy thing to accomplish using a variety of methods.

Seed

Only *P. villosa* and *P. lusitanica* self-pollinate their own flowers. All other species can be self-pollinated by hand to produce seed set.

The flowers of butterworts are designed to be pollinated by "long-tongued" insects and animals such as butterflies and hummingbirds. The repeated in-and-out actions of their mouth parts, to get at the nectar deep in the spurs, effectively pollinates the plants.

When you closely examine the flower of a butterwort by peering down its "throat," you will notice a small, apronlike pad on the ceiling. This is the sticky female stigma. Hidden immediately behind this, and completely out of view, are the pollen anthers. To pollinate, use a toothpick or tiny paintbrush. Insert this past the stigma, and with a gentle, upward swipe, withdraw. If you examine the pollinating object, you will usually notice a small amount of pollen grains on it. Carefully reinsert, dabbing the pollen onto the front-facing apron or skirt of the stigma. If you wish to cross-pollinate flowers (to produce hybrids or to cross several of the same species), dab the pollen onto the stigmas of the other blooms without bypassing the stigma, which will risk self-pollination.

The corolla, or petals, will wither and fall off within a few days after successful pollination. Over a few weeks the small seed pod will swell, eventually turn brown, and split, revealing many seed. Collect immediately. Seed can be stored a few months in the refrigerator. For best results, sow as soon as possible.

To germinate, sow the seed sparsely on the species' preferred soil medium. Keep damp, humid, and in bright light. Germination usually occurs in weeks.

Gemmae

Temperate species that form winter resting buds are easily propagated by the large amount of small "baby buds" that are produced around the base of the "mother bud" during late winter. These gemmae are easy to remove with forceps just prior to the plant's spring growth. Place each cone-shaped gemma pointy-side-up on the plant's preferred soil mix. As spring approaches, they will send out roots and leaves, and can be semimature by the end of the first season's growth.

Leaf cuttings

All Mexican species that form succulent winter rosettes can be easily multiplied by this method. Use the small, dry leaves of the plant, just prior to or during the new growth of larger, carnivorous leaves. Using forceps, gently grasp each leaf to be removed without bruising it too much, and with a soft tug the leaf will pull from the rosette very easily. Up to half of the winter leaves can be removed without injury to the mother plant.

Lay these leaves right-side-up on the soil without burying them. Pure vermiculite is an excellent medium to use. Keep slightly damp and humid: a propagating seed tray with a clear plastic dome or a pot covered with a plastic bag both work well. Keep in medium-bright light. Budded plants and roots will rapidly appear at the base of the leaf. Promptly discard any leaves that rot.

The young plants can be potted and grown normally within a few months time.

— 10 —
THE BLADDERWORTS
(UTRICULARIA)

"I was forced to the conclusion that these little bladders are in truth like so many stomachs, digesting and assimilating animal food."

—MRS. MARY TREAT, 1873

BLADDERWORTS ARE THE STRANGEST and probably the most highly developed plants in the world. Nothing about them is familiar or makes them akin to other flowering plants except their flowers and ability to photosynthesize. In fact, bladderworts are so weird that a parade of famous botanists over the last two hundred years have puzzled not only over the complexity of their truly amazing traps, but what to call their various body parts. Do they have leaves? Stems? Roots? These simple questions left scientists scratching their heads, but a study of the animal-catching, pinhead-sized traps reduced the investigators to a cross-eyed stupor.

Bladderworts make up the largest genus of carnivorous plants and are the most widespread. They grow on every continent of the world, and are missing only from the most frozen Arctic regions and the oceanic islands. At last count, there are 214 species. Highly adaptable, bladderworts may be found in Alaskan swamps that are frozen most of the year; in quiet acidic ponds in sunny Florida; in wet, mossy South American trees; in fast-moving African streams; in seasonal Australian deserts; or even living in other plants such as the bromeliads. Some bladderworts survive ice by turning into dormant, hairy turion buds. Others survive heat and drought by changing into underground tubers the size of a grain of rice. Others are annuals, dying off

An easy aquatic species to grow, *Utricularia gibba* will thrive in a container as small as a cup.

after a season's growth and coming back from seed.

In horticulture, *Utricularia's* most popular attributes are their flowers. In fact, when the plant is not in flower, a neighbor's reaction to your pot of precious bladderwort might be, "What an ugly pot of slime!" A month later, that same neighbor will exclaim, "What a lovely display of miniature orchids!" and promptly beg for a cutting.

Bladderwort flowers may be as tiny as an ant or as large as a medium-sized butterfly—and often as beautiful as the latter, but rarely as homely as the former. Most bladder-worts—or utrics, as hobbyists call them—have blooms somewhere from an eighth of an inch to two inches in diameter. They are often truly orchidlike in appearance and offer a rainbow of colors: white, pink, purple, violet, yellow, and red—and often in multicolored combinations. Related to *Pinguicula,* the flowers of bladderworts are somewhat similar in structure. They have spurs and two petal lobes, an upper and a lower, often in various shapes. The lower petal is usually the larger and more showy. Flowers may appear singly or in groups.

Typically the species grow in sunny, wet areas. Around 15 percent are true aquatics, free-floating in quiet ponds. The rest find their homes in permanently or seasonally wet or waterlogged sand, mud, or mosses, commonly in bogs and swamps or along lake margins. Several are epiphytes, growing on mossy trees, and at least one grows on barren wet rocks under waterfalls.

In the most general of descriptions, utrics form creeping or floating stems that are usually thin and hairlike. They are completely rootless. Most of the plant is under ground or in water. The majority of the species produce leaflike appendages, called photosynthetic stolons, that protrude along the soil surface. These may be a fraction of an inch long or much larger (up to several inches), the latter resembling true leaves. Aquatic varieties often have thin, branching leaves not much different than their stems. The entire plant may be only a few inches across, while some aquatic varieties may grow several yards long. When flowers appear, they grow up from the stems, protruding above the soil or water surface.

But it is the bladder-trap that makes *Utricularia* the wonder of nature.

Scattered along much of the plant's underground or aquatic stems and leaves are hundreds to thousands of tiny bladderlike traps. The traps are usually the size of a pinhead—or can be smaller than the period at the end of this sentence. In some species they are more substantial, perhaps an eighth of an inch or a quarter inch across. A newly discovered species found in Australia (unnamed at this writing) has relatively enormous bladders approaching a half inch in diameter.

These tiny traps are now known to catch small swimming prey in as fast as ten to fifteen thousandths of one second!

As early as 1797, a gentleman named Sowerby noticed the bladders on an aquatic species and assumed them to be flotation devices. He also saw small insects in the bladders, but thought the creatures were just "lodging" there. During the mid-1800s, many botanists examined the plants but were often unaware of each others' findings until years later. Ferdinand Cohn found prey in the traps of dried herbarium specimens. In 1875, he put water fleas (daphnia) into an aquarium of live plants, and by the following day, all of the daphnia were inside the bladders. Charles Darwin thought insects forced their way into the traps. But it was the botanist Mary Treat, an American, who first observed that the prey were sucked into the traps through a small door in an instantaneous, vacuumlike manner.

The early twentieth century had botanists slowly piecing together the

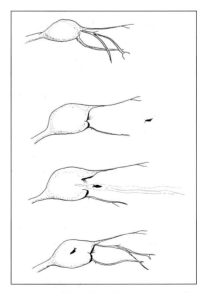

Upon touching the trigger hairs at the bladder traps door, tiny prey are sucked inside faster than the blink of an eye.

Utricularia cornuta in mass flower in southern Alabama

complex nature of the bladderwort trap, and Francis Lloyd, in his 1942 *Carnivorous Plants,* realized that over a dozen separate things occurred when a bladder caught prey—and most of them much faster than the blink of an eye.

The bladders are usually kidney-, pear-, or tubular-shaped. They are attached to the plant by a small stalk. The traps are hollow and transparent, their walls only two cells thick. At one end of the trap is a small door, which can only open inwardly. When closed, an oozy mucilage around the door keeps it watertight. When set, the bladder's walls are concave; a strong vacuum exists within it.

Outside the bladder's door are several long, filament-like hairs that usually form a funnel to guide prey toward the door. Glands exist around the closed entranceway, which may secrete a lure. Typical prey are microscopic organisms such as paramecium and cyclops, and larger prey such as rotifers, water fleas, worms, and mosquito larva. The biggest prey include newly hatched fish fry and tadpolettes.

Minute trigger hairs sit at the trap door's entrance. A mere touch of one of these hairs and—whoosh! The door swings open and the prey and any surrounding water are sucked inside due to the trap's vacuum. The door slams shut. The prey is suddenly trapped inside its transparent, vegetable prison.

Water is pumped out of the trap through the door within minutes. Again, the mucilage seal makes the bladder a watertight vacuum. As soon as twenty minutes later the trap is reset and ready for its next meal. One bladder can catch over a dozen prey.

Inside the bladder, glands secrete digestive juices that cover the prey. Within hours, the victim dissolves. Other glands absorb this nutrient soup.

Larger creatures caught by the traps suffer a particularly gruesome death. Tadpoles and mosquito larvae are often caught by their tails.

They struggle helplessly to free themselves as they are slowly digested alive. As the trap resets itself, the prey's agonized thrashing will set off the trap again…and again…and again, until only their heads protrude from the trap, too large to be sucked in through the door.

In 1989, Peter Taylor of England's world-renowned Kew Gardens, in his impressive *Utricularia* monograph, reduced the number of recognized species from 250 to 214. Since bladderworts are such a large genus, and since most of the species are rare or unknown in cultivation, here I will review some of the easier and more popular representative species. While curiosity about the traps is of interest primarily to those of a scientific bent, most hobbyists enjoy utrics for the flowers. Many species make fine windowsill and terrarium specimens, often putting on their flower show for months at a time. Others are beautiful in bog gardens, adding delicate color to the architectural boldness of plants such as *Sarracenia*. Still others thrive in greenhouses, their bright flowers rivaling orchids in beauty. Methods of growing utrics in ways that will highlight their tiny traps are outlined on page 233.

TERRESTRIAL BLADDERWORTS

These species are simple to grow and when in flower include some of the finest. They are native to all the world's climate zones, and some are pan-climatic. Typically they grow in permanently wet, peaty sands that are sometimes flooded with shallow water, and they are frequent companions to other carnivorous plants. The small bladders feed on various swimming and crawling creatures that inhabit their waterlogged soils, such as fungus gnat larvae and tiny worms. Usually they produce carpets of short photosynthetic stolons along the soil surface, something like blades of grass pressed flat to the ground. Their flowers may be minute to substantial, held close to the soil or on stems several inches tall.

Utricularia subulata

Like *Drosera capensis,* this bladderwort has a reputation of becoming a weed in collections due to its massive production of powdery seed. It is native to much of the world: Canada, south into South America, Africa, and Southeast Asia. They carpet the soil with fine, hairlike stolons or leaves barely a quarter of an inch in length, and they appreciate occasional flooding. The multiple flowers appear in waves during warmer weather, on fine, purplish stalks that seem almost invisible. The bright flowers are sulfur

Tiny drops of glue can be seen on some of the flower stalks of *Utricularia subulata,* a pleasant weed of carnivorous plant collections.

yellow, and about a quarter of an inch across with a large lower lip. The sight of masses of these flowers is particularly beautiful. Two things are peculiar about this species: sometimes the delicate flower stalks produce tiny drops of viscid glue along their length (probably to protect the blooms), and the plants can also produce large quantities of seed pods without having flowered, a process known as cleistogamous flowering. This species is excellent in bog gardens, terrariums, greenhouses, or on windowsills.

Utricularia livida

This very popular species comes from warm-temperate to subtropical climates in south Africa and Mexico and is tolerant of light frost. The leafy stolons are short and blunt, often covering the soil surface. They flower continuously when the weather is warm and sunny. The lovely one-third-inch flowers appear in rows of several along delicate seven-inch stalks. The large lower lip is apronlike, turning from white to violet in sun, with a yellowish streak at the spur's throat. They rarely produce seed, but spread rapidly through soil. A beautiful plant for the windowsill, terrarium, and greenhouse, and in bog gardens in suitable climates.

Utricularia sandersonii

From South Africa, this species is extremely popular due to its unusually pretty, rabbitlike flowers (which make the plant popular at Easter). Like *U. livida,* this species is suitable on windowsills and in terrariums, greenhouses, and in bog gardens in suitable climates. The short scapes hold up to half a

Utricularia livida, a wonderful free-flowering bladderwort.

Miniature orchid-like flowers, with faces of angry little bunny-rabbits, make *Utricularia sandersonii* a very popular plant. This one has grown in its tiny container for several years.

Utricularia graminifolia flowers prolifically in late summer and autumn.

dozen blooms, each about a half inch across. The upper petal divides into two earlike lobes. The lower, skirted lobe seems facelike due to its purple and yellow markings. The long, curved spur bends forward under the petals. A form with wider, bluer flowers blooms only occasionally.

Utricularia graminifolia

This Asian species grows from Japan to India. It flowers prolifically in late summer and autumn. The blooms are held a few inches above the ground, with an attractively colored puffed lower lobe of pale pinkish blue.

Utricularia bisquamata

A variable miniature from South Africa, this species flowers often and spreads from seed. The tiny flowers are beautifully multicolored in yellow, violet, orange, and white. There is also a form with larger flowers, as well as a tinier white form. It is also tolerant of light frost.

The tiny but colorful blooms of *Utricularia bisquamata*

Utricularia cornuta

This U.S. species grows from the Great Lakes into the southeast. The brilliant yellow flowers are similar to those of *U. subulata* but are much larger and are on tall (twelve-inch) stalks. It enjoys occasional flooding, with mass flowering as the water recedes. Excellent in the bog garden. *U. juncea* is also from the United States and almost identical, but smaller.

Utricularia resupinata

This species is found in parts of eastern Canada and the United States, as well as Cuba and Central America. It flowers after flooding recedes. The purplish and ruffled-looking flowers appear on short stalks and have a yellow throat.

Utricularia dichotoma.

Utricularia pubescens

This unusual tropical form is found in South America, Africa, and India. The peculiar soil-surface stolons look like tiny, dark green, circular buttons. The shy flowers are large and lilac colored with yellow and white near the throat, on ten-inch stems. Best kept warm in terrariums, warmhouses, and hothouses.

Utricularia dichotoma

A handsome species from Australia, the tall flowers look like lovely purple fans touched with yellow at the throat, and usually appear in twos. It appreciates waterlogged conditions and a frost-free environment.

Utricularia praelonga

From Brazil, this species produces two types of stolons: one like thin blades of grass several inches long, the other circular and flat on the ground. The large yellow flowers appear on tall sprays up to twenty inches tall. Protect this plant from frost. It should be flooded occasionally.

Utricularia tricolor

This South American species has one-inch-long, kidney-shaped stolons held close to the soil. The lovely flowers are almost one inch across, pale violet with a ruffled skirt, and possess a puffed palate with yellow and white at the throat. This species also enjoys flooding, and should also be protected from frost.

Utricularia arenaria

This African species frequently produces tiny purple flowers touched with yellow. It spreads through seed and survives light frost.

Utricularia multifida

This Western Australian species is an annual, so flowers should be pollinated and seed collected. The large and beautiful flowers are pink, the lower petal divided into three rounded, incised lobes. This species was once called *Polypompholyx multifida,* but is now considered to be part of the *Utricularia* genus.

Utricularia calycifida

This tropical form from South America does best in terrariums and hothouses. The unusual ground stolons look like teardrop-shaped leaves and are handsomely streaked in purple. The neat flowers are held close to the stem, and are purple with yellow markings. There is also a white-flowered form with pure green leaves.

Utricularia calycifida **is an excellent terrarium plant.**

SEASONAL BLADDERWORTS

Australia is home to a large number of unusual bladderworts that grow only during the wet season. In terms of climate, they may be considered tropical or Mediterranean-like. They survive through seed or tuber production. Most of these interesting species are only recently entering cultivation, usually through seed. For more information on their climates, refer to the woolly and tuberous sundew varieties (see pages 145 and 152).

Utricularia menziesii

This lovely species from southwestern Australia is a cool winter-grower, surviving hot dry summers by forming tiny tubers under the soil. It has a surface rosette of small, green leaves. The magnificent flowers are bright red with an underhanging, pendulous spur.

Utricularia dunstaniae and Utricularia capilliflora

These two weird bladderworts are annuals from tropical, monsoonal northern Australia. Their tiny flowers are extremely peculiar—they look like insect heads. The flowers themselves are dull colored and minute, but the two upper petals look like long, thin insect antennae! It is believed that gnats pollinate the flowers.

Utricularia fulva

A beautiful northern Australian plant, the substantial flowers have seemingly ruffled petals of pale yellow, with brownish red speckling at the palate.

Utricularia chrysantha

Thick and stocky flower stalks hold several pretty blooms that are bright yellow with white lower lobes. From northern Australia.

Utricularia leptoplectra

This handsome species, also from northern Australia, has bluish violet flowers. The large lower lobe is deeply incised, giving the flowers the appropriate appearance of dangling boomerangs.

Utricularia lasiocaulis

Large, colorful flowers mark this northern Australian species. The upper and lower lobes, violet pink in color, are fanlike with a spot of yellow at the throat.

TROPICAL BLADDERWORTS

These are all from the Caribbean, Central America, and South America, with many native to the tepui table-top mountains of Venezuela. They typically grow terrestrially, or in mossy pockets of leaf and bark debris in trees or on cliff sides, and may die down to tubers during a drought. Most are popular greenhouse and terrarium plants. Some species may adapt to windowsills. Many are highland tropicals and are untroubled by nightly lows into the forties, but for the most

Utricularia alpina

part they prefer warm houses and hothouses. Most produce large, showy, orchidlike flowers.

Utricularia reniformis

By far the most pleasing species to grow, this plant flowers in my warm house virtually non-stop from spring until fall. The leafy stolons are several inches tall on stiff petioles, the kidney-shaped blade one to two inches across. The flower spikes are over twelve inches high, the several, long-lasting blooms one and a half inches

The large orchid-like flower of *Utricularia reniformis*, a simple epiphytic species to grow.

across. They are pinkish violet, with a large lower skirt and puffed palate noticeably marked with two golden lines. The bladders are also large. The plant dies away each winter to underground tubers, at which time I keep the soil barely damp. This species should excel on the windowsill.

Utricularia longifolia

A popular species with large, leafy, strapped-shaped stolons several inches long. The bladders are large and often grow out of pots through the drainage holes. The large flowers are pink to violet, with a fanned skirt. The puffed palate has a prominent golden yellow streak. This species also has a dry winter rest period.

Utricularia alpina

This is a beautiful species when in flower. The leaf stolons are several inches long, paddle-shaped, and pointy. The large flowers are creamy white with a yellow blotch on the palate. This also dies down in winter to oval, opaque tubers when the soil should dry out.

Utricularia quelchii

A beautiful and rare species from the tepui Mt. Roraima (on the border of Venezuela and Guyana). The stolons are short, stiff, and

Utricularia quelchii

teardrop-shaped, with gorgeous purple red flowers that are oval and skirt-like. A period of drier dormancy is necessary.

Utricularia asplundii

Also from the tepui mountains. The stunning flowers are white with three lower, pointed lobes, and the palate is flushed violet with two prominent gold streaks.

Utricularia jamesoniana

Another rare species from the tepui mountains, the flowers have a purple, ruffled, skirted lower lobe with golden stripes on the palate. The incredible pendulous spur hangs below, thick and purple.

Utricularia campbelliana

This species has small leafy stolons and large flowers bright red in color.

Utricularia humboldtii

This is one of the strange species of utrics that is commonly found in the water wells of large bromeliad plants growing on the tepui table mountains. It also grows terrestrially. Not only are the bladders very large (up to a quarter of an inch) but the flowers are the biggest in the genus at nearly two inches across. They are pink, with a large, undulating skirt, and a golden white palate. The foliage stolons are erect, stiff, and teardrop-shaped. The seed of this plant are bizarre, as the small green embryo is clearly visible in a transparent, flattened casing. The seed, when released, must immediately be sowed in water or they will dry out and die. Within twenty-four hours the seedling germinates as a tiny, star-shaped plantlet that grows rapidly. Surprisingly simple to cultivate, *U. humboldtii* succeeds in cool houses and warm houses. I like to grow them in water-logged bowls of long-fibered sphagnum moss.

Utricularia humboldtii has the largest flowers in the genus.

Aquatic Bladderworts

Free-floating, aquatic bladderworts are better known to the general public (through television nature programs) because these are the easiest of the bladderwort species to film. They are not necessarily the easiest to grow, primarily because popular varieties can reach enormous size and require wading-pool-sized containers. Another hassle in cultivation is algae growth, which can inhibit utrics, and thus far there are no known treatments that kill algae without harming the bladderwort. Daphnia help control algae while providing the plants with food. So do tadpoles—but they will eat utrics when they run out of algae.

Most aquatic utrics in cultivation are temperate species, and most form hairy dormant buds called turions during cold temperatures. They usually grow in quiet, shallow ponds of acidic water. Some of the plants flower en masse when water tables drop; a few form dormant buds at times of drought. The foliage of the plants often alternates along the floating stems, producing whorls of threadlike leaves and other branches that produce the bladders. The often pretty flowers grow on stems sent above the water surface.

Utricularia gibba

If you wish to grow only one aquatic, it should be this species. It is by far the simplest to grow, surviving years in a container as small as a cup or bowl or even as an amphibious species in waterlogged peat. It also does well in the home or classroom on sunny windowsills or under grow-lights. It even grows in the water trays of potted plants. The species grows in much of the world, in both temperate and tropical climates, usually in shallow water. It never goes dormant, and plants frozen solid return to growth when temperatures increase. The plants are small and fibrous, with half-inch bright yellow flowers with a skirt and a puffed palate delicately penciled in red veins. The upper lobe forms an overhanging bonnet, and the spur looks like a curved tail.

Utricularia vulgaris and Utricularia macrorhiza

These two species are very large and very similar. The former grows in Europe, the latter from North America west into China. Their stems can exceed ten feet in length, and the bladders are large, up to a quarter of an inch. *Utricularia macrorhiza* often has bladders that change in color as they age: from green to red to black. The flowers are superficially similar to those of *U. gibba,* but larger. Their dormant turions are walnut-sized and hairy. This species likes a great deal of room—an appropriate container you should use would be a children's wading pool. A pool of these plants with tadpoles, frogs, aquatic insects such as backstrokers, water beetles and striders, daphnia, and water lilies or duck weed can provide an ecosystem that offers hours of hypnoid fun.

Utricularia minor

A tiny species that grows in much of the Northern Hemisphere, this plant enjoys peaty slurries and has small, pale, yellow flowers.

Utricularia purpurea

This large plant grows from eastern Canada to Cuba, and will only go dormant during freezes. It produces no foliage, only whorls of bladder traps. The flowers are beautiful: deep purple with a balloonlike palate.

Utricularia inflata

This unusual plant is common in the southeastern United States and has also been found, oddly, in Washington State. Similar to *U. macrorhiza,* it is strange because the flower stem is supported by a rosette of hollow flotation tubes, starlike in shape. The large yellow flowers grow upwards from this. *Utricularia radiata* is similar but smaller. These plants go dormant only during freezing temperatures.

Utricularia volubilis

This species from Western Australia is an annual. It grows in winter ponds that dry out in summer. The plant is often anchored in sandy soil that is water covered, and has bladders as large as a quarter of an inch. The lovely fan-shaped and purple flowers are paired at the end of a scape that twirls around reeds and grasses. Pollinate for seed. The seed can be sown in large bowl with wet sandy peat at the bottom. After germination, gradually add water over the course of a few weeks until it is several inches deep. Provide bamboo skewers or thin branches for the flowers to climb.

Utricularia reticulata

This tropical aquatic from Asia is often found in rice paddies. Its flowers also climb. They are a charming blue, with a paler inflated palate marked with dark lines.

CULTIVATION *(See Parts One and Two for further details)*

Most bladderworts are very easy to grow and propagate, and make nice companion plants to other CPs.

Soil recipes	Aquatic varieties: One cup of peat well-mixed into each gallon of water. Tropical: A good mix is one part fine orchid bark, one part long-fibered sphagnum, one part peat, and one part perlite. Terrestrial: Use a mix of one part peat to one part sand.
Containers	Plastic containers with drainage holes work best for terrestrial and tropical species. Most terrestrials also do well in undrained containers. If you wish to view the bladders on terrestrials, grow them in glass containers with removable black plastic sheeting or construction paper wrapped along the outside of the glass below the soil level. The traps will be visible when the dark covering is removed. Large aquatics require pools or tanks that hold a minimum of fifty gallons of water. Smaller species succeed in containers that hold roughly one gallon of water.
Watering	Use the tray system for the terrestrials. Many appreciate periodic flooding and will do best in undrained bowls so the water level can rise and fall beyond the soil level. Tropical species enjoy drained containers (these can be set in shallow trays) that are watered overhead, keeping the soil wet. If you're growing a species that goes dormant in winter, keep the soil only barely damp during that season. Aquatic species may need their peaty water changed if algae becomes severe. Gently rinse off the plants before introducing them to fresh water.
Light	Sunny to partly sunny conditions for most species. Sun induces flowering.
Climate	For outdoor growing, refer to the descriptions of individual species suitable to your climate zone.

Feeding	Aquatics can have daphnia (water fleas) and other microscopic life introduced to their water containers. Local, natural ponds are a good source of these. The other varieties will feed on fungus gnat larvae and microscopic life that often grow on their own. If you flood your terrestrials, introduce daphnia.
Fertilizers	Utrics appreciate light fertilizer about once monthly during their growing season. Acid, orchid, or epiphytic fertilizers at one-quarter strength can be misted onto the foliage. Aquatics can have the water sprinkled similarly.
Greenhouses	Refer to the species' climatic preference to see what species are appropriate for your greenhouse. Most terrestrials and tropicals thrive in warm houses and cool houses. Large aquatics do best outdoors.
Windowsills	Many terrestrials make fine sunny windowsill plants, particularly *U. livida* and *U. sandersonii*. *Utricularia gibba* is a good aquatic species to try. Of the tropicals, *U. reniformis, U. longifolia,* and *U. humboldtii* may succeed.
Terrariums / Grow-lights	Warm-temperate, subtropical, and tropical terrestrials do very well in lighted tanks. *Utricularia gibba* does nicely in a small glass jar in a potted tank.
Outdoors	Refer to the individual descriptions of species for suitable plants in your climate.
Bog gardens	An excellent place for terrestrials; they add color when in bloom. Larger bogs can have waterfilled depressions or moats that can allow you to grow smaller aquatic varieties.
Transplanting	Most species are easily transplanted early in the growing season. New colonies of utrics should be started every two to three years.
Pests and diseases	Aphids can attack the photosynthetic stolons; use an appropriate insecticide or flea collar. Slime mold should be scraped off terrestrials. Algae can be problematic for

be scraped off terrestrials. Algae can be problematic for aquatics, but daphnia help clear the water and feed the plants. Note that if algae are too sparse, tadpoles will eat utrics. Never use algaecides—change the water when infestation is great.

PROPAGATION

Propagating bladderworts is easy. Early in the growing season, simply remove sections of the plant and introduce these sections into fresh medium. That's it! With terrestrials, a section of soil, including surface stolons, of one or two square inches will do the trick. With tropicals, likewise, remove a section that includes the larger foliage stolons. Aquatics can simply have pieces separated, usually a few inches long.

To produce seed, most need to be pollinated. Refer to *Pinguicula* pollination techniques (see page 217), as those flowers are similar. Insert toothpicks or needles (for tiny flowers) into the throat and spur, with an upward swipe, several times. Seed can be sowed on their preferred medium early in the growing season.

Leaf cuttings also work well with those species that produce leafy stolons. Simply pluck the stolons from the plant and treat as you would sundew leaf cuttings (see pages 165–166). Larger leaves, such as those of *U. longifolia,* can be cut into smaller pieces about one to two inches long.

THE TROPICAL PITCHER PLANTS

(NEPENTHES)

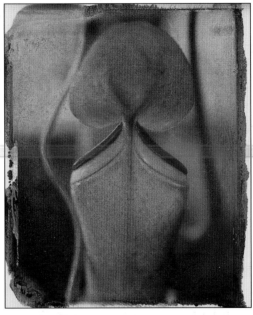

Nepenthes albomarginata

"Can anyone see such marvelous things, knowing them to be only plants and feel no wonder?"

—*Gardeners' Chronicle*, 1849

IF THERE IS A ROYALTY among carnivorous plants, that distinction surely lies with the *Nepenthes*.

Ever since their discovery by Europeans in the middle of the seventeenth century, tropical pitcher plants have inspired awe and wonder in anyone who has laid eyes on them. *Nepenthes* have a rich botanical and horticultural history, and the plants themselves are a virtual ecosystem of give and take with nature. The genus has the only species known to have devoured whole rats. And they are hauntingly beautiful, their pitcher traps often as elaborate and gaudy as artistic creations by humankind.

While primarily a plant of Southeast Asia, the first description of a species, *N. madagascariensis,* was given in 1658 by the then French governor of Madagascar, Etienne de Flacourt. He described in a book on the history of the island a strange plant with "a hollow flower or fruit resembling a small vase, with its own lid, a wonderful sight."

The second species described was *N. distillatoria* from Sri Lanka. When Carl Linnaeus first saw dried specimens of the plant, he was euphoric. He recalled Homer's *The Odyssey,* and the drug "Nepenthe" that Helen of Troy threw into flasks of wine to alleviate soldiers' sorrow and grief. Linnaeus wrote, "If this is not Helen's Nepenthes, it certainly will be for all botanists. What botanist would not be filled with admiration if, after a long journey, he should find this wonderful plant. In his astonishment past ills would be forgotten when beholding this admirable work of the creator!" Thus in 1737 the genus received its Latin name. It is ironic that *N. distillatoria* is one of the simpler species of *Nepenthes,* compared with the elaborate ones that had yet to be discovered, and that Linnaeus had no idea of the carnivorous nature of the plant, let alone any intoxicating influence the plant has on its prey. Like many others for years to come, he assumed the unusual pitcher leaves to be water-holding devices to help the plant survive drought.

It wasn't until the following

Nepenthes khasiana

century that *Nepenthes* had their heyday. Several things occurred to precipitate their rise in horticulture. One was imperialism, as Europeans began to explore and colonize Southeast Asia. In the 1700s orangeries were developed to grow the royal fruit Citrus for kings, and glass greenhouses were being built soon thereafter, enabling Europeans to grow exotic plants that were being discovered around the world. The Royal Botanic Gardens at Kew was started in England. In 1833 Nathaniel Ward invented the "wardian case," a sealed glass container that made it easy for exotic plants to survive long ocean voyages to England. In 1845 came the elimination of excise taxes on glass, resulting in cheaper and better greenhouses. Economies also boomed, so the middle and upper classes could afford such luxuries.

Nurseries also opened—for the first time plants were mass-produced for their ornamental value and sold to the public who could afford them. Among the first was the pioneering Loddiges Nursery in England, which introduced *N. khasiana* in 1825. James Vietch & Sons became the leader of such nurseries by the middle of the century. Hugh Low and Co. was another. These nurseries financed expeditions to faraway places such as Borneo, where exotic plants were collected and introduced into horticulture, *Nepenthes* being as sought after as palms, orchids, rhododendrons, and other ornamentals.

Also influential were the gardening magazines. Journals such as the *Gardener's Chronicle* and *Curtis's Botanical Magazine* featured articles on the cultivation of *Nepenthes,* with beautiful illustrations and advertisements from suppliers.

By the late 1800s, *Nepenthes* were much in vogue. Most conservatory greenhouses on the estates of the wealthy boasted *Nepenthes* hanging from the rafters, tended by a gardening staff only the rich could afford. Fancy hybrids were winning silver and gold medals at flower shows. New species were being discovered and introduced.

After the turn of the century, all of this came to an end. World wars, economic depression, fuel shortages—soon the dark, early years of the twentieth century led to dark and empty greenhouses everywhere.

NEPENTHIANA

A study of tropical pitcher plants is virtually a who's who of early botany and horticulture. The following is a list of some of the personalities entwined among the vines of Nepenthes:

⚘ Entienne de Flacourt: The French governor of Madagascar who first described seeing pitcher plants in 1658.

⚘ George Everhard Rumph: The famous tropical botanist known as Rumphius described *N. mirabilis* as 'Cantherifera' in a book written in the late 1600s.

⚘ Carl Linné or Carl Linnaeus: The father of scientific nomenclature gave the genus the name *Nepenthes* in 1737.

⚘ William Curtis: Started *Curtis's Botanical Magazine* in 1787. It is still in publication.

⚘ Sir Joseph Banks: Was involved with the early development of Kew Botanic Gardens and introduced *N. mirabilis* there in 1789. Banks also discovered *Cephalotus* while on Cook's tour of Australia.

⚘ Father Joao Loureiro: A Portuguese priest in Vietnam, describes *N. mirabilis* as *Phyllamphora mirabilis* (Marvelous urn-shaped leaf) in 1790.

⚘ Sir Stamford Raffles: Was founder of Singapore and started the Botanic Garden of Buitenzorg in Bogor, Indonesia. *N. rafflesiana* is named after him. Early 1800s.

⚘ C. G. C. Reinwardt: Was the botanist of Raffles' garden. *N. reinwardtiana* commemorates him.

⚘ Dr. William Jack: Discovered *N. rafflesiana* and *N. ampullaria* in Singapore around 1819. A surgeon for the East India Company, he befriended Sir Raffles when the latter was governor of Sumatra.

⚘ Conrad Loddiges and his son, George: Were the first to introduce *N. khasiana* into cultivation (in 1825) through their Loddiges Nursery of Hackney, England. They were the first to make use of wardian cases to import *Nepenthes* and other exotics.

⚜ P. W. Korthals: A Dutchman, publishes the first monograph on *Nepenthes* in 1839, describing nine species.

⚜ Joseph Paxton: Began publishing the *Gardeners' Chronicle* in 1841, which helped popularize *Nepenthes* in cultivation.

⚜ Hugh Low: Son of the owner of Hugh Low & Co. nurseries in England, Hugh Jr., in the mid-1800s, made three expeditions to Mt. Kinabalu in Borneo. He discovered four famous *Nepenthes: N. lowii, N. rajah, N. villosa,* and *N. edwardsiana*. He also introduced *N. x hookeriana* into cultivation.

⚜ Sir Harry Veitch: Prominent member of the family that ran the Veitch Nurseries. *N. veitchii* is named after the dynasty, while Sir Harry is the namesake of *N. x harryana*. He introduced many species and hybrids of *Nepenthes* into cultivation. The Veitch Nurseries employed several of the most prolific *Nepenthes* hybridizers, among them Messrs. Dominy, Seden, Court, and Tivey. Many of their introductions survive today and some bear their names.

⚜ Thomas Lobb: An employee of Veitch Nurseries, he collected many new species of *Nepenthes*.

⚜ John Dominy: Also an employee of Veitch Nurseries, in 1862 he introduced the first commercial hybrid, *N. x dominii,* plus many others.

⚜ Sir Joseph Hooker: Son of Sir William, he became director of Kew Botanic Gardens in 1865. A friend of Darwin, he proved the carnivorous nature of *Nepenthes* and wrote the second monograph listing thirty-three species in 1873. *N. x hookeriana* is named for his father.

⚜ Charles Curtis: Another Veitch employee and collector, he discovered *N. curtisii (N. maxima),* which was named for him.

⚜ Marianne North: Famous botanical artist, *N. northiana* bears her name because Harry Veitch saw her painting of it and realized it was a new species. Today, a gallery of her work remains on display at Kew Botanic Gardens.

⚜ Frederick Burbidge: A collector for Veitch, he wrote the well-known *Gardens of the Sun* in 1880 (still in print). He discovered and named *N. burbidgeae* for his wife.

⚘ Maxwell Masters: An editor of *Gardeners' Chronicle,* Veitch Nurseries named their beautiful hybrid *N. x mastersiana* for him and the work he did publicizing *Nepenthes.*

⚘ James Taplin: An Englishman who moved to America, he produced many hybrid *Nepenthes* for George Such Nurseries in New Jersey in the late 1800s.

⚘ J. M. Macfarlane: Wrote a revised monograph on *Nepenthes* in 1908, listing fifty-eight species.

⚘ B. H. Danser: In 1928, wrote a monograph on *Nepenthes* reducing the species count to forty-eight.

⚘ Matthew Jebb and Martin Cheek: In 1997, these two botanists at Kew Gardens revised the genus, listing eighty-two species.

Nepenthes are tropical pitcher plants that usually grow as climbing or scrambling vines. Most species are found in Southeast Asia, their center of distribution being the island of Borneo, but isolated populations are found as far off from this center as northeastern India, Madagascar, the Cape York Peninsula in northern Australia, and New Caledonia. There are currently estimated to be around eighty species.

Nepenthes are not typically jungle plants, but prefer more open and sunny ridges, slopes, meadows, fields, and stunted forests. Only 30 percent of the species are found in lowland areas where the days are hot and the nights warm. The majority of *Nepenthes* are highland or mountain plants, preferring warm days with cool nights. Humidity and rainfall are both high in the habitats supporting the plants.

Nepenthes are found in a variety of

A giant form of *Nepenthes rafflesiana*

soils that are permanently wet throughout the year, although some survive droughts or brief drier seasons. The soils are kept moist by frequent rainfalls, foggy mists, or by seeps and springs. Some *Nepenthes*
are native to marshes or swamplands. The soil itself is often a shallow
layer of leaf litter, decomposing bark and twigs, and mosses, including
sphagnum. Although this loose and airy soil is generally acidic, it may
overlie a foundation of ultra basic rock like serpentine, or sandstone, or
even alkaline limestone. Some *Nepenthes* grow epiphytically, their roots
in mossy, leafy debris caught in the branches of trees. Sometimes the
plants will grow in wet sand or gravelly seeps. Common companion
plants are ferns, grasses, shrubs, and stunted trees. As with most carnivorous plants, these habitats are low in nutrients, and moving water
carries away what little minerals are in the soils.

The seed of *Nepenthes* are very thin and filiform, and so lightweight
they can be carried off by the wind—their pri-
mary method of dispersal. Soon after germination, tiny rosetted plants are formed,
and after one year's growth the entire
plant may be a mere one inch in diameter, the tiny pitchers erect at the end
of broad, leaflike petioles. As the
plant grows year after year, the
rosette spreads to a diameter of a
few inches in the smallest species
to a few feet in the largest. The
extensive root system is very brittle and hairlike.

The leaflike petioles are oval
to lance-shaped, and have a
prominent midrib vein down the
center. At the end of the leaf this
midrib extends into a tendril, the
tip of which is the immature
pitcher. Not all leaves form pitchers,
but in those that do, the tendril
lengthens and the tip begins to grow
and swell, ballooning into a hollow, sealed
pitcher. When mature, the lid pops open,

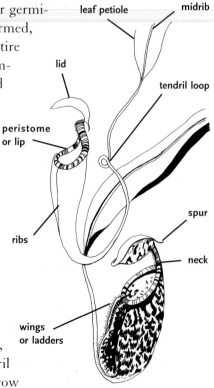

The upper and lower pitchers of
Nepenthes rafflesiana

and the trap quickly reaches its full development. The lip or peristome unfolds, and the often bristly wings form "ladders" along the front. The pitcher quickly colors up in the sun, glistening with nectar droplets and often gaudy patterns to lure unsuspecting prey. These lower pitchers produced by the rosette sit on the ground facing outward. They are usually tubby and squat. When the pitchers open they already have digestion fluids in them, and will secrete more once the plant starts to catch prey. It can take weeks to months for a pitcher to develop, and its lifetime may be similar.

A rosette of ground pitchers may take five to ten years to mature. Then the climbing stem begins to grow. The leaves of the climbing stem look similar to those of the rosette, but the tendrils and pitchers can be dramatically different. As the tendril elongates, it slowly moves about, groping through the air for something, like a branch or twig, to grab hold of. (This movement is best seen in time-lapse photography.) The tendril then forms a single loop, whether or not it finds anchor. But, to form a hanging pitcher, support is usually needed. The tip of the tendril then swings upright like a hook, and it quickly swells into a pitcher. These upper or climbing pitchers can be so radically different in appearance from the lower ground pitchers they can seem to be of another species. They join the tendril from the rear rather than side of the trap. They are usually more graceful and funnel-shaped than the bulkier lowers, and they lack bristly wings along the front. In some species they are less colorful than the ground pitchers, while others are more so.

Nepenthes produce climbing stems for the purpose of having their flowers higher in the air and sunshine than the surrounding vegetation. The climbing stems may be fairly short in some lower-growing *Nepenthes,* such as *N. ventricosa.* In others they may grow several feet to several yards in length, scrambling over bushes or climbing into trees. After flowering, the stems usually continue to grow, and may flower repeatedly for several years. Meanwhile, down below, new shoots appear at the base of the stem. These rapidly develop into large rosettes of new ground pitchers. A wonderful thing about *Nepenthes* is that usually every year a new rosette is formed that eventually becomes a climbing stem. Thus most species are a continuously rejuvenating mass of ground rosettes and pitchers with many climbing stems and hanging pitchers of various ages.

Male and female flowers are found on different plants, but look

The flowers of a male *Nepenthes*

similar to each other. They are more odd than beautiful, but in some species can be colorful and attractive. The long flower stalks arise from the stem and are held upright. Each stalk has dozens to hundreds of small, densely packed blooms. Each bloom is a single flower, but occasionally they are joined in twos and threes. The individual flowers have short stalks and do not have true sepals or petals. Instead they have four short, teardrop-shaped tepals, and from this stands the small male anther or female stigma, depending on the sex of the plant. Stigmas are usually sticky and green, while the anthers are capped with a head of yellow pollen. Wind probably carries most pollen to female plants, but the tepals produce nectar to entice pollinators such as ants, beetles, and small flies. About 70 percent of plants in the wild are male, while 30 percent are female, thus males are also more common in cultivation. When pollinated, the female ovary swells, turns brown, and cracks open, releasing hundreds of fine, threadlike seed, the embryo a small bulb in the center. One flower spike can produce thousands of seed.

But it is the pitchers that make *Nepenthes* so famous. True leaves, the pitchers may be small and dainty to large and almost woody. They also have a fascinating life of their own, and apparently are more than just stomachs for the plant—they are a complete ecosystem of life and death.

The whole plant is covered with nectar glands that supply food for insects such as ants. Nectar is heavier along the tendril, and rather copiously produced by the pitcher, particularly along the ladderlike wings, around the liplike peristome, and under the lid. The lid never moves once it has opened, as is commonly supposed, but instead prevents rain from entering and diluting the contents too quickly. Some species have small or narrow lids that freely allow rainwater into the trap, and act primarily as a nectar-baited lure.

Insects, primarily ants, visit the pitchers in great numbers. They are led by nectar and color patterns to the underside of the lid and the slippery peristome. For many insects, the nectar has an intoxicating effect. After feeding for a while, some insects can appear to be in a drunken stupor, walking or spinning in circles. Many of these lose their foothold, falling from the lid or peristome into the depths of the trap.

When a pitcher first opens, the secreted solution inside is fairly neutral in pH. But as insects are caught, their struggles apparently signal the pitcher to secrete acids and enzymes in large quantity. This liquid is often thick and almost syrupy, so the prey sink quickly and drown.

The interior of the trap is divided into two zones. The upper is the waxy zone, where most insects find it impossible to climb, their feet becoming clogged with a slippery substance. The lower digestive zone is covered with hundreds to thousands of large glands clearly visible to the naked eye. These glands secret the juices that rapidly dissolve the soft parts of the prey. A fly can be digested in a couple of days. The glands then reabsorb nutrients from this soup. The carcass or exoskeleton sinks down to the growing graveyard of corpses at the bottom of the trap.

Strangely enough, tropical pitcher plants don't eat all insects and animals that visit their fanciful and dangerous traps. In fact, over 150 creatures, during at least some part of their life, make the pitcher plants their home or otherwise have a mutually beneficial relationship with the plants.

The simplest of these "friendships" can be found with ant

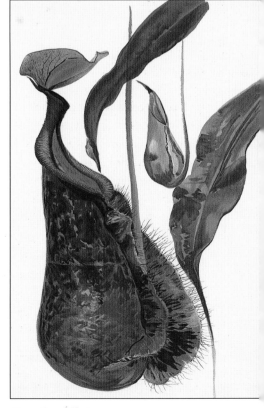

Nepenthes rafflesiana

colonies that make their nests near *Nepenthes.* While countless ants are caught and eaten by the plants, it has been found that at times of drought (when nectar is otherwise scarce), the pitcher plants sustain the ant colonies by offering sugary nectar for them to feed on. What effect the drugs in the nectar have on the ants is not yet known. It may be that only nectar of the pitcher causes intoxication, and not from other parts of the plants.

Numerous mites and microscopic organisms, plus mosquito and fly larva, live completely unharmed in the digestive juices of the plants, even when the acidity of the juice is as low as 3.0 on the pH scale. These creatures act as scavengers and may possibly help the pitchers with digestion.

A species of golden ant is known to drill holes into the thick, hollow tendrils of *N. bicalcurata,* where it raises its young. The adult ants feed on trapped prey. Drummer ants are well known on some species of *Nepenthes.* These solitary ants claim a plant as their own, and when threatened, beat their abdomens on the lids of the pitchers to scare off intruders. If Drummer ants fall into the trap, they can easily and mysteriously escape.

The red crab spider is a common resident of *Nepenthes,* sometimes living in up to 35 percent of their ground pitchers. It attaches itself to the interior of the trap by a small thread. It will swing on this and snatch flies that fall into the digestive juices, and has even been known to "fish" mosquito larvae out of the fluid. Amazingly, when threatened the red crab spider will plunge into the juices, only to haul itself out by its safety line when the threat has passed!

The pitchers of *Nepenthes* seem to go through stages of productivity as they age. Early in their life, they catch insects for the plant's benefit. But as they get older, their contents may become diluted with rain, or deteriorate and dry out. Many insects and other creatures then move in, feeding on the carcasses of the prey or making nests out of the once deadly traps. Recycling at Nature's best.

Humans, too, have utilized *Nepenthes* for more than their beauty.

Travelers have often used older pitchers filled with rainwater as a source of drinking water. As repulsive as it may sound, even insect-debris-laden water is refreshing to those suffering thirst in the tropics! The pitchers can also be cleaned out and used as water scoops.

Various medicinal uses have been beneficial to native inhabitants of

Southeast Asia. The sterile solution in unopened pitchers has been used as an eyewash, an asthma reliever, and a painkiller during childbirth. (I once applied the fluid to a mild skin burn, and was amazed at the immediate relief.) The roots of *Nepenthes* have also been used to regulate menstruation and to help reduce fevers. Various parts of the plants have also been used for indigestion, heartburn, stomach ailments, and dysentery.

The climbing stems of *N. ampullaria* were once commonly used like rope to bind fences and other construction. Today, larger pitchers are still used as cooking tools: rice is often cooked inside the pitchers, some believing the taste of the grain to be enhanced in this way.

WORLD DISTRIBUTION OF *NEPENTHES*

Region	Total Number of Species	Endemic Species
Borneo	32	24
Sumatra	21	11
Malay Peninsula	11	3
Philippines	10	7
New Guinea	10	5
Sulawesi	9	5
Indochina	5	4
Australia	1	0
New Caledonia	1	0
Sri Lanka	1	1
Assam, India	1	1
Seychelles	1	1
Madagascar	2	2

THE LOWLAND SPECIES

Species that grow below 3,000 feet are considered lowland. They experience hot days, warm nights, and continuous high humidity.

Nepenthes gracilis

This fine and graceful scrambler is native to Borneo, Sumatra, Malaysia, and Sulawesi, and in some of these areas is still a common roadside weed. The leaves are long and narrow, up to about eight inches. The small lower pitchers are two to three inches tall, cylindrical with a tubby base, with fine, eyelashlike wings and a thin, circular peristome and lid.

The upper pitchers are similar but lack wings and can be twice as large. Several forms exist. The common is green with many red spots along the upper half of the pitcher. Another beautiful form has pitchers a full, deep red. Easy to grow and an excellent beginner's plant, it is perfect for the room-temperature terrarium, and can have its fast-growing narrow vines pruned back severely to encourage bushier growth. Easy to root in water.

A red form of *Nepenthes gracilis* growing in Singapore

Nepenthes rafflesiana

This magnificent species is extremely variable, with many forms native to Borneo, Sumatra, and Malaysia. A large grower, it is a showpiece in the hothouse, or, when young, in larger, warm terrariums. The leaves can be fairly broad and one to two feet in length. Several forms have been named, but are confused in horticulture. Different forms have been hybridized, giving birth to a wide variety of handsome offspring.

This species characteristically has bulky lower pitchers with a thick, striped peristome; fine, sharp teeth; pronounced wings; and a tall, spiny neck where the peristome joins the lid. The lid is often large and vaulted, with two prominent keels running lengthwise. Upper pitchers are usually as ornamental as lowers, but can be very elongated and funnel-shaped.

The typical forms have pitchers four to five inches tall with pale green backgrounds that are very heavily splotched in reds or purples. Some that are fully red with light green speckling and greenish wings were named *N. rafflesiana* var. *nigropurpurea* by Masters in 1882. *N. rafflesiana* var. *nivea,* collected by Burbidge, has creamy colored pitchers with red speckling and white hairs on the stem, while in *N. rafflesiana* var. *nivea elongata* the pitchers are longer and more narrow. Jumaat Adam, in 1990, described *N. rafflesiana* var. *alata,* which has ornamental, frilly wings on the lower portion of the tendrils. This variety itself can be variable, with red-blotched pitchers to pitchers predominantly green, outlined with purple in the peristome and wings. The most remarkable forms of *N. rafflesiana* have huge purplish pitchers over one foot in length, with tendrils that can be very long, dropping their heavy pitchers from above greenhouse benches all the way to the ground, a distance of nearly

Two forms of *Nepenthes rafflesiana.* On the left is a green form. On the right is *N. rafflesiana* var. *nivea elongata* just opening.

five feet. Giant plants are known from Sabah, Malaysia, and another from Malaysia is nicknamed "Singapore Giant". A dwarf form, called *N. rafflesiana* var. *minor* by Beccari, may be lost in cultivation.

Nepenthes ampullaria

This is another common, variable, and startling species from Borneo, Sumatra, the Malay Peninsula, and New Guinea. This species primarily produces numerous ground pitchers that are round and squat, resembling bird eggs. They are usually one to three inches high, but can be larger. The unique peristome sits at the top of the pitcher, circular and funnel-shaped. The lid is narrow and strapped, deflected from the opening and offering no protection from rain, which the pitchers readily collect. Two prominent wings sit at the front of the tubby pitcher. The leaves of the climbing stem rarely produce pitchers, but when the stem is very tall, clusters of pitchers can suddenly appear along its length.

Several varieties exist. In one, the pitchers are entirely green. The most common has green pitchers liberally spotted in red. There are several striking red forms, among them *N. ampullaria* 'Cantley's Red', which is scarlet with light green flecking.

Nepenthes ampullaria is excellent for the terrarium.

Nepenthes mirabilis from Irian Jaya on New Guinea. This new variety has been nicknamed "John Holmes."

N. ampullaria is very popular for warm terrariums, as the climbing stems can be easily pruned back, resulting in clusters of ground pitchers. The plants also pitcher nicely in shadier conditions.

Nepenthes mirabilis

This is the most widespread species of the genus, its many forms found from southern China to northern Australia, including Malaysia and the Philippines. Its leaves typically are paper-thin with slightly fringed margins. A small grower, it makes a nice terrarium plant. The upper and lower pitchers are usually similar: cylindrical with a bulbous bottom, round mouth and lid, flattened peristome, and colored green to suffused with red. An interesting form called *N. mirabilis* var. *echinostoma* has a marvelously wide, oversized peristome that is flat and striped. A plant from Vietnam widely circulated as *N. anamensis* appears to be a form of *N. mirabilis,* and has been known to grow on windowsills.

N. mirabilis loves wet swampy conditions, but avoids acidic peaty soils, preferring more alkaline areas. It is often seasonally flooded in nature, and has even been known to colonize coastal, brackish swamps.

Nepenthes bicalcarata

This amazing plant is famous for its sharp, saber-toothed fangs that hang from the rear of its lid, making it appear rather dangerous. Native to Borneo, it prefers shaded peat swamps, and can grow to enormous dimensions. The stem is thick, with long, broad leaves two feet in length. The lower pitchers average six inches tall, are round and squat, are almost woody in texture, and have prominent wings. They are green to coppery orange or reddish in color. The broad peristome joins to form a tall neck capped with a large lid. The two hard, sharp fangs are an outgrowth of the peristome and overhang the pitcher's mouth. Nectar sometimes drips from these, giving the appearance of oozing venom. Ants find the fangs difficult to negotiate, and often fall from them into the digestive pool below. It has also been suggested that the sharp fangs prevent small mammals from stealing prey from the trap. The upper pitchers are similar, but lack wings and are yellow green in color.

The lower pitcher of the vicious-looking *Nepenthes bicalcarata*, its sharp fangs overhanging its mouth. The frightened tillandisa is *T. butzii*.

N. bicalcarata is easy to grow but needs hot, humid conditions. When young it succeeds well in terrariums, but does best in roomy hothouses and stove houses. Long a favorite with collectors, it is another showy, fantastic plant that never ceases to amaze people who see it.

Nepenthes albomarginata

A small growing scrambler from Borneo, Sumatra, and the Malay Peninsula, the pitchers are cylindrical and around six inches long, with an oval mouth and lid, narrow peristome, and reduced wings. The beauty of this plant is the prominent white ring below the peristome, which almost appears hand painted. Most forms have grayish green pitchers, but a lovely Malaysian form has red lower pitchers.

Nepenthes reinwardtiana

This tall scrambler also comes from Borneo, Sumatra, and the Malay Peninsula, and sometimes grows epiphytically in trees. The smooth, curvaceous pitchers have negligible wings, and are long and thin, with a slight waist. The slanted mouth is oval with a thin peristome and oval lid. Its hallmark are two curious, waxy "eye spots" that usually appear on the upper interior back wall of the pitcher, which may be a lure for prey. There

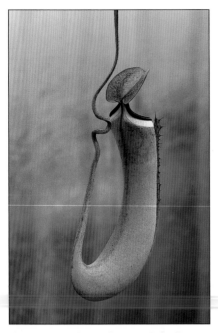

The upper pitchers of *Nepenthes albomarginata*.

Nepenthes northiana, a striking lowland species with enormous and beautiful pitchers.

is a common green form, and a more striking red form.

Nepenthes truncata

A spectacular plant from the Philippines, this large, coarse species has unusual leaves that are squared or truncated at their ends. The enormous pitchers have smooth green exteriors, with colorful interiors heavily mottled in reds, pinks, and purples. The lower pitchers are fat and cylindrical with prominent wings. The slanted mouth is large with a colorful and wide peristome that may be fluted along its edge and striped or golden orange. The lid is domed and held horizontally. The pitchers may reach fourteen inches in length.

Nepenthes northiana

This is the showy species made famous by Marianne North's colorful painting. It grows on limestone cliffs in Sarawak and is nearly extinct, but tissue-cultured plants have now re-entered cultivation. The giant lower pitchers reach 14 inches in height, are bronzy green, heavily splotched with red. The slanted, large mouth has a huge fluted peristome pale red with purplish stripes. The lower pitchers are fat and squat, while the similar uppers are more cornucopia-shaped. I have found a good alkaline medium for it to be two parts coarse vermiculite, to one part each of perlite, pumice and sand. Avoid peat moss or sphagnum, which stunts its growth. A plant known as *N. decurrens* is believed to be synonymous.

Nepenthes merrilliana

From the Philippines and Sulawesi, this is another large species with heavy, squat, flat-bottomed lower pitchers. They are green, with prominent wings, and a wide, gaping mouth.

Nepenthes veitchii

This beautiful species from Borneo is found from sea level to about 4,000 feet, so some forms can be considered highland plants as well. The squat pitchers are green with strong wings. Its main attribute is its tremendously flared, nearly vertical peristome that is reminiscent of the gills of a fish. The peristome is the predominant feature of the plant. It can be green to golden brown, or, in some spectacular forms, beautifully striped in red. The oval lid seems to hang precariously at the top. This species often climbs up trees, its leaves hugging the trunks.

Nepenthes hirsuta

This small scrambler from Borneo is covered with dark, bristly hairs. The most popular form in cultivation has handsome, cylindrical pitchers heavily colored a dark brownish red, with a thin peristome and stems colored purplish black. A nice plant for the terrarium.

The upper pitchers of *Nepenthes veitchii*.

Nepenthes hirsuta is a small growing specimen perfect for the warmer terrarium.

Nepenthes thorelli

From Indochina, this species has been frequently used to produce popular hybrids, particularly in Japan. The lower pitchers are oval-shaped and tubby, and a lovely crimson color. The uppers are elongated, very slim, and a pale yellow green.

LOWLAND HYBRIDS

Nepenthes, like *Sarracenia,* hybridize in the wild, and some that were originally thought to be species are now known to be natural crosses. Hybrids have also been artificially produced for over 150 years, thus there are hundreds in circulation.

Unfortunately, CP lovers face problems with the nomenclature of *Nepenthes* hybrids similar to those of *Sarracenia.* Since no official registry was ever organized for *Nepenthes* (the International Carnivorous Plant Society has registered only cloned cultivars since 1978), the first time a particular hybrid was produced it may or may not have received a fancy "group" name. Sometimes single individuals were chosen and given varietal or cultivar status, thereafter reproduced vegetatively as clones.

Thus, as an example, the cross of *N. mirabilis* x (*rafflesiana* x *ampullaria*) was never given a fancy hybrid name by which all similar crosses thereafter would be called. However, many individual offspring of this cross have been named, making them cultivars. So we have *N.* x *wrigleyana, N.* x *coccinea, N.* x *compacta, N.* x *eyermanni, N.* x *lawren-ciana, N.* x *morganiana, N.* x *paradisae, N.* x *patersonni, N.* x *ratcliffiana, N.* x *robusta, N.* x *splendida,* and *N.* x *stewartii,* all varieties chosen from offspring of the above mentioned hybrid produced by many people over many years—and most, incidentally, probably lost to cultivation.

Fortunately, some modern growers, such as Clyde Bramblett and Bruce Lee Bednar of southern Florida, have been following a more organized program of hybridization. New crosses that they develop receive a fancy group name, and outstanding individuals are then given a fancy varietal title.

Here I will review a few popular hybrids—some official cultivars, but most not.

Nepenthes x trichocarpa

This natural cross between *N. gracilis* and *N. ampullaria* was thought to be a species until recently. A pretty and delicate little plant, it is excellent in warmer terrariums. The small ground pitchers are tubby and spotted (resembling fat *N. gracilis* pitchers), while the uppers are more tubular and pale.

Nepenthes x hookeriana

This is the natural hybrid of *N. rafflesiana* x *ampullaria*. A large and vigorous plant, the lower pitchers are usually green with much red spotting, and have a heavy, squat, "boxy" look to them. This hybrid was very popular in the nineteenth century for use as a parent in other crosses. The many results have given us a wide range of plants that have somewhat similar compact and colorful pitchers that are still popular today. Some of these are:

Nepenthes x wrigleyana

This is *N. mirabilis* x (*rafflesiana* x *ampullaria*), and has thick, cylindrical pitchers, light green with much red spotting.

Nepenthes x morganiana

This is the reverse cross of the above, with fat, tubby pitchers and lighter red spotting.

Nepenthes x lawrenciana

This is a rather similar cross.

Nepenthes x coccinea

Again, the same cross but with deep red pitchers lightly marked with green. Very handsome and popular.

A lower pitcher of Nepenthes x morganiana

N. x coccinea

Nepenthes x boissiense

This is (*gracilis* x *khasiana*) x (*rafflesiana* x *ampullaria*) and has rather bottom-heavy lower pitchers, very pale green with light red flecking.

Nepenthes x superba

This is a more richly colored sibling of the above.

Nepenthes x henreyana

This is the same but with pitchers predominantly red.

Nepenthes x williamssii

This is a sibling of *N.* x *henreyana* with similar dark red pitchers.

Nepenthes x chelsonni

This is (*rafflesiana* x *gracilis*) x (*rafflesiana* x *ampullaria*), resulting in red and green tubby pitchers with a wider mouth and larger floppy lid.

Some other popular Victorian hybrids still can be seen in collections and botanical gardens today, such as:

Nepenthes x intermedia

This cross of *N. gracilis* x *rafflesiana* is similar to *N. rafflesiana* in its neck and its red, blotchy, bulky pitchers.

Nepenthes x dormanniana

This is *N. mirabilis* crossed with (*gracilis* x *khasiana*), the lower pitchers well spotted but with a green peristome and wavy wings.

Nepenthes x dominii

This is *N. rafflesiana* x *gracilis*. The bulky lower pitchers are very crimson, which contrasts well with the green mouth and large, domed greenish red lid.

Some Victorian hybrids produce enormous, magnificent pitchers that are still the highlight of many botanical gardens and private greenhouses. Two exceptional clones are:

Nepenthes x mixta

This cross between *N. northiana* and *N. maxima* produces huge pitchers up to a foot long. The pale green traps are heavily streaked with red, and the large, slanted mouth has a wide, luscious peristome that glistens bright red. Upper pitchers are equally impressive but more funnel-shaped, like giant cornucopias. Produced by Tivey in 1893. A more richly colored form is called *N.* x *mixta* var. *sanguinea*. Another is *N. mixta* var. *superba*.

Nepenthes x dyeriana

This is another showstopper. A cross between *N.* (x *mixta*) and *N.* (*rafflesiana* x *veitchii*), the pitchers reach fourteen inches, and are green with many red/purple/brown streaks. The large peristome is candy cane–striped, turning bronze in good light. Amazingly, this clone has recently been found to do well on windowsills. Released by Tivey in 1903.

From 1918 to 1956, the Missouri Botanical Gardens housed one of the largest *Nepenthes* collections in the world, under the direction of George H. Pring. Three cultivars were named from a cross of *N.* [(*rafflesiana* x *hirsuta*) x (*rafflesiana* x *ampullaria*)] x (*rafflesiana* x *hirsuta*). All have tubby, squat pitchers of similar shape,

The magnificent lower pitcher of *Nepenthes* x *mixta,* a showy hybrid for the hothouse.

but with coloration differences. They are *N.* x 'Lieutenant R. B. Pring', *N.* x 'St. Louis', and *N.* x 'Henry Shaw'. If anyone still grows these cultivars, both the author and Missouri Botanical Gardens would like to hear from you.

Three hybrids from France are noteworthy. A natural hybrid of *N. mirabilis* x *thorelli* was introduced from Cambodia by Mr. Marcel Lecoufle and named *N.* x *lecouflei.* He crossed this plant with *N.* x *mixta* var. *sanquinea* and introduced the beautiful *N.* x 'Ile de France'. The cylindrical lower pitchers are flushed pink in the upper part, with streaks of chocolate red, and the flat peristome is striped green and crimson. Upper pitchers are paler. Another, raised by Mr. Yvon Vezier, is *N.* x 'Ville de Rouen', a cross between *N.* x *superba* and *N.* x *mastersiana,* a highland hybrid.

In Japan in the twentieth century, more *Nepenthes* have been hybridized than ever before, far surpassing the numbers of Victorian hybrids. Of the many crosses produced from 1914 to 1939 by both individuals and commercial nurseries, almost none survived the hard winter of 1940, or the war and bombings that quickly followed.

Unfortunately, the Japanese follow their own rules of nomenclature—so duplicate crosses in the West have different names!

Since 1950, hybridization in Japan has resumed, with many beautiful results. Few of these are in circulation outside of that country, but trade is on the increase. One of the best crosses in worldwide circulation is *N. x rokko,* which I will discuss under highland plants, below. Of predominately lowland ancestry, a few are worth mentioning:

N. x *nagoya* = *N.* (x *mixta*) x *thorelli*

N. x *oisoensis* = *N.* (x *mixta*) x *maxima*

N. x *minamiensis* = *N.* (x *mixta*) x (x *wrigleyana*)

N. x *mizuho* = *N. rafflesiana* x (x *dyeriana*)

Probably the most prolific modern hybridizer in the world is Dr. K. Kawase of the Kosobe Botanical Garden at Kyoto University in Japan. He has produced many dozens of crosses (163 between 1973 and 1983) and has named them all alphabetically after Koto, which means "Old Capital" (Kyoto). Thus we have an amusing list that includes *N.* 'Aglow Koto', *N.* 'Balmy Koto', *N.* 'Delectable Koto', *N.* 'Dreamy Koto', *N.* 'Ecstatic Koto', *N.* 'Feverish Koto', *N.* 'Fruity Koto', and *N.*

Nepenthes x 'Ile de France', upper pitcher

'Giddy Koto', all the way to *N.* 'Zonal Koto'. Many of these plants are in wide circulation, but space does not allow me to review them here. Many of these hybrids have been bred from highland species, offering a wide variety suitable to cooler growing conditions. The Koto series are group names, not cultivars, so individual plants can be variable.

For many years, two nurserymen in southern Florida, Bruce Lee Bednar and Clyde Bramblett, have hybridized many dozens of *Nepenthes,* producing some of the finest plants seen since the Victorian era. In August 1992, Hurricane Andrew had a devastating effect on some of their greenhouses, and many plants were blown into the Everglades, never to be seen again.

Their cooperative venture has since recuperated, and their hybridization program has resumed. They give their crosses group names, from which they occasionally choose varieties, listing the seed-bearing females first. Some of their more popular crosses are listed here.

Nepenthes x excellens

This cross between *N.* x *rokko* and *N.* x *mixta superba* is similar to the latter parent but with an even larger and flatter peristome of brilliant color. Two varieties are *N. excellens* var. 'Superba' and *N. excellens* var. 'Jessica Lauren'.

Nepenthes x David Parkyn

The striking pitchers are cylindrical with a slight waist, yellow with maroon stripes. The cross is *N.* (x *oisoensis*) x [*thorelli* x (x *wittei*)].

Nepenthes x madisonii

This is *N.* (x *oisoensis*) x *ventricosa*. The hourglass pitchers are tinted pink/orange/yellow with red speckling and a red, scalloped peristome.

Nepenthes x dianiana var. 'rex'

This is an offspring of *N.* (x *splendiana*) x (x *mixta*). The distinctive pitchers are speckled pink and have large wings and a tall, vaulted peristome.

Nepenthes x dwarf peacock

This is a miniature plant with teardrop-shaped pitchers, multicolored in reds, pinks, and purples. The parents are *N. thorelli* x (x *savannah rose*).

Nepenthes x East Everglades

This is the cross between *N.* (x *splendiana*) x (x *redlanderii*). The pitchers have a bright green background with dark red stripes and a round peristome.

Nepenthes x hareliana var. 'Red Skelton'

This bony-looking plant has long, thin leaves with skinny, skeletal pitchers dark maroon in color. The cross is *N.* (x *hachijo*) x [*thorelli* x (x *dyeriana*)].

Nepenthes x sheridaniana

This is *N.* x *splendiana* x *ventricosa*. The pitchers look like a plump, elongated hourglass, with heavy, blood-red spatters and a red, spiked peristome.

Another lowland hybrid worth mention was produced by Marie Baumgartl of Marie's Orchids, in California. She bred a vigorous plant of *N. truncata* x *alata* with a plant called *N.* x "Sens", an unknown hybrid found growing in a botanical garden in Sens, France. The resulting offspring were named *N.* x *Frieda Crisp*. I was so impressed with these plants I chose three outstanding clones, which were named *N.* x 'Marie', *N.* x 'Frau Anna Babl', and *N.* x 'Nora'. All three of these clones are marked by bright red peristomes with white interior pitchers, the exteriors variably colored with pink blush to heavy streaks of purple.

THE HIGHLAND SPECIES

Seventy percent of *Nepenthes* are tropical highland or mountain plants, growing at elevations of 3,000 to 10,000 feet above sea level. Above the lowland heat of the rain forest, the mountain climate can be considerably cooler and wetter, especially at night. Day temperatures average in the seventies, and by early morning drop into the sixties and fifties or even cooler, but frost never occurs except at the highest of levels. The mountains are often shrouded in cloud cover, the nights frequently misty or rainy. As a result, the ground, rocks, and stunted trees are typically covered with thick growths of sphagnum and other mosses. These elevations are known as elfin or mossy forests, and when the sun breaks through the thick clouds, it is usually brief and in the breezy afternoons. This is the *Nepenthes* zone.

Nepenthes khasiana

The first species introduced into cultivation in 1825, N. khasiana is an endangered plant from the Khasi Highlands of Assam in northeastern India, the only Nepenthes native to that country. It is an extremely cool-tolerant plant, unaffected by brief lows in the thirties, and large plants in cultivation have been known to return from their stems after freezes down to twenty degrees—but they certainly prefer it warmer. The species is very adaptable to windowsills, and succeeds well as an outdoor plant in climates such as the immediate coast of California, where winters are frost free and summers cool and foggy. It also adapts to warmer, humid climates such as that found in Florida, but grows faster in winter when the nights are cool. A large plant, the stems can grow several feet long, with large leaves. The eight-inch pitchers are handsome, cylindrical and slim, with an oval mouth and lid. The upper pitchers can be heavily suffused with red coloration. There is a fairly prominent reddish band below the thin peristome. Males and females are common in cultivation, so seedlings are often produced, but it is very difficult to strike from cuttings. Tissue-cultured plants are making this easy species more common.

Nepenthes ventricosa

From the Philippines, this wonderful species is as adaptable as *N. khasiana*. It is a low grower, with compact leaves growing along the gradually scrambling, branching stems. The lovely pitchers are tubby and rounded, with a constricted waist and no wings. The mouth is wide and oval, with a beautiful scalloped-pink peristome, thick, tightly ridged, and sharp-toothed. Variable, the best forms have lower pitchers up to five inches, suffused in carmine with crimson blotches. Upper pitchers are pale greenish yellow and smaller. The flowers can also be handsome and colorful. An excellent plant for the windowsill and terrarium, it is also tolerant of brief temperature drops near the frost level.

Nepenthes alata

A common and widespread species from the Philippines, this species is extremely variable, and also grows in the lowlands. Many forms exist in cultivation. The common one has slim pitchers with a slight waist and a bulbous bottom, the lower pitchers with fringed wings. The peristome is thin, with an oval mouth and lid, but overall the pitchers are bland, with only a slight flush of pink. In a plant I grow called 'Highland Form', the pitchers are rather similar but more flushed with red. Other varieties may have green pitchers with attractive red peristomes. Forms called "boschiana mimic" look nothing like the very rare *N. boschiana* from Borneo, and instead simply have a more bulbous bottom. (*N. boschiana* is a species similar to *N. maxima,* and has only recently been rediscovered.) A "hairy" or "pubescent" form of *N. alata* has large lower pitchers that are fuzzy and streaked with red.

By far the best variety of *N. alata* is *N. alata* var. 'Spotted Form' from

This form of *Nepenthes alata* is often called spotted or striped and is one of the easiest *Nepenthes* to grow, often succeeding on windowsills.

Luzon in the Philippines. This is a beautiful plant and very adaptable to warmer or cooler conditions, often excelling on windowsills or outdoors in warm-temperate and subtropical climates. The lower pitchers are plumper than the typical, with strong wings, and are heavily streaked and splotched with red, sometimes entirely cherry red with darker spots. This contrasts well with the pale interior of the trap. Upper pitchers are more funnel-shaped but also nicely colored. The peristome is thin.

Nepenthes maxima

This rather gorgeous pitcher plant is widespread and variable, growing from Borneo through Sulawesi to New Guinea. Mostly from the high-

lands, where in New Guinea some forms can experience frost, it can also be found in lowland areas. Typically the lower pitchers are six to eight inches tall, but can be larger. They are heavily blotched and streaked in crimsons on a pale green to olive background. Wings on the lower pitchers are prominent. The mouth is oblique, with an enormous, fanciful peristome that can be widely flared and fluted, colored pink to wine red. The interior pitcher is pale with reddish spots. The lids are often held upright, are oval to triangular in shape, and colored green suffused with reddish streaks and spots. Most curious is the hooked boss at the underbase of the lid, and a thin, filamentous "tooth" hanging from the tip. Usually the upper pitchers are smaller, extremely funnel-shaped, and lacking much color. A fine plant for

The magnificent lower pitchers of *Nepenthes maxima*

terrariums and windowsills, this is one of the most popular species and is very easy to grow. It is also tolerant of brief cold snaps near the frost level.

Nepenthes fusca

Another beautiful plant, this species from Borneo is closely related and similar to *N. maxima*. The pitchers, up to ten inches, are much narrower, the peristome slightly so. One form, which I call "Coppermouth," has a coppery orange peristome while the pitcher is blotched and spotted in brownish red. The more popular variety has long, cylindrical pitchers heavily marked in purplish red, with a stunning peristome so purple maroon it looks almost black. The unusual lids are very narrow and triangular. Upper pitchers are short and very funnel-shaped, sometimes spotted, with unusually narrow and downward-curved lids.

Nepenthes stenophylla

Related to *N. maxima* and *N. fusca,* this attractive species has long, narrow pitchers of a pale yellow green color with sparser purple blotches. The mouth and lid are circular, the narrow peristome striped purple and green. The heavily marked lid has a boss similar to its relations. Upper pitchers can reach a foot long.

Nepenthes sanguinea

This vigorous, fast-growing Malaysian species has large, plump pitchers up to a foot tall, a big oval mouth with a large, upturned lid, medium peristome, and prominent wings. The magnificent 'Red Form' has lower pitchers fully scarlet on their exteriors, with pale to spotted interiors and a cherry-red peristome. The upper pitchers are funnel-shaped and plump, pale green, with red spots along the upper portion of the trap, and a striped peristome. Other forms of *N. sanguinea* have uniformly yellow green pitchers, sometimes with red stems. This species may be a good windowsill candidate.

Nepenthes macfarlanei

From the Malay Peninsula, this variable species has heavy, fat pitchers with large mouths that are oval to

Nepenthes fusca, lower pitchers. This form comes from Mt. Kinabalu.

Nepenthes sanguinea, an easy and fast-growing highland species. This is a lower pitcher of the large red form.

teardrop-shaped, thick peristomes red to purple in color, and medium wings. The lids are large and oval. The lower pitchers can be pale brown to reddish tan, with irregular reddish to purple spots. Upper pitchers can also be large, usually a beautiful creamy yellow with interior red spots, heavily striped peristome, and red-blotched, large oval lids. See terrarium photo page 42.

Nepenthes gracillima

Also from the Malay Peninsula, this slender species has long, tubular, six-inch pitchers. The wings are reduced to two long ribs, making the pitcher appear flat-fronted. The lower pitchers have sloping, teardrop-shaped mouths with a thin red lip, pale interior and oval, horizontally held lids, and are reddish brown to blackish in color. Uppers have a more circular mouth and are often olive gray. A very pretty plant for terrariums.

Nepenthes tentaculata

Another small grower excellent for terrariums, this variable species comes from Borneo and Sulawesi. The flat front of the pitchers have handsome, bristly wings; the slanted mouth is almost triangular with thin lips. Usually the lids have tentacle-like hairs on the top of the lid, but not always. The pitchers are usually four to six inches long, and may be green, spotted, or red. See terrarium photo page 42.

Nepenthes tobiaca

Some taxonomists consider this Sumatran species to be a form of *N. reinwardtiana,* but to the hobbyist they appear quite different. Their pitchers are small, and they can scramble considerably when given the room, like a highland counterpart to *N. gracilis.* One form has small, brownish red, tubby pitchers on the ground, with uppers green with some red spots. Another form is all green and rather boring. The peristomes are slim; mouths and lids circular. This plant is happy in the terrarium or on the windowsill, and on my porch survived to the freezing level but died when frosted.

Nepenthes carunculata

This very colorful plant is from Sumatra. The lower pitchers are mahogany red to almost chocolate, with beautiful, wine-colored, flared peristomes. Upper pitchers are boring and green. Nice in tanks, the pitchers are under six inches long. (See terrarium photo page 42.)

Nepenthes spectabilis

This species from Sumatra has beautiful pitchers that are plump and cylindrical, with a creamy yellow background, purplish blotches, and dark peristome. The striped mouth of the upper traps can be almost vertical.

Nepenthes spathulata

From Sumatra, this handsome plant has squat lower traps green in color with a wine-red peristome flared and wavy, almost rivaling that of *N. veitchii*. The upper pitchers are green and funnel-shaped and much less attractive. Easy to grow, it may get too large for a terrarium, but may succeed on windowsills. Cuttings easily root in water.

Nepenthes clipeata

On the verge of extinction, very few plants remain of this spectacular species due to overcollection and forest fires. It grows only on one cliff side on Mt. Kelam in Borneo, but has recently entered cultivation. The leaves are oval, and the tendrils bearing the pitchers come not from the leaf tip but its underside. The purplish pitchers are flask-shaped and can reach a foot in height. The peristome is striped and the unusual lid is a domed canopy over the oval mouth. The beauty of the plant is the way in which the pitchers seem to hover in air beside the leaves, their tendril attachments hidden from view.

Nepenthes madagascariensis

The first *Nepenthes* discovered was very rare in cultivation until recently, when it entered tissue culture. From Madagascar, its best feature is its upper pitchers, narrowly funnel-shaped, tinted claret, and with a yellow peristome and large oval lid. Lowers are often red and more typically tubby.

Left to right, the lower pitchers of *N. spectabilis*, *N. glabrata*, and *N. ventricosa*

The giant lower traps of *Nepenthes spathulata*

The dainty upper pitchers of *Nepenthes infundibuliformis* are shaped like miniature wine glasses.

Nepenthes infundibuliformis

Possibly a Sulawesi form of *N. maxima,* the lower pitchers are similar but squatter and orange brown in color. The tiny upper pitchers are startling—barely three inches tall, they are shaped like miniature wine glasses, with oval mouths and a very narrow lid. The pitcher rapidly constricts to the tendril, its interior sticky like flypaper, the digestive juices at the bottom viscid like syrup. This species has also been called *N. eymai.*

Nepenthes muluensis

From Mt. Mulu in Borneo, this charming small grower has five-inch cylindrical traps heavily blotched with purple on a creamy yellow background. In good contrast, the oval peristome and lid are almost pure white.

Nepenthes ephippiata

New to cultivation, this rare species from Borneo is most unusual, slightly resembling *N. lowii* and *N. rajah* (see below). The tubby pitchers are squat, slightly constricted at the waist, and about six inches tall. The large mouth has a narrow peristome. The main feature is the huge vaulted lid, the underside covered with peculiar, short tendrils. The coloration is fabulous: the outer pitcher is pale crimson while the interior is blood red. The lids are green with a red margin, turning fully red with age.

Nepenthes inermis

This is one of the strangest of pitcher plants. From Sumatra, the unusual upper traps are only one or two inches tall, papery thin, funnel-shaped with no peristome, and a thin, filamentous lid. They are pure green in color. It is believed that nectar on the tiny lid paralyzes small insects, which drop to the inner wall of the funnel trap and slowly slide into the digestive juices by means of a sticky, lubricating fluid.

Nepenthes glabrata

One of the daintiest and prettiest of the *Nepenthes,* this species comes from Sulawesi. The leaves are very narrow and lance-shaped. The small lower traps are smooth and tubby, barely one or two inches tall. The peristome is yellow, with a small oval mouth and lid. The pitcher background is lemon green, delicately marked with some red streaks as though hand painted. The upper pitchers are similar but larger and more cylindrical. Sometimes, tendrils and pitchers appear without leaves from the basal stems. In strong light some forms of the plant can turn purplish black. Certainly this species is a prize for any terrarium.

The upper pitchers of *Nepenthes glabrata* almost appear hand-painted.

Nepenthes hamata

When people ask me which is the scariest-looking and most dangerous *Nepenthes,* I usually point in the direction of this one, which sends shivers down most animal spines. A recent introduction from Sulawesi, it has also been called *N. dentata,* and was described in 1984. The lower pitchers are reminiscent of *N. maxima* and *N. fusca,* long and narrow, heavily blotched in purple, and with prominent wings. The upper lid is hairy. It is the highly evolved peristome that is so disturbing, for the lip has transformed into a row of long, curved hooks, sharp as knives, that overhang the pitcher's mouth. In the lower pitchers these teeth are purple black. The upper pitchers are pure green and the hooks particularly long—somewhat like a torture device from the Inquisition. One can only guess what

The upper pitchers of *Nepenthes hamata* can send chills down animal spines.

Nepenthes *villosa* on Mt. Kinabalua

this plant may be evolving into. Pray that it doesn't start walking.

Mt. Kinabalu is Borneo's tallest and most famous mountain. Many of the species I have discussed grow there, but there are a few *Nepenthes* that grow nowhere else, or are found only on other nearby peaks. These include some of the most notorious and beautiful of the tropical pitcher plants.

Nepenthes burbidgea

A lovely species, it is native to Mt. Kinabalu and the adjoining Mt. Tamboyukon. The lower traps are up to a foot long, ovoid and stout, with moderate wings and a broad peristome, while the uppers are short, plump, and funnel-shaped. The coloration of the uppers is spectacular, the background a pale yellow white, marked with sparse, irregular rosy blotches. The peristome is striped with red and pale yellow. The large lids are heavily spotted in purple. Burbidge, its discoverer, described them as "pure white, semi-translucent like eggshell, porcelain-white with crimson or blood-tinted blotches." I have found this species easy to grow with nightly lows around sixty degrees. Cooler temperatures and the plant is reluctant to pitcher.

Nepenthes villosa

From the higher elevations of Mt. Kinabalu comes this popular, ground-scrambling species, where nighttime temperatures can drop to forty degrees. Upper and lower pitchers are similar. They are plump and roundish, up to eight inches tall, red orange in color, and covered with an animal-like pelt of fur. The lid is large and held horizontally. The spectacular peristome looks like a row of raised claws, sharp as razors and yellow in color. This is a slow-growing species that is easy to grow. Chilly nights in the fifties, with cool days, are required.

Nepenthes edwardsiana

From both Mt. Kinabalu and Mt. Tamboyukon, this species is very similar to *N. villosa,* but the pitchers lack the furry pelt and are long and cylindrical. It is also a climber, up to forty feet, whereas *N. villosa* scrambles on the ground. The pitchers are golden to flushed red, the teeth of the peristome a similar series of raised hooks with downward-curved barbs. The long neck raises the lid far above the mouth.

Nepenthes macrophylla

Closely related to the above, this recently described species comes from Mt. Trus Madi, a neighbor of Mt. Kinabalu. The leaves are huge, up to two feet. The pitchers are more stout than those of *N. edwardsiana,* with a wide, gaping mouth. The teeth of the peristome are shorter and blood red.

Nepenthes lowii

Discovered by Hugh Low on Mt. Kinabalu, this famous plant also grows on several other tall peaks on Borneo. It may be the strangest of all *Nepenthes,* thanks to its bizarre upper pitchers. The lower traps are fairly normal and cylindrical, reddish brown, with a medium wide peristome. The oval lid is held horizontally and hints at peculiarities to come: under the lid hang many long, pointed appendages, like thin vegetable stalactites.

The stems grow tall, up to forty feet. The upper pitchers, up to several inches long, look like weird, constricted gourds. The peristome is entirely lacking, the mouth wide and gaping. The pitcher suddenly narrows to an extreme waist, then balloons to a bulbous bottom. The exterior of the trap is pure green, while the interior of the yawning mouth is shiny red to purple. The large

The mysterious eggs amid the bristles of the lid on **Nepenthes lowii**. Do they lure tree shrews for food?

The bizarre upper pitchers of **Nepenthes lowii**. Toilet bowls for birds?

lid of the upper pitcher is held vertically. It has the same strange, bristly projections as the lower trap lids. In cultivation, *N. lowii* is easy to grow.

A strange mystery surrounds this plant. Often, in the bristles of the lid, an oozy white substance is secreted, often taking the form of egglike beads. It does not attract insects. Professor J. Harrison, in the early 1960s, assumed they were snail eggs, and reportedly saw small tree shrews eating them. That *N. lowii* catches these small mammals has yet to be documented. It wasn't until plants entered cultivation that the "eggs" were discovered to be a product of the plant by grower Cliff Dodd and myself. Botanist Charles Clarke has observed birds and shrews feeding on the "eggs," while their excrement falls into the pitcher!

Nepenthes rajah

When Hooker described this species, also discovered by Hugh Low on Mt. Kinabalu, he wrote, "This wonderful plant is certainly one of the most striking vegetable productions hitherto discovered...", and it remains so to this day. Also found on Mt. Tamboyukan, *N. rajah* grows along the ground as a scrambler. The large leaves are blunt and truncated, and the tendril originates from the middle underside. The enormous pitchers are oval-shaped, almost woody in texture, red to purple in color, with a large, gaping, oblique mouth. The thick, fluted peristome is blood red. The interior of the tublike traps is pale green to pink and has no waxy zone, being entirely covered with large digestive glands. The giant lid is vaulted, red above and lime green below. The pitchers can be over a foot in length, and can hold over two quarts of digestive juices, but there have been specimens known to hold four quarts. The flower spikes can also be impressive, standing as tall as four feet. Climbing stems are rare.

Nepenthes rajah at the Park Headquarters on Mt. Kinabalu

N. rajah is the only pitcher plant truly documented as having caught rats. It is believed the mammals were in search of water when they fell in and drowned.

HiGHLAND HYBRiDS

Until recently, hybrids of highland *Nepenthes* have been rather rare in cultivation. Lowland plants have always been more popular to grow, because it's easier to heat greenhouses in winter than to cool them during warm summer nights. Also, areas where cool summer nights prevail (all of the lands west of the Rockies) were much less populated in the Victorian era when growing *Nepenthes* was so much in vogue. This has changed, of course, particularly with the invention of air-conditioning and evaporative coolers, which are helpful in reducing summer heat in greenhouses to temperatures more pleasing to mountain plants. Interior terrariums, especially in basements, have also added to the growing interest in breeding more vigorous and beautiful hybrids that are happy in cooler temperatures. Some of the following crosses have lowland ancestry, and thus can also do well in warmer conditions.

Nepenthes x ventrata

This hybrid, which is also tolerant of lowland conditions, is a vigorous plant with graceful, curvaceous pitchers intermediate between its parents *N. ventricosa* and *N. alata.* Variable parents give rise to variable offspring, so some are boring and green, while those from more colorful parents are bronzy and pleasing. A good terrarium and windowsill candidate.

Nepenthes x emmarene

This handsome cross between *N. khasiana* x *ventricosa* is happy in warm conditions yet is also tolerant to the frost level. The short pitchers are squat and cylindrical, tinted red with darker vertical streaks. Superb on windowsills or in humid, frost-free climates outdoors.

Nepenthes x rokko

A Japanese hybrid of *N. thorelli* x *maxima,* the clone I grow myself is one of my favorite *Nepenthes.* Lower pitchers reach eight inches, with a scalloped red peristome and many red streaks and spotting. Upper pitchers are funneled and green, with less color. A vigorous plant, its stems can climb seven feet in one year. It thrives in humid, frost-free climates and as a houseplant, but is too large for tanks. It also succeeds in lowland conditions.

Nepenthes thorelli x (x wittei)

My clone of this plant is a very vigorous and handsome hybrid similar to *N.* x *rokko* but darker in color.

Highland Hybrids

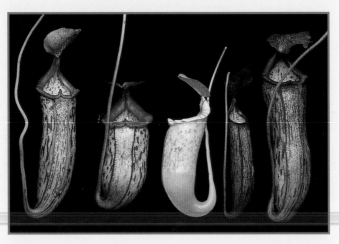

Related hybrids, left to right: *Nepenthes* x *rokko;* lower and upper pitchers of N. (x *rokko*) x *thorelli;* N. x Santa Mira var. 'Jack Finney;' and N. *thorelli* x (x *wittei*)

Nepenthes x *tiveyi*

Nepenthes x *mastersiana*

Nepenthes (x rokko) x thorelli

A variable plant, the clone I grow has beautiful lower pitchers that are squat and tubby, with a large, heart-shaped peristome ruby red in color. Much red markings cover the pitchers, the lid is oval and the wings strong. The upper pitchers are a buttery yellow with pale pink splotches. Superb on windowsills.

Nepenthes x Santa Mira

This was my own cross between *N.* [*thorelli* x (x *wittei*)] x (x *rokko*). All of the offspring were similar to their attractive parents, but even more richly colored. One clone, N. x 'Santa Mira' var. 'Jack Finney' produces numerous dark red pitchers with extra large floppy lids. Jack Finney is the author of *Invasion of the Body Snatchers* and Santa Mira was the location of that invasion in the 1956 film version of the novel.

Nepenthes x mastersiana

In 1883, Court produced this for Vietch Nurseries by crossing *N. sanquinea* and *N. khasiana,* and it was one of Sir Harry's favorite. It has large cylindrical pitchers with an oval mouth and lid, and the coloration is vibrant, especially in the cultivar *N.* x *mastersiana* 'Purpurea'. Try this one on a windowsill, or in cool greenhouses and terrariums.

Nepenthes x tiveyi

An utterly beautiful hybrid of *N. maxima* x *veitchii,* it has colorful pitchers and a rainbow peristome of large, flared proportions. Gorgeous, and suitable for warm or cool tanks.

Nepenthes sanquinea x macfarlanei

A beautiful plant with chocolate-red pitchers and red peristome—offset by a pale interior—it does best in cooler conditions.

Nepenthes x harryana

Named for Harry Vietch, this natural hybrid looks much like its similar, beautiful parents, *N. villosa* x *edwardsiana.*

Nepenthes x kinabaluensis

Discovered by Lilian Gibbs (the first woman to climb Mt. Kinabalu) in 1910 and named by Shigeo Kurata in 1976, this is a natural hybrid between *N. rajah* and *N. villosa.* Requiring cool conditions, the large pitchers measure one foot, are yellow with an orange blush, and have a gaping mouth with a scalloped, well-toothed, red peristome. The pitchers have a slight furry pelt and huge vertical lid.

Nepenthes x *kinabaluensis* on Mt. Kinabalu

Nepenthes x 'briggsiana' var. 'Peter D'Amato'

Nepenthes x trusmadiensis

A rare hybrid of *N. macrophylla* and *N. lowii,* it was discovered by Johannes Marabini and John Briggs in 1984 on Mt. Trus Madi. A fantastic plant, the huge pitchers are cylindrical to funnel-shaped, pure green, and with a spectacular green-and-red, sharp-toothed peristome. The yawning mouth reveals a beautifully red-blotched interior. The lid is large, dome-shaped, and held vertically.

Nepenthes rajah x burbidgea

One of the most breathtakingly beautiful of the natural hybrids, it comes from Mt. Kinabalu. The one-foot pitchers are tubby, with a pale, rose pink background heavily splashed with purplish marks. The large, undulating peristome is striped crimson and plum. The large lid is heavily streaked and smeared with dark red.

Nepenthes lowii x stenophylla

Discovered in 1985 by John Briggs on Mt. Mentapok in Borneo, this closely resembles *N. stenophylla* but has dusky, red-streaked pitchers with bristles under the lid.

Nepenthes stenophylla x veitchii

This hybrid has been recently found in a few locations in Borneo. It is a beauty, with wine-red pitchers marked in burgundy, and a gorgeous, large, fluted peristome, golden-yellow with a few burgundy stripes.

Nepenthes x briggsiana

This lovely and vigorous hybrid of *N. ventricosa* x *lowii* was created by

Johannes Marabini in Germany, and can be rather variable. The pitcher shape is wide-mouthed with a thin-toothed peristome, narrowing to a waist, with a bulbous bottom. The lid is large and held upright. One variety, named *N.* x 'Peter D'Amato' by Bill Baumgartl, has smaller pitchers solidly colored blood red. Other clones have rather sizable pitchers with paler coloration.

Nepenthes x Judith Finn

Produced by Marie's Orchids in California, this is a breathtaking hybrid of *N. spathulata* x *N. veitchii,* both famous for their wildly flared peristomes. The variable offspring were named for the popular assistant manager of Berkeley Botanical Gardens at the University of California, a longtime CP enthusiast. Several varieties of this cross may soon achieve clonal status.

CULTIVATION *(See Parts One and Two for further details)*

Soil recipes	*Nepenthes* enjoy loose, open soil that remain wet to moist but allows drainage of excess water. They are tolerant of a wide variety of soil mixes. The best include a portion of long-fibered sphagnum, the rest of the medium being a combination of coarse materials. My deluxe recipe is one part each of the following: long-fibered sphagnum, peat moss, perlite, pumice, lava rock, vermiculite, fine orchid bark, and charcoal. An easy and reliable alternative is: one part peat or long-fibered sphagnum, one part fine orchid bark, one part perlite, one part vermiculite. Another good mix is one part sphagnum to two parts osmunda fiber.
Containers	All containers must have drainage holes. Place a thin layer of sphagnum at the bottom of the pot to prevent the gradual loss of soil through the holes. This will also retain some moisture should the soil accidentally become too dry. Plastic pots work well, as do terra-cotta or glazed ceramics. Even better are wooden boxes or orchid baskets. Avoid metal zinc baskets, which poison *Nepenthes*. Four-inch pots suit young plants; six- to ten-inch pots (or larger) suit mature plants.

Light	Most *Nepenthes* enjoy very bright, diffused light or partly sunny conditions. Lowlanders often can take bright shade. Greenhouses generally require 50 percent shade cloth.
Climate	All *Nepenthes* are tropical plants, roughly divided into lowlanders and highlanders. Lowlanders require temperatures in the sixties and seventies at night, eighties and nineties during the day. Colder temperatures, even briefly, may stunt or kill them. Highland species require temperature drops at night. Highlanders do best in the fifties and low sixties at night, in the seventies and low eighties during the day. Many highlanders tolerate brief nighttime drops to the forties, if day temperatures rise. Exceptions are mentioned under the species listing. Humidity must be high all of the time, above 60 percent. Highland plants can experience more humidity fluctuations, with the highest humidity at nighttime.
Feeding	Any suitably sized insects can be fed to these pitcher plants, such as crickets, sow bugs, and mealworms. Dried insects are also excellent.
Fertilizers	Nepenthes appreciate fertilization. During the warmer months, apply twice monthly. In winter, once a month will suffice. Apply as a foliar feed, or also through the soil if plants are heavily watered at other times with pure water. Use a 50 percent solution of an orchid or epiphytic fertilizer. Avoid Miracid, which can stunt many Nepenthes.
Greenhouses	*Nepenthes* grow best in greenhouses. Lowlanders require stove houses or hot houses; highlanders do best in warm houses, but some tolerate cool houses. Many can be grown together at roughly sixty degrees minimum, eighty-five degrees maximum. While many highland varieties can tolerate hothouse conditions, lowlanders can be damaged at cooler temperatures. Hybrids are much more tolerant of temperature fluctuations, but are heavily influenced by their parentage.

Watering	In greenhouses, avoid the tray system entirely and place the containers on benches or hang them so that water can freely drain away. In terrariums and on windowsills, place the pot in a shallow saucer and water overhead as soon as the water in the saucer evaporates. Don't allow the pot to sit in deep water for extended periods. Greenhouse plants should be watered every day, or before the soil dries out. Always water overhead. If the medium dries out, the pitchers may shrivel and brown very quickly, even if the leaves and stems survive.
Windowsills	A surprising development in recent years has been experimental growing of *Nepenthes* on windowsills—with often wonderful results. Bright light to partly sunny conditions are necessary, and high humidity with frequent misting is helpful. Of the many plants found to thrive in good conditions, I can recommend *N. alata* "Spotted," *N. khasiana,* and *N. ventricosa* as the first to try. Some lowland hybrids with highland ancestry are also possible, such as *N. x dyeriana.* See the individual listings of species for further recommendations. If the plants don't pitcher, low humidity and light are usually why. The tendrils of upper pitchers will need something to grasp.
Terrariums / Grow-lights	Larger tanks are an excellent way to grow *Nepenthes.* Lowlanders may require heating pads to maintain a sixty to seventy degree minimum. Highlanders will thrive in homes that are chilly at night: fifty to sixty degrees. Choose smaller species, and prune back extensive climbing stems. The best species to try are *N. ampullaria,* *N. x trichocarpa, N. alata, N. mirabilis, N. gracilis,* *N. ventricosa, N. glabrata,* or young plants of larger species—but these will eventually outgrow the space. Lowlanders can take warm and steamy tanks; highlanders appreciate good air circulation and misting at nighttime.
Outdoors	If you live in a tropical climate similar to their native habitats, *Nepenthes* make wonderful potted outdoor plants, especially near latticework or trellises in partly

sunny areas where they can climb. In humid subtropical or warm-temperate climates, outdoor growing can be tricky, due to seasonal fluctuations, so plants are best moved indoors or to greenhouses for winter. In places like southern Florida, many lowlanders and hybrids succeed year round outside, but you must protect them during rare winter chills. On the immediate coast of California, in the frost-free fog belt, many highland species can thrive. As a rule, they despise frosts and periods of hot temperatures with low humidity.

Bog gardens	*Nepenthes* are not suitable in bog gardens.
Pruning and transplanting	Mature *Nepenthes* can survive many years in large pots, but will require pruning of larger stems. This will also encourage new basal shoots to develop, and the cuttings can be used for propagation. Typically, mature plants develop one or more basal shoots annually. These form ground rosettes for one or two years before beginning to climb. It you prefer lower-growing plants with ground pitchers, pruning stems will not harm the plant. Never remove a climbing stem until a basal shoot has developed. Climbing stems require something to climb: other plants, hangers, pipes, lattice, and so on. Very old plants that need repotting should have all stems and most basal rosettes removed. Discard old soil and trim away excess roots, then soak in Superthrive and repot.
Pests and diseases	The primary pests of *Nepenthes* are thrips and scale, and rarely mealybug. Systemic insecticides work best. Flea collars help in terrariums. Sometimes the plants are bothered by a fungus that causes rusty spots on the leaves. Treat with a fungicide.

PROPAGATION

Nepenthes *are easy to propagate by seed and stem cuttings.*

Cuttings

Propagating Nepenthes from stem cuttings is the fastest way to obtain large plants, and the only way to multiply cultivars besides tissue culturing.

Along the climbing stem, and adjacent to each leaf base, are dormant nodules or shoots. Occasionally these grow on their own, producing branching stems. If the growing point of a stem is removed, nearby shoots start to grow, replacing the removed portion.

Some growers take cuttings a little at a time, removing the growing point for propagation and waiting until new shoots sprout before removing that next section. Alternatively, a whole climbing stem may be removed and divided into sections. Sections of the stem should have from one to three leaves attached. If multiple leaves are attached, remove the lowest. Remaining leaves should be cut in half. The lower portion of the cut stem is then treated with a fungicide/rooting hormone such as Rootone (a powder) or Dip and Grow (a liquid), following the manufacture's instructions. Insert the cuttings into pots of medium. A good medium to use is pure long-fibered sphagnum, or vermiculite, or a combination of the two. Rock wool is superb for rooting *Nepenthes.* The entire block of rock wool can be planted in soil once the cutting has rooted. Keep the medium damp at all times and place the potted cuttings into a propagation case, terrarium, or similar enclosed tank to ensure very high humidity. Place in bright light, but out of direct sun, at a temperature range similar to that of the mother plant. Mist frequently, keeping the medium damp. Rooting can be enhanced by leaving pitchers on the cutting and filling them with water.

Cutting a *Nepenthes* vine for propagation.

Rooted cuttings with
emerging shoots,
ready to be potted

Within weeks to months the cutting should root, and the dormant bud sprout. It can then be transplanted and grown normally. Not all cuttings may survive. Remove dead ones from your propagating case. Superthrive and fertilizers can be used once the cutting has rooted.

There is a hormone available to promote growth of dormant shoots on plants, and these are often advertised in orchid magazines, such as *Orchid Digest*. These shoot promoters are usually pastes applied to the dormant bud. They are helpful to promote new shoots on a stem, which can later be removed as cuttings to be rooted. They can also be applied to cuttings with dormant buds, in addition to rooting hormones along the cut stem.

Some vigorous *Nepenthes* can be rooted in plain pure water, if all other conditions (such as high humidity) are right. Change the water frequently.

There are other ways to propagate stem-growing plants like *Nepenthes*, such as layering and air layering. Consult good books on gardening and houseplants for more techniques such as these. The above methods are still the most popular.

Pollination

To produce seed, male and female plants need to be in flower at the same time, or pollen can be stored in the freezer up to one year for future use. When they bloom, individual flowers open several at a time, working their way up the spike. To pollinate, pollen from a male flower needs to be transferred to the stigmas of females. One method is to remove a ripe male flower by clipping it and, using forceps, dab the pollen onto the stigmas. Alternatively, one can shake the male spike over a sheet of plastic or aluminum foil. Ripe pollen will fall, and can be collected with a small paintbrush and transferred to the female. Flowers continue to open up the spike over a few weeks' duration. It is best to repeat pollination to assure good seed set. When you're successful, the female ovaries will swell over several weeks, turn brown, and crack open, revealing seed. Pollen can be stored in foil packets in the freezer. Be sure to label flower spikes that have been pollinated, as well as any stored pollen.

Seed

Nepenthes seed is short lived and should be sown as soon as possible. It can be stored several weeks in the refrigerator (do not freeze seed), but this can kill seed of lowland species. Good mediums to sow seed onto include milled sphagnum, a mix of peat and sand, or vermiculite. Keep the soil damp and sow sparsely. High humidity, as in a covered seed tray, is required. Keep the seed in an environment similar to that of the parents, but out of the direct sun. Grow-lights are useful—keep the seed within several inches of fluorescent tubes.

After the seed has germinated, remove the cover. Allow seedlings to grow until small rosettes are formed (six months to one year). Gently remove them and transfer to small individual pots of their preferred soil recipe. Watering seedlings with a weak solution of Superthrive will encourage good root growth. Fertilizing should be done with care, using a quarter strength solution the first year, once monthly.

Tissue culture

This works well using seed as the generating source, and has recently resulted in many once rare species becoming common and affordable. Vegetative tissue culture is still being perfected.

— 12 —
OTHER SAVAGE PLANTS FROM THE DEMENTED MIND OF MOTHER NATURE

Not all carnivorous plants are showy, ornamental specimens, and not all are as popular as the Venus flytrap or *Nepenthes*. A few, in fact, may not fit the stricter definitions that define a true carnivore, namely, plants that don't produce their own digestive enzymes: *Heliamphora, Darlingtonia,* and *Byblis liniflora* may lure, catch, kill, and absorb insect prey, but do so with the help of bacteria or other life forms to aid in digestion. Are they carnivorous, semicarnivorous, or subcarnivorous? These answers may elude us, and may not be as black or white as botanists would hope. Some species may be entering or leaving a carnivorous phase in their long, endless history of evolution. A sudden mutation of this or that gene, or an ecological cosmic catastrophe from outer space, may quickly speed up evolutionary jumps and turn a petunia that uses sticky hairs to defend itself against bugs into a petunia that eats those bugs.

In this chapter I will review some of the more obscure plants of the savage garden. A few of these may fit the full definition of true carnivorous plants, others may be subcarnivores that digest by proxy. Some may be not as popular because they appear less dramatic, or because you would need a microscope to see the drama unfold. Most are still sought after by the hard-core collector, but you'll probably never see them at your local garden center. The majority are easy to grow, while one or two can be rather challenging. While all are in cultivation, a few are so rare that live plants in a pot may be counted on one hand.

THE WATERWHEEL PLANT
(ALDROVANDA)

The waterwheel, *Aldrovanda vesiculosa,* is a true aquatic carnivore that is currently believed to be a direct relative of the Venus flytrap.

I have always been impressed by young boys who visit my carnivorous plant nursery and eagerly ask where the Aldrovanda are. When I show them, their happy little faces become shadows of disappointment. "I thought it was a lot bigger," they say, as I hand them a magnifying glass. I tell them that the plant they saw on TV or in a science book was no doubt photographed under a microscopic lens. "Better look quick," I add, "because in a month it may be dead!" Alas, as fascinating as waterwheels may be to the hobbyist, they are somewhat difficult to keep long-term in cultivation.

Aldrovanda

But *Aldrovanda* is a fascinating little plant. It was first discovered in India by Leonard Plukenet in 1699. In 1747, Italian botanist Gaetano Monti described it as Aldrovandia from plants found near Bologna by Dr. Carlo Amadei. Linnaeus misspelled it in 1753 as *Aldrovanda,* listing it in his *Species Plantarum.*

Waterwheel plants are fond of placid, acidic ponds and lakes throughout much of the world. They are found in most of Europe, Africa, India, Australia, and Japan, where it recently became extinct in the wild. In Europe, the plants are vanishing due to pollution. The plants float just below the surface of water, often amid reeds, cattails, and other water-loving plants. In temperate areas the plants go dormant as tightly rolled buds in winter, whereas in the tropics they grow year round.

Waterwheels are rootless. They typically have stems about four to six inches long, one end growing while the other dies away. The leaves appear in whorls of six to nine. Each leaf has a broad petiole that ends in a small trap. Around the trap are long, pointy bristles, believed to prevent the trap from being damaged by other vegetation as the plant freely floats about in the water. The whorls of leaves are compactly grown along the stem, a dozen or more along its length. Small, single, white-petaled flowers appear above the water's surface in summertime.

The tiny trap is barely one-twelfth of an inch across, and is remarkably like that of a Venus flytrap. It looks like a green, translucent clamshell. Along its free margins, each lobe is lined with numerous tiny hooked teeth. Inside the trap are long, filamentous trigger hairs, about forty in each trap. The inside of the traps is liberally peppered with digestive glands.

Tiny swimming creatures, like water daphnia and eel worms, enter the trap for unknown reasons. No lure has been detected. Regardless, upon touching one or more trigger hairs, the trap quickly shuts. The tiny teeth interlock, imprisoning the prey. Slowly the margins of the trap squeeze together, until the prey is forced to the base of the trap near its hinge, and most water is expelled. The trap seals itself with a viscid secretion. Then digestive enzymes and acids are secreted, and the victim dissolves and is absorbed. Each trap can catch several meals.

As I mentioned, *Aldrovanda* is not an easy species to maintain long-term in cultivation. Ironically, while the plant is now extinct in the wild in Japan, botanists there have managed to reproduce it in laboratories, so these clones are the most commonly available in horticulture.

The plants are best grown similarly to the aquatic bladderworts—in water that has about one cup of peat per gallon. I strongly recommend larger containers that can hold a minimum of five to ten gallons of water. They should be grown outdoors in a partly sunny environment. Algae is one of *Aldrovanda's* worst enemies, second to tadpoles. To keep your plants alive, change the water whenever algae builds up. Water fleas will feed the plants and help clear the water. Reportedly, the addition of other water plants, such as duck weed, helps *Aldrovanda* survive cultivation. The plants can be easily propagated by breaking them apart. The subtropical form from Japan usually remains in growth when it's kept above fifty degrees, but will go dormant in colder temperatures, returning in spring. Never allow them to freeze solid.

TWO CARNIVOROUS BROMELIADS

Bromeliads are a large order of plants found in tropical and subtropical regions of the Americas. A few varieties have become popular garden-center and grocery store plants. Bromeliads can grow epiphytically on trees or terrestrially on the ground. Their leaves are usually held in a tight, upward rosette, the base of the leaves forming a tank where rainwater is collected and held. It has always been assumed that bromeliads benefit from leaf debris and the occasional insect—when such things fall into these water-holding tanks, they break down and decompose, supplying the plant with extra minerals. But it wasn't until recently that evidence was offered showing some of these plants had taken the next step or two forward along the path to carnivory.

In 1984, Professor Thomas Givnish showed that *Brocchinia reducta,* a terrestrial bromeliad from the Guyana Highlands of South America, showed features of a carnivorous plant. Not surprisingly, this species shares its home with *Heliamphora,* growing on and around the tepui table mountains of Venezuela and Guyana.

Brocchinia reducta give off a sweet, honeylike aroma that lures bugs. No nectar is actually produced. The leaves are coated with a wax that easily crumbles under insect feet, making a foothold a difficult accomplishment. Insects fall into the pool of water the leaves hold in their tank, where they drown and are broken down by bacterial action. Hairlike trichomes at the base of the tank readily absorb the minerals of the dissolved prey.

Since frogs enjoy making their homes in the plant, as is frequently seen in both cultivation and in the wild, I wouldn't be surprised if they helped digest prey for the plant: perhaps the frogs' fertilizer-rich droppings are a reward to the plant for

Two carnivorous bromeliads. On the left is *Catopsis berteroniana*, on the right is *Brocchinia reducta.*

providing a good home, much the way I suggested for *Heliamphora* (pages 111–112).

Brocchinia reducta, growing in sunny, wet grasslands or high on the tepuis, usually has tightly held leaves of a lovely golden yellow. In cultivation, the leaves are usually more openly held, and more grayish green in color. The plants reach about fourteen inches tall. Branching spikes of flowers are inconspicuous, but when the plants do flower, as with many bromeliads, the mother plant dies and is replaced by numerous offshoots.

A second bromeliad, *Catopsis berteroniana,* has also recently been described as insect-eating. It grows as an epiphyte on trees, and is found in Florida and parts of Central and South America. This species has an open crown of pointy leaves. A powdery wax is so abundantly produced that the plant can appear almost white. It works in the same manner as the *Brocchinia.*

I have found both species to be very easy to grow. They succeed outdoors in warm-temperate and subtropical climates that are frost free. Brocchinia does well in pots of soil that are two parts peat to one part each of sand and perlite (or lava rock). *Catopsis* grows well attached to branches or sitting in a pot of fine orchid bark and lava rock. Cool houses and warm greenhouses are perfect for them. Don't grow them on the tray system. Instead, sprinkle them frequently overhead with water, keeping the soil damp and well drained. Some mild epiphytic or orchid fertilizers about once monthly will greatly benefit them. Propagation is best by division of their gradually produced clumps, but don't remove any offshoots until they are at least one quarter the size of the parent. Tissue-cultured plants are becoming available, so these uncommon species should soon become more popular.

THE CORKSCREW PLANT
(GENLISEA)

Corkscrew plants are extremely odd carnivores that entered cultivation in the 1980s. There are estimated to be around twenty species growing in tropical Africa, Madagascar, and South America. They are closely related to *Pinguicula* and particularly *Utricularia,* although the traps of *Genlisea* are unlike those of any other carnivorous plant in the world.

Genlisea grow in habitats similar to and often with bladderworts and even sundews. They grow as terrestrials or semiaquatics in wet to waterlogged peaty sand. All the species are very similar in leaf and trap structure, so identification usually relies on flower structure, which is rather similar to that of bladderworts.

The plants produce small rosettes of spade- to strap-shaped leaves flat on the soil surface, from one to three inches across. The strange traps are underground, about two to six inches long. They resemble a two-pronged fork or corkscrew. A cylindrical stalk extends downward from the base of the plant. Midway down, this swells into a hollow, bulblike digestive chamber, the "stomach" of the trap. It then continues downward as a tubelike structure, then abruptly branches into two corkscrewlike appendages. At the base of the fork where it branches appears a slit-like mouth. This slit continues in a spiral fashion all the way down both prongs of the trap.

Tiny creatures, similar in size to the prey of waterwheel plants and bladderworts, can enter this slit at any point along its length. What lures, if any, attract the prey is presently unknown. There is some evidence that a vacuumlike suction helps to draw in victims. Once within the slit, these tiny creatures find themselves in a tubelike tunnel.

Genlisea as grown by Geoff Wong

They cannot escape because the slit is lined with bristly hairs that force them to continue upwards along the tube of the prong. This one-way journey to death leads them all the way up the bristle-lined tube and into the digestive chamber. Imprisoned, the prey are dissolved by digestive juices.

Genlisea are simple plants to grow. Since they are tropical, minimum temperatures should be sixty degrees. They enjoy waterlogged conditions, so I prefer to grow them in undrained containers several inches deep, such as brandy snifters. The soil should be sphagnum, pure peat or peat and some sand, filling the container nearly to the brim. Keep the soil wet to flooded. Grow them in very bright to partly sunny conditions. They do nicely in hothouses and warmer terrariums.

Unfortunately, while the plants are simple to grow in the above manner, you cannot see the traps! Geoff Wong won "Best of Show" at the San Francisco Flower Show for his *Genlisea* shown in the photograph on the previous page, which was a very clever way to cultivate the plant in a way that made the traps clearly visible. The rosette of the plant grows in sphagnum moss in a box that sits on a clear plastic container filled with water. The bottom of the box can be any plastic screened material that will hold the sphagnum while allowing the traps free access into the water below. Plastic strawberry baskets from grocery stores are a good source of screening to hold the moss. The traps will grow downward from the moss box into the transparent water container.

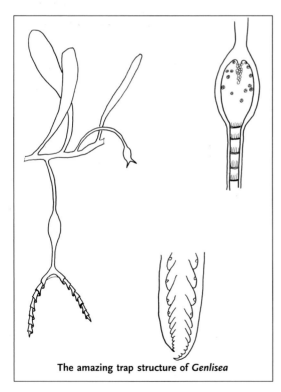

The amazing trap structure of Genlisea

Genlisea send up small, pretty flowers that look rather similar to those of some bladderworts. The flowers of the species are usually yellow or violet, although white forms are known as well. Several species are now in cultivation. My favorite is *G. hispidula* from Africa, which has dark pink blooms. I have had plants of this species growing in the same large goblet for many years in my hothouse. Other easy species are *G. repens* and *G. pygmaea,* both yellow-flowered plants from South America, and *G. violacea,* a violet-flowered plant.

If you grow your corkscrew plant in water, introduce daphnia to feed them. Otherwise, an occasional foliar mist of fertilizer on the rosette leaves will keep them happy.

Propagation is easily accomplished by leaf cuttings. Gently pluck a few leaves from the surface rosette, including the white base. Lay these flat on peat or sphagnum, keeping the soil very wet. Each leaf will grow into a new corkscrew plant.

THE DEVIL'S CLAW
(*IBICELLA LUTEA*)

This is a new and old carnivorous plant. Apparently, in 1916, an Italian botanist named E. Mameli conducted experiments on this species, then known as *Martynia lutea.* She proved its carnivorous nature by feeding it egg whites and insects, noting how the food dissolved and was absorbed by the plant. Unfortunately, she published her work in an obscure university publication that no one read.

In 1993 her paper was rediscovered and the species reexamined. Probably related to *Pinguicula,* this and other similar species from the Pro-

boscidea family of unicorn plants and devil's claws catch insects with sticky glands, but don't produce digestive enzymes. Some, like *Ibicella lutea,* grow on desert fringes, making it one of the few varieties that grow in dry habitats.

Ibicella lutea grows in South America but has been introduced to the Sonoran Desert of Mexico and has been naturalized in southern California and Arizona. The plants are annuals, the seed germinating with the arrival of the summer thunderstorms. They grow rapidly in the summer heat, thick fleshy stems scrambling along the ground for a few feet. The leaves, up to several inches long, grow scattered along the stem. They are spade-shaped with strong veins. In structure,

The seed pod of the devil's claw.

the plants are vaguely similar to geraniums or some varieties of bego-
nias, or melon plants.

The whole plant—stems, leaves, even the sepals of the flowers—
are covered in tiny glandular hairs. Under a magnifying glass, these
glands appear almost identical to the hairs on butterworts and rainbow
plants. The plant glistens in sunlight and feels sticky to the touch. There
are also flat sessile glands that secrete the juices that dissolve the prey.
The plants catch numerous tiny insects the size of gnats and midges.

The flowers of *Ibicella lutea* are large and funnel-shaped like a bell
or trumpet, with ruffled petals. Rather handsome, the corolla tube is
yellow green on the outside and bright yellow inside with some red
spots along the palate.

The creepy-sounding common name, devil's claw, comes from the
awesome seed pods the flowers produce at the end of the growing season. They look like some horrific insect jaws, black and spiny. Native
Americans often sell them to tourists as curios, and grow related species
for food and textile materials. The clawed seed pods are probably
adapted to be dispersed by larger mammals such as coyote, antelope, or
bighorn sheep, the pods attaching themselves to fur.

Ibicella lutea is an easy plant to grow—if you can get the hard,
black, quarter-inch-sized seed to germinate. The plant can be grown in
most climates that have a long hot summer. They often do well as a
regular garden plant, grown similarly to tomatoes or melons and excellent as a control for whitefly. In a pot, use some houseplant soil mixed
with plenty of sand, perlite, and lava rock, similar to a mix for cacti.
Water heavily and allow the soil to freely drain and become slightly dry
between watering. Lots of sun and heat in summer are helpful.

To treat the rock-hard seed I can recommend several methods—
but be warned that germination can take a year or longer. You can pour
boiling water over them (but do not soak in boiling water). Try crack-
ling them slightly with a hammer or soak them a few days in water (a
drop of Superthrive per cup of water might help).

The plants die after setting seed, and seed should be stored in the
refrigerator.

RORIDULA

Roridula is a genus of two species from South Africa that are on the verge of extinction. The plants look so similar to sundews they were briefly included in that genus in the nineteenth century. Francis Lloyd, in his 1942 book *The Carnivorous Plants,* dismissed them from the true carnivores because they do not produce their own digestive juices. The species are now considered subcarnivores, like *Byblis liniflora,* and they rely on assassin or capsid bugs to digest their prey for them.

Both species are scrubby, branching plants up to two or three feet tall. The thin, woody stems are crowned with a dense cluster of leaves. *R. gorgonias* grows near the cooler, foggy coast and has long, thin, lancelike leaves. *R. dentata* looks similar, but the leaves are serrated like a large-toothed saw, and it grows further inland. Both species have pink, five-petaled flowers with bright yellow stamens.

The leaves are covered with stiff, glandular hairs, but they have no power of movement as do those of the

Roridula gorgonias

sundews. The glue is more resinous than the viscid glue of *Drosera.* So many insects are caught on the plant—even prey as large as bees—that a lure is suspected, but none has been found.

As mentioned in the Introduction, only recently has it been shown that assassin bugs do the digestion of prey for the plant. Hordes of these tiny bugs live on the plant, able to walk all over the glands without being caught. When prey is trapped, the bugs close in, stabbing their needle-like mouths into panicking, struggling victims. Slowly they suck their juices dry, leaving a shriveled carcass. Later, the assassin bugs secrete clear drops of nutritious fluid onto the leaves, which is then absorbed by the plant like a foliar fertilizer.

Roridula is very rare in cultivation thus far, but tissue culture should soon make the plant more available. I grow it successfully in a mix of two parts peat to one part each of sand, perlite, and lava rock, as the plants reportedly grow in wet seeps of rocky soil in otherwise semiarid heathland. I water them overhead, allowing drainage but keeping the soil wet. Avoid fertilizer in the soil; one grower reported to me he killed a few plants this way. My own plants lost their leaves after I applied a foliar feed, but later developed offshoots. The plants can take cool weather, but you should avoid frost. Seed easily germinates on damp soil. I have also grown a hybrid of the two species, which looked rather similar to *R. gorgonias.*

TRIPHYOPHYLLUM PELTATUM

This odd plant was discovered in 1907 and although several botanists recognized its similarity to other known carnivores, it wasn't until 1979 that Sally Green and others made observations in the wild and at Kew Botanic Gardens that proved the plant is carnivorous. Strangely enough, the plant eats insects during only one stage in its life.

Triphyophyllum grows only in west Africa—Sierra Leone, Liberia, and the Ivory Coast—and is on the verge of extinction. Its name relates to the three types of leaves it produces during the course of its life.

In its juvenile stage the plant produces a woody stem up to three feet high, topped with a crown of lance-shaped leaves fourteen inches long. It looks rather like a *Cordyline* or *Dracaena* plant during this early growth.

It is then that the leaves change to a carnivorous nature. The midrib of the flat leaves extends into an upright, wiry leaf that looks and behaves much like a leaf of the dewy pine, *Drosophyllum.* These fili-form leaves have stalked gluey glands that catch many crawling and fly-ing prey. Flat, sessile glands secrete juices that digest the prey. These carnivorous leaves may be entirely threadlike, or may be transitional, flat in its lower portion and filiform at the tip. The plant probably becomes carnivorous to accomplish its next feat—a climbing, flowering stem—which no doubt requires a supplement of nutrients.

This climbing stem can reach an astounding 150 feet in height, where it blooms in the sunlight at the top of the forest canopy. The leaves of the stem look surprisingly like *Nepenthes* leaves, lance-shaped with a strong midrib. Here the midrib does not produce tendrils and pitchers, but instead two short hooks, which it uses to climb up the surrounding vegetation. At the top, small clusters of fragrant white flowers appear. These turn into large seed, four inches across, that look like bright red umbrellas. Detached, they float away in the wind.

I have never known anyone who has grown *Triphyophyllum*. It would require a very tall stove house with minimum temperatures in the seventies. It has an extensive root system in poor soils, and experiences a wet and a dry season. Reportedly, if the climbing stem is pruned the plant reverts to its carnivorous stage.

APPENDICES

iN ViTRO CULTiVATiON OF CARNiVOROUS PLANTS

Ron Gagliardo, Atlanta Botanical Garden

It seems nearly a requirement of the carnivorous plant grower to also be a plant propagator. Seeds, leaf cuttings, and division are traditional but often slow methods of reproduction. But in recent years the demand for plants has far exceeded the supply so new techniques have been developed. Thus the appearance of a sometimes mysterious method called "tissue culture." In many cases, tissue-culture propagation has become the norm for some species and has nearly replaced conventional methods. Despite the now common description of "tissue cultured" that we see on price lists or in catalogs, it remains an enigma to some. Here I will introduce the concepts and techniques of plant tissue culture, followed by the applicability of tissue culture for mass producing carnivorous plants. I will then present some thoughts on conservation and the challenges that lie ahead for in vitro carnivore endeavors.

What is Plant Tissue Culture?

Plant tissue culture is a propagation technique performed under sterile conditions, usually within a glass vessel such as a flask or test tube. The term "in vitro" means "in glass." The flask contains the plant and a suitable growing medium consisting of a solution of organic and inorganic salts, a carbon source of energy (sugar), and hormones to manipulate the cultured cells to perform as needed. The entire mixture is solidified using agar (an extract from the cell walls of seaweed) or other agents. In pure laymen's terms, it can be called "Jell-O with fertilizer." The hormones used generally fall into two classes: 1) auxins, which promote root formation and 2) cytokinins, which encourage multiplication and axillary bud production. The type, ratio, and exact amounts of each hormone added can vary depending on what is required. Too much of either is usually detrimental, resulting in deformities such as gnarled shoots or profusion of axillary buds (common among some *Nepenthes* grown on too much cytokinin). With the incorporation of sugar into this medium, there is the high probability that if the container is opened to air, fungal spores would enter and contaminate the culture. For this reason, the medium is sterilized by means of heat and pressure in an autoclave or pressure cooker. Manipulations that involve opening the container are done only in a laminar flow hood or glove box. The flow hood is basically a large air cleaner. It contains a HEPA (High Efficiency Particle Absorption) filter that catches minute particles from the air and creates a nearly sterile environment. Sterility does not end here, however. It is important that the plant tissue itself be sterile when initiating the culture, or else the normal contaminants that occur on the non-

sterile plant surface would wreak havoc in the flask. There are several ways to start a plant tissue culture, the most common being from seeds, followed by leaf sections, and finally a more difficult technique of dissecting out a growth tip or apical meristem. The initial plant material that is used (called an explant) is surface sterilized (usually with a dilute bleach solution) prior to introduction onto the sterile medium. Seeds are generally

Carnivorous plant propagation in vitro

the easiest to clean, however some, such as those of *Drosophyllum* or *Sarracenia,* have many rough edges and grooves that hide potential sources of contamination. Actual plant tissue is susceptible to damage during the disinfection process, but with care, leaf cuttings (particularly of *Drosera, Pinguicula,* and *Dionaea*) can be used. The most problematic method involves the removal of the entire shoot containing the apical meristem or growth center. This technique is a must when one desires to multiply a specific clone or cultivar of a plant since seed of these should not be used. The hurdle in this case is removal of fungal and/or bacterial contaminants that seem to be nearly always present inside the plant tissue. Following cleanup, the shoot may continue to grow normally and appear sterile until the internal infection seeps out to contaminate the culture! Seeds, leaf cuttings, and other explants can be resterilized and placed on fresh media until a clean culture is established. Most carnivorous plants will grow and multiply quickly once started, but it generally takes about a year to achieve significant numbers of plants. After the plants have sufficiently grown, multiplied, and rooted, they can be established back into soil conditions. It is important to take precautions for this process to succeed. While growing in vitro, the plants are under ideal nutrient and moisture conditions and are often rather delicate. It is important to maintain a high level of humidity for a period of several weeks following removal from flask as the plants "toughen up."

Mass Production

One of the most beneficial aspects of plant tissue culture as a propagation tool is the ability to produce literally tens of thousands of plants quickly and at relatively low cost. The foliage plant industry has depended on these techniques for decades, and it's safe to say that the vast majority of the tropical foliage plants seen on the market today were born in a laboratory. Thus, we see very uniform quality and price among these plants. The same can be said for carnivores. In the past ten years, several laboratories in the United States, the Netherlands, India, and Australia have produced millions of Venus flytraps for the trade. Imagine what a relief that is to the dwindling populations left in the wild! This alleviation of collection pressures on the remaining populations of carnivores in the wild is probably the greatest benefit of tissue culture. Currently, there are many carnivores being mass-produced using tissue-culture methods, including *Dionaea, Drosera, Pinguicula, Sarracenia, Heliamphora,* and *Nepenthes.* Today, one can walk into a local garden center and find very rare *Nepenthes* in a small domed pot for several dollars. And finally, with this book, you'll be able to grow it successfully!

Role of Plant Tissue Culture in Plant Conservation

The ability to produce thousands of plants in little time helps make plants available and discourages people from collecting from the wild, but how else can tissue culture assist in plant conservation? Botanical gardens worldwide are starting to understand some of the advantages of tissue-culture techniques and are working to integrate those into pre-existing conservation programs. For example, where conventional seed propagation may take months or even years to generate a specific *Sarracenia* or *Nepenthes* species, tissue culture offers a way for researchers to quickly produce uniform plants to experiment with. Germinating the seeds in vitro has produced seedlings that are far more vigorous than their soil-sown counterparts. By cloning sexed individuals, we can increase the numbers of male or female plants available and later strengthen the gene pool through pollination. Because they are exempt from some CITES restrictions, tissue cultures are also good vehicles for exchanging plant material between countries. Hopefully, an increased cooperation between botanical gardens and private individuals worldwide will insure that these species do not leave us permanently before humankind comes to its senses and makes a more vigorous effort to protect their rapidly disappearing natural habitats.

RESOURCES

I.

If you have found this book interesting and wish to learn more about the world of carnivorous plants, there is only one thing you need to do: join the International Carnivorous Plant Society!

As a member, you will receive their colorful and slick publication, *The Carnivorous Plant Newsletter*. Published quarterly, this journal contains articles for both lay people and scientists, including many color photographs, a seed bank, and plenty of advertisements for nurseries and vendors dealing with carnivorous plants. You will also find fascinating information on field trips, newly discovered species, cultivars, regional societies around the world (often with their own publications), CP conventions, computer websites and data bases, interviews with growers, plus the latest on conservation.

Annual membership fee is $20.00 for U.S. members, $25 foreign, and can be sent to:

ICPS, Inc.
3310 East Yorba Linda Blvd., #330
Fullerton, California 92831-1709

II.

That young people find carnivorous plants fascinating is an understatement, and it is a subject the author has lectured and written about frequently. While basic botany is the first subject that usually comes to mind (children will find the anatomy of a flower more interesting if that flower is a Venus flytrap than, say, a tulip), there are numerous subjects that can be investigated using carnivorous plants as the catalyst. Some of these include the study of diverse topics such as: the many theories of evolution, the scientific method, geography, natural history, climate, astronomy, travel, computers, pen-pals, economics, politics, art and photography, carpentry, biochemistry, medicine, ecology, and entomology, just to name a few!

Michael Szesze, a teacher specializing in secondary science, has developed an extraordinary program utilizing carnivorous plants in educating children, which has been adopted by some Maryland school districts. It's not only fun, but it stresses rational thinking, and can be helpful for parents as well as educators. For information on his *Activity Book for Carnivorous Plants,* you can contact Mr. Szesze at his email address:

Szesze@redix.net

or write to him care of

Calvert County Public Schools
Attn: Michael Szesze
1305 Dares Beach Road
Prince Frederick, Maryland 20678

III.

The devastation and disappearance of carnivorous plant habitats throughout the world is currently beyond alarming.

This tragedy rang a particularly personal note for the author a few years ago, when I returned to the site where I had first discovered carnivorous plants as a child, as mentioned in the introduction of this book. Accompanying me on my return to the lakeside habitat in southern New Jersey was my young nephew, who wanted to see the place where his uncle found the strange plants that had changed his life so many years before.

What we found was a scene of numbing horror. The once picturesque setting of southern white cedars, sphagnum moss, pitcher plants, and sundews was now a bulldozed clearing, scraped clean by the machines which sat idle that dark Sunday afternoon, beside a debris pile of trees and vegetation the size of a small mountain. A sign said, "Coming Soon! Lake View Homesites!" My nephew picked up the shriveled leaf of a *Sarracenia purpurea.* When he asked me if it was a pitcher plant, I told him yes, it was. Cleared to the water's edge, we found no living plants at all.

This is a scene that has occurred countless times to nature lovers and carnivorous plant enthusiasts around the world and with growing frequency. In the United States, over 95 percent of the original carnivorous plant habitats along the southeastern coastal plain are gone. That includes virtually all of our *Sarracenia* species, as well as the Venus flytrap. In fact, at the current rate of destruction, the Venus flytrap, according to Dr. Thomas Gibson of the University of Wisconsin, will be extinct in the wild in roughly the next century. Dr. Donald Schnell, one of the founders of ICPS, is frequently asked by enthusiasts for easily accessible roadside habitats so they may see *Sarracenia* in the wild. In 1980, he offered a list of twenty sites. By 1995, his list had been reduced to three. In southwestern Australia, most *Cephalotus* habitats are now golf courses and housing tracts. In southeast Asia, *Nepenthes* are fast disappearing due to clear-cut deforesting, and as a result some mountain habitats are experiencing climate change, with longer and more frequent droughts. *Aldrovanda* is already gone in Japan, and is vanishing in Europe. *Darlingtonia* bogs along the Oregon coast are being drained and filled for convenience stores and condominiums. The depressing list goes on and on.

There is hope. One of the finest organizations dedicated to preservation is The Nature Conservancy, a non-profit group that buys and manages endangered habitats. When becoming a member, one can request that your donation be used to protect specific threatened ecosystems, such as wetlands which are home to carnivorous plants. You will be helping to save many other species of life as well. Atlanta Botanical Gardens also has an excellent conservation program. For information, write to:

The Nature Conservancy
1815 N. Lynn Street
Arlington, VA 22209

Atlanta Botanical Gardens
Box 77246
Atlanta, GA 30357

IV.

If you were caught digging up Venus flytraps in North Carolina—or collecting their seed—did you know you could face up to $50,000 in fines and/or one year in prison? If you took a vacation in Borneo and dug up some roadside *Nepenthes,* then were caught trying to smuggle them into the United States—did you know you could face two years in federal prison, plus $10,000 in fines, plus an equal amount in attorney fees? Plant lovers beware! Laws protecting threatened or endangered species are a serious matter, and should not be taken lightly.

The laws regulating trade of some endangered carnivorous plants can be a headache-inducing confusion of bureaucratic red tape, but remember these laws are meant to help the survival of endangered species. Here I will offer a very brief review of a few of these laws and list some agencies where information and permits can be obtained so trade in these species can be done legally.

For a more detailed review of these laws I suggest you read Christopher Belanger's excellent article that appeared in the *Carnivorous Plant Newsletter,* 1995 (Volume 24, Number 3).

CITES

The Convention on International Trade of Endangered Species (CITES) came into existence in the early 1980s. Many countries participated in the development of these laws to protect endangered species from being collected from the wild populations of one country and then shipped to another—usually for commercial reasons. For example, it has been estimated that up to 250,000 Venus flytraps were being removed from the Carolinas and shipped overseas per year prior to CITES. With CITES, commercial producers who ship flytraps overseas must obtain permits to do so proving that the plants were commercially propagated. These laws govern personal, non-commercial international trade as well.

CITES divides species into two sections: those endangered with extinction are listed under Appendix I, those that are threatened with possible future extinction are listed under Appendix II. Plants under Appendix I require both permits from the receiving country as well as export permits from the country of origin. Plants listed under Appendix II do not require an import permit but only an export permit from the country of origin.

Appendix I species are:

Nepenthes rajah and *N. khasiana, Sarracenia oreophila, rubra* ssp. *alabamensis* and *rubra* ssp. *jonessi.*

Appendix II species are:

All *Byblis* species. *Cephalotus f., Dionaea m., Darlingtonia c.* All *Sarracenia* species not under Appendix I. All *Nepenthes* species not under Appendix I.

Appendix II species are exempt from CITES regulations if material being shipped internationally is seed, pollen, or tissue cultured material in flasks.

For CITES permits or further information contact:

United States Department of the Interior
Office of the Management Authority
U.S. Fish and Wildlife Service
4401 N. Fairfax Drive, Room 420C
Arlington, Virginia 22204
Phone (800) 358-2104

In addition to the CITES permits, if required, all plant material being imported to or exported from the U.S. are required to have Phytosanitary Certificates showing that the plant material is free of pests and diseases and are being shipped in artificial soils. Usually exporting nurseries provide such Phyto Certificates, or they can be obtained through local agricultural departments. For further information in the United States, contact:

U.S. Department of Agriculture
APHIS-PPQ
Port Operations Permit Unit
4700 River Road, Unit 136
Riverdale, Maryland 20737-1236
Phone (301) 734-8645
Fax (301) 734-5786

Individual countries have their own laws pertaining to trade of endangered species domestically. In the United States most of these regulations fall under the Endangered Species Act (ESA). Currently there are four species listed that are covered by the ESA: *Sarracenia oreophila, S. rubra* ssp. *alabamensis, S. rubra* ssp. *jonesii, Pinguicula ionantha.*

These species cannot be removed from wild populations. It is also against the law to import or export these plants, or ship or trade them between states without permits. Permits to legalize such trades can be obtained through the same address for acquiring CITES permits listed above.

There is another permit available in the United States for commercial trade of endangered species. Once obtained, the commercial enterprise dealing in endangered species must, among many other requirements, report to the government any individual who purchases their plants. The Native Endangered and Threatened Plant Interstate Commerce Permit can be obtained through:

U.S. Department of the Interior
Office of Management Authority
U.S. Fish and Wildlife Service
1875 Century Blvd.
Atlanta, Georgia 30345

It should be mentioned that while the ESA currently pertains to the four above named species, other species have been proposed to be added under the Act. These include *Dionaea m., Pinguicula planifolia, Sarracenia leucophylla* and *rubra* ssp. *wherryi.*

Since almost all Venus flytraps *(Dionaea)* now commercially sold in the U.S. are tissue cultured and traded in the millions, one can only wonder how nurseries and the government could cope with the reporting of all individuals who purchase the plants to the government. One can only hope that reason will overcome insanity and certain exemptions will apply.

As a final note, it should be realized that many countries and states have their own laws meant to protect their native species from wild collection. For example, Mexico prohibits the collection of their native flora, including *Pinguicula,* without permits, and while the Venus flytrap is not yet federally protected in the United States, the State of North Carolina does offer protection under their own laws.

ABOUT THE AUTHOR

Peter D'Amato has been growing flesh-eating plants for over three decades. His nursery, California Carnivores, houses the largest carnivorous plant collection in the world. You can reach them at:

California Carnivores
2833 Old Gravenstein Highway South
Sebastopol, CA 95472
Phone: (707) 824-0433
Fax: (707) 824-2839
www.californiacarnivores.com

SUGGESTED READING

Clarke, Charles. *Nepenthes of Borneo.* Kota Kinabalu, Sabah, Malaysia; Natural History Publications, 1997.

Darwin, Charles. *Insectivorous Plants.* London: John Murray Publishers, 1875. (out of print)

Juniper, Robins, and Joel. *The Carnivorous Plants.* London and San Diego: Academic Press, 1989.

Lloyd, Francis Ernest. *The Carnivorous Plants.* New York: Dover Publications, 1976. (out of print)

Lowrie, Allen. *Carnivorous Plants of Australia.* 3 vols. Nedlands, Australia.: University of Western Australia Press, 1987, 1989, 1996. (Volume 1 out of print)

Phillipps, Andrea & Anthony Lamb. *Pitcher Plants of Borneo.* Kota, Kinabalu, Sabah, Malaysia: Natural History Publications, 1996.

Schnell, Donald E. *Carnivorous Plants of the United States and Canada*. Winston-Salem, N.C.: John F. Blair Publisher, 1976.

Slack, Adrian. *Carnivorous Plants*. Cambridge, Mass.: MIT Press, 1988. (Out of print)

_____. *Insect-Eating Plants and How to Grow Them*. Sherborne, U.K.: Alphabooks, 1986. (Out of print)

PHOTOGRAPHY AND ILLUSTRATION CREDITS

All plants shown in this book were grown by the author and/or his company, California Carnivores, unless otherwise noted.

Photos on pages xiii, xiv, xix, 3, 8, 12, 17, 19, 20, 24, 27 (aphid damage), 35, 36, 47, 50, 65, 66, 67, 68, 77, 81, 83 (*leucophylla*), 84, 86, 89, 92, 94, 96 ("sand mountain"), 111, 121, 122, 123, 128, 133, 138, 140, 141 ("Giant"), 143, 151 (all but flowers), 152, 154, 156, 159 (*ramellosa*), 163, 164, 182, 185, 190, 194 (*grandiflora*), 199, 203, 204 (flower), 206 ("*gigantea*"), 207 (*potosiensis*), 208, 212 (*agnata x gypsicola*), 215, 220, 229 (*reniformis*), 244, 249, 250 (*ampullaria*), 252, 253, 255, 257, 258, 262, 263 (*sanguinea*), 265, 268, 272 (group and *x* mastersiana), 274, 285, 291, back cover and spine by Jonathan Chester/ Extreme Images, Inc..

Photos on front cover and pages xvii, 14, 38, 42, 73, 78, 88, 91, 134, 137, 142, 148, 157, 183, 204 (lava), 209, 212 (clump forming), 241, 263 (*fusca*), 266, 267 (*glabrata*), 269 (upper), 272 (*x tiveyi*), 280, and 289 by Sharon Bergeron.

Photos on pages 74, 99, 103, 110, and 236 were taken by Jonathan Chester/ Extreme Images, Inc., of photos orginally taken by Sharon Bergeron, and rendered into color transfers.

Photo on page 1 by Peter D'Amato.

Photos on pages 27 (mealybug damage), 76, 151 (flowers), 159 (*stolonifera*), 206 (*agnata* rosettes), 212, (Rizzi), 226, 230, and 252 (*albomarginata*), by Marilee Maertz

Photos on pages 27 (thripe damage), 58, 63, 75, 132, 135, 145, 147, 158, 196, 206 (dubious *agnata*), 207 (*esseriana*), 224, 225 (*sandersonii* and *graminifolia*), and 261 by Chuck Ratzke

Photo on page 52 by Rob Gardner

Photos on pages 53, 54, and 295 by Ron Gagliardo

Photos on pages 55, 229 (*quelchii*), 250 (*mirabilis*), and 252 (*northiana*) by Bill Baumgartl. The first of these was grown by the photographer, the second two were photographed in natural habitat.

Photo on page 57 by Jana Olson Drobinsky

Photos on pages 62, 93, 139, 141 (flowers), 212 (mola), and 160 by Chuck Powell

Photos on page 71 and 222 by Larry Logoteta

Photos on pages 80 and 97 by Larry Mellichamp

Photo on pages 83 (*Sarracenia oreophila*) by David Johnston

Photos on pages 87, 104, 131, 169, and 197 by Richard Doub

Photo on page 96 (Red Ruffles) by Tom Kahl

Photos on pages 106, 144, 194 (*longifolia* and *macroceras*), 198, 206 (true form *agnata*), 225 (*bisquamata*), and 227 by Ron Parsons

Photos on pages 117 and 251 by Glen Rankin

Photos on pages 146, 283, and 287 by Joe Mazrimas. Plant on 283 also grown by Joe Mazrimas; plant on 287 grown by Geoff Wong

Photo on page 162 by Rocks Miner

Photo on page 174 by Geoff Wong, grown by photographer

Photo on page 193 by Juerg Steiger. Plant grown by Juerg Steiger.

Photo on page 267 (*hamata*) by Lee Maddox. Plant grown by Tom Gibson.

Photo on page 269 (*lowii* in habitat) by Noel Gielechem

Photos on pages 248 and 270 by Erin Petersen North

Photo of author on back cover by Renee Lynn

Paintings on pages 61, 82, 84, 120, 125, 127, 129, 153, 167, 168, 180, 188, 191, 193, 198, 201, and 208 and line drawing on page 165 by Scott Bennett

Line drawings on pages 100, 101, 131, 166, 169, 203, 221, 228, 242, 279, and 288 by Judith Finn

Illustration on page 60 from Danser's monograph; colorization by Candace Elliot

INDEX